Women and Power in Zimbabwe

Women and Power in Zimbabwe

Promises of Feminism

CAROLYN MARTIN SHAW

UNIVERSITY OF ILLINOIS PRESS
Urbana, Chicago, and Springfield

© 2015 by the Board of Trustees
of the University of Illinois
All rights reserved

1 2 3 4 5 C P 5 4 3 2 1
♾ This book is printed on acid-free paper.

Library of Congress Control Number: 2015950095
ISBN 978-0-252-03963-8 (hardcover)
ISBN 978-0-252-08113-2 (paperback)
ISBN 978-0-252-09772-0 (e-book)

Contents

List of Illustrations   vii

Acknowledgments   ix

Introduction   1

1. Sticks and Scones: The Homecraft Movement in Colonial Zimbabwe   13
2. Flame, Nyaradzo, and Pretty: Black Women and Girls in Harare with Reason to Hope   47
3. Women against Government: An NGO under Stress   85
4. Mercy, Mercy, Mercy: Middle-Class Working Wives and Mothers in Harare   121
5. Reflections: Promises of Freedom and Feminism   167

Notes   173

Works Cited   183

Index   191

Illustrations

MAP

Sub-Saharan Africa, featuring Zimbabwe and the Central African Federation   xii

FIGURES

1. Women in church uniforms, around 2005   25
2. A *n'anga*, member of the National Traditional Healers Association, 2000   28
3. Jekesa Pfungwa/Vilingqondo (JP/V) member, 2001   40
4. A university graduate and her friends, 1984   48
5. Amy Tsanga at a meeting on the women's movement in Zimbabwe, 2000   65
6. Traditional dance performance, 2000   78
7. Miss Summer Breeze and her mother pose for a photo, 2000   79
8. Sheila Chikoore and the Workers' Theater Group, 1985   92
9. Dorothy Gona, labor and women's rights activist, 1985   113
10. A secretary interviewed at lunch, 2001   123
11. Maids at the back of the university flats, 1984   144
12. Rural entrepreneur and his two wives   147

Acknowledgments

Many people and many years, many celebrations and many disappointments went into the making of this book. I would like to acknowledge the women in Zimbabwe who were willing to put thoughts into words in answer to my questions and the members of NGOs who opened their doors to me. Young women and men in the city keenly engaged my concerns, all the while teaching me about what mattered to them. My colleagues who chewed over ideas with me and my neighbors in University of Zimbabwe housing who took me into their confidence and who allowed their children to freely visit my home were crucial to my getting a feel of what life was like for them. Those who supported this project include the wonderful professional staff at the National Archive of Zimbabwe and the secretaries and lecturers in the African Studies Department at the University of Zimbabwe.

This book project traveled with me around the world. Starting at my home university, Don Brenneis, Shelly Errington, and Dan Linger read early drafts of some of the chapters. Jim Clifford and May Diaz stepped in at vital moment to keep the project on track. Other colleagues in the anthropology department were unfailingly encouraging—Olga Najera-Ramirez, Loki Pandey, Judith Habicht-Mauche, Lissa Caldwell, and Anna Tsing. As graduate research assistants, Michelle Rosenthal and Kristen Cheney helped organize my archive and track down data. On-campus discussions with Aaron Montoya and Sarah Chee about their research in Mozambique and South Korea often led to my musing about women and life in Zimbabwe. Happily, they engaged and read my work, much to its benefit. Melissa Hackman, a recent graduate from our program at the University of California, Santa Cruz, has cheered me on throughout this process and also provided excellent critiques of my work. In the town of Santa Cruz, a former student, now a writing teacher, Andy Couturier, with his asymmetric writing process, moved me to try a new way of putting ideas together. In Chicago and Gainesville, Florida, I was inspired by the work of Florence Babb, Mary Moran, Fran Mascia-Lees, Martin Manalansan, and Louise Lamphere as well as critiqued by Luise White and Marit Ostebo. Anthropologists from around the country who gave me a stage to present portions of the book or who shared their insight with me include Brackette Williams, Betty Harris, Barbara Joans, and Naomi Katz. In Hong Kong, my writing partners, Virginia Mack and Susan Fiksdal, looked at my work with fresh eyes and asked new questions. Sarah Rabkin's able editing helped ready the manuscript for the publisher. Finally, this well-traveled manuscript found a wonderful home at the University of Illinois Press, where acquisitions editor Daniel Nasset read it and found anonymous reviewers willing to give constructive criticism of the project. What a joy it was to find that they grasped what I was doing and knew how I could build on it. The University of Illinois Press has been good to me: they encouraged my participation in the production process; Barbara Wojhoski gently massaged my prose; and Jennifer Holzner picked through my photos and ideas and came up with a cover design that I could not have imagined. Jennifer Comeau had just the right degree of structure and openness in managing the book's production.

My friends and family may not be familiar with the contents of this book, but their love and care have sustained me in its making. Bill Shaw, who has been with me through the thirty years that this book covers, never lost confidence in my ability to finish the book; though he completed a dozen books in the time it took me to finish this one.

The book contains a revised version of my article "Sticks and Scones: Black and White Women in the Homecraft Movement in Colonial Zimbabwe," *Race/Ethnicity: Multidisciplinary Global Context*, 1 (2), 253–78. Map 1 was drafted by © OpenStreetMap contributors. Photos of Dorothy Gona and Sheila Chikoore appear in chapter 4 with permission of the photographer, Birgitta Lagerstrom.

Women and Power in Zimbabwe

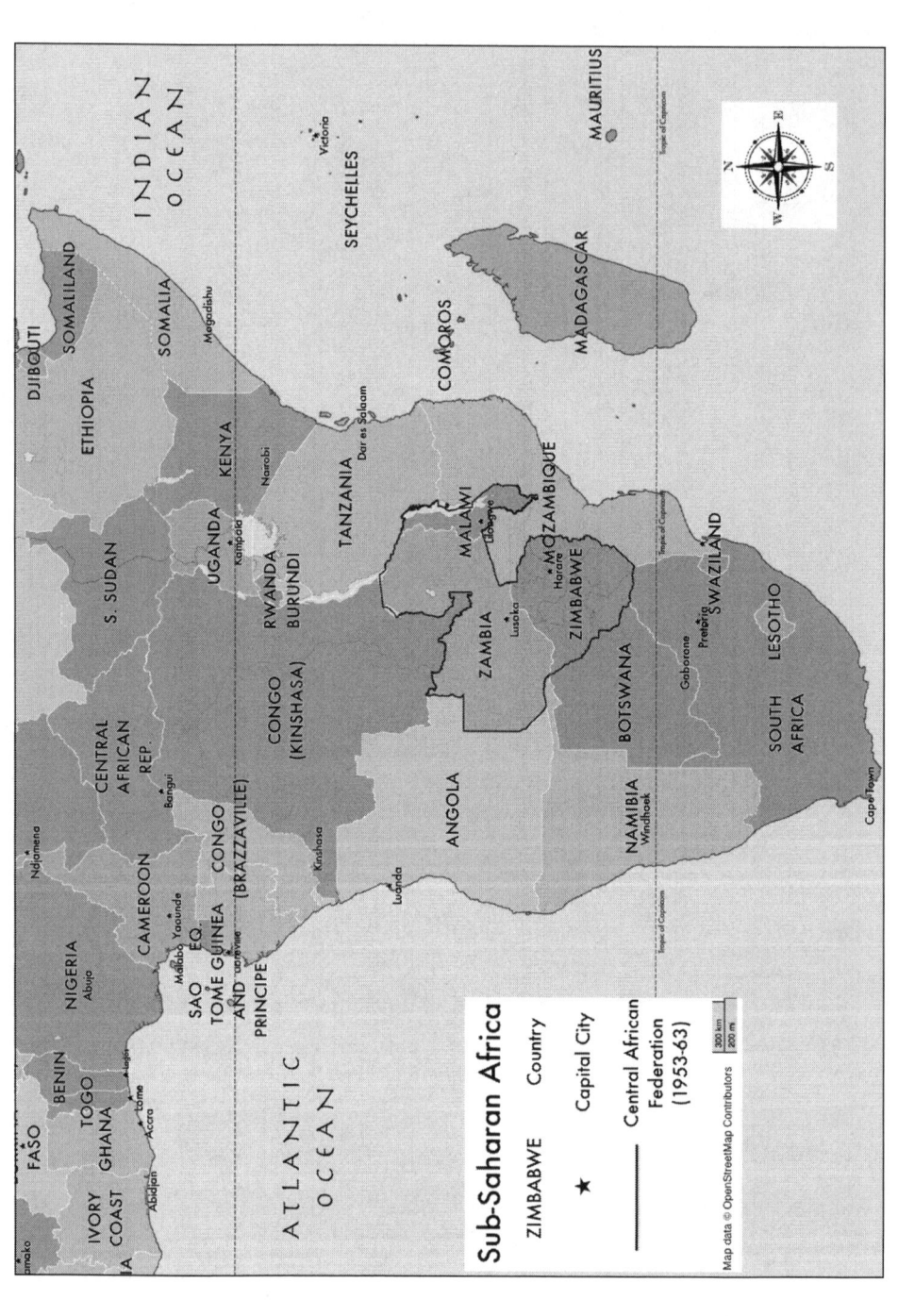

Introduction

> "What it is," she sighed, "to have to choose between self and security."
> Tsitsi Dangarembga, *Nervous Conditions*

This book is about fulfilled and unfulfilled promises. It examines the promise of feminism to empower women and bring social and political equality to both men and women. I try to convey the varied effects of feminism in Zimbabwean social life, focusing on instances that seemed to promise women a better life and led them to believe in their own potential to influence politics. Women felt that they had been promised gender equality, and many continue to feel the betrayal of the government's promise to care about them.

In 1980 Zimbabwe came into existence to the strains of Rastafarian singer-songwriter and political icon Bob Marley's revolutionary anthem, "Zimbabwe":

> Every man got a right to decide his own destiny,
> And with this judgment there is no partiality.
> So arm in arm, with arms, we will fight this little struggle.

In the struggle against a white supremacist regime in the settler colony of Rhodesia, two separate and competing liberation armies marched toward a single socialist goal, which included the emancipation of women, with women combatants in war and empowered mothers in the countryside as their prime examples of success. But Zimbabwe did not live up to its promise. By the end of its first decade, the Zimbabwean state, under the leadership of Robert Mugabe, had denied freedom of movement and assembly to urban women, had allowed deep corruption among its officers, and had massacred tens of thousands of its own citizens, primarily members of the ethnic group predominant in the other liberation army that had helped bring independence. Incredibly, a short-lived prosperity followed this upheaval, but that ended in an awful downward spiral of increasing inflation and brutal state-orchestrated violence. What happens to feminism under these varying conditions? In this book, I argue that black women in Zimbabwe were paradoxically primed for feminism during the colonial period. Though women's resolve was greatly tested just where they thought they had their best allies, especially in the armed forces during the liberation struggle, feminism held the lure of a better life for many. As the luster of independence wore off, feminism seemed like cruel optimism, fighting for a better life when the government had become the enemy of the good. Women responded to this in different ways. Some made accommodations to the new regime; others confronted it head on, while most combined feminist ideals with more-conventional feminine powers.

Zimbabwe was once celebrated by feminists and progressives in the West for its liberation ideology, which included principled stands in favor of economic justice and gender equity. While the rest of the world learned later of the dismal failure of Zimbabwe's promise, many women in Zimbabwe felt its betrayal early on. A central question of this book concerns what happens to women when such promises fail. More specifically, it asks what feminism's promises are, how a feminist outlook developed within the Zimbabwean context, and how it has led to innovation and to conventionality. Explicitly feminist ideology and, to a much lesser degree, practices came to the country during the Zimbabwean liberation war, when rural women's resources and skills (especially in preparing foods and transporting goods) pushed them to the fore and a few thousand young women left home to join the battle. During the war, women warriors suffered gender discrimination and sexual abuse. After independence, women who looked for change took varying paths to find better lives, including reclaiming domesticity, working for the government, forming cooperatives, creating income-generating projects, and establishing or participating in nongovernmental organizations (NGOs) to enhance development. Though rural villages, as opposed to cities, were most affected by the war effort, after independence rural women's daily routines changed little. Yet for some, feelings and attitudes did change: they were emboldened to proclaim singly and in groups that independence did not come for men alone. As inviting as an overt campaign for feminism may be, women's crusades for equal rights, political empowerment, and personal agency did not displace women's exercise of power based on more conventional models, especially the moral superiority of the sacrificing mother and the obedient wife. Although some women took pride in their accomplishments outside the home and in their sexual freedom, other women primarily sought security in the embrace of fathers, brothers, husbands, and sons as providers and protectors. And they craved the approval of the women they lived with, whether in the families into which they were born or the ones into which they married. To tell the story of women's hopes and heartaches, I use history, ethnographic fieldwork, literature, and Zimbabwean women's own writings.

Zimbabwean novelist Tsitsi Dangarembga, whose first novel, *Nervous Conditions*, signposts this exploration of feminism and its promises, embeds her approach to feminism in theories that emphasize women finding their own voice, appreciating their sensuality, and developing antipatriarchal skills and resources.[1] Her work exposes the hidden contradictions in the opposition of self and security that many women feel when articulating their wishes and acting on their desires. My book takes up many of the issues raised in *Nervous Conditions*, a coming-of-age story that centers on two cousins: a shy yet ambitious rural black girl who discovers feminism for herself, and her spirited urban cousin who sinks into mental illness as she confronts the limits of black female autonomy under Rhodesian colonialism. In the novel, a character ponders "what it is . . . to choose between self and security," but Dangarembga troubles the opposed categories of self and security (1988, 101). The author deftly counterpoises women and girls who negotiate this tension between self (self-expression, self-fulfillment) and security (economic and social protection) in different ways. The discipline of the female mind and body exacted in Zimbabwean society pushes women to contain themselves, to make themselves small by kneeling, to lower their voices, to be respectful, and to remember their place. Women who do not contain themselves are called "loose." Choosing security not only means having the respected status of wife and mother, being a woman of good reputation, and having the possibility of housing and money provided by a husband and his family; it also means accepting the husband as the ultimate decision maker and very likely living with his emotional distance, physical cruelty, and infidelities. Choosing self not only puts a woman in charge of herself, but also brings isolation from conventional society, the loneliness of the sole decision maker, and the onus of carrying all the weight on one set of shoulders.

Dangarembga's protagonists know or come to know what they want; they exercise agency in acting on their desires, but sometimes they are unable to escape the force of the discourses that represent women who act on their own will as un-African, sinners, prostitutes, or loose women. In her play *She No Longer Weeps*, Dangarembga portrays a tragic example of a woman who refuses to marry the unfaithful father of her child, and who achieves distinction as a lawyer but turns murderous in a child-custody battle when her former lover threatens to use her history of sexual license against her (1987). Dangarembga's protagonist fulfills some of the promises of feminism in choosing not to become a silently suffering wife and in acting on her career and sexual desires, yet she has grown cold. In this revenge play, no one ends happily; as the protagonist takes a knife to castrate her former lover, she also destroys her father and herself. If there is blame placed in this piece of fiction, it is on the society that has become "violent, corrupt, and sadistic" and on women and men who promote patriarchal principles (1987, 43). Dangarembga shows that the terrain in which feminism must find a way to flourish includes the binaries of obedience versus self-assertion, social acceptance versus social isolation, and sexual containment versus sexual pleasure. Considered this way, the choice between self and security is a false dichotomy. The self—even a liberal, individualized self—comes into being through social networks and grows through the continual exercise of choices within social and cultural contexts. Nonetheless, the tension between self and security resonates with many Zimbabwean women, who are taught to minimize self in order to gain the security of husband and family.

In the incident from my experience in Zimbabwe's capital city that I describe below, a woman is faced with just such a choice, but in this instance she has to choose whether to protect her health or be seen as a bad wife. This occurred twenty years after Zimbabwe's 1980 independence. At that time, the AIDS pandemic was raging, abetted, in part, by President Mugabe's denial of its existence in the country:

> A beautiful young married woman with three daughters, Chipo was the subject of much gossip. Her daughters were always borrowing food and supplies from neighbors, who complained that Chipo was mismanaging her household. Chipo was plump and had a head full of her own hair, but she was in the hospital for one thing or another; she said she had gallstones and intestinal problems. The neighbors did not believe her stories about why she was in the hospital. Most people knew that her husband had AIDS, and they were watching to see the symptoms in her. Two of his girlfriends already had that skeletal look that folks associate with AIDS. When one of them, the mother of his only son, came to the apartment building demanding to see her boyfriend, Chipo got into a physical fight with her and sent her on her way unsatisfied. As her husband's condition worsened, Chipo grew angry at him for not taking his medicine—he said that he could not drink if he took it. Now he was dying of tuberculosis (TB) in the hospital, and though the strain of TB was virulent, family, friends, and neighbors expected Chipo to spend long hours at his bedside every day. The doctor told her to minimize contact with him, but she refused. Already suspected of being loose because of her vitality and beauty, she said that if she did not sit by his bedside every day, she would be suspected of "killing" him.

It is not surprising that a woman wants to spend time at the bedside of her dying husband. Why this story is significant is that it exemplifies the disregard of self that is expected of a good wife, the acts by which she performs the good wife role, and the fear of being called "loose" that pushes her to hazard her own health. Chipo is a good wife: she fights for her man, she is resigned to her husband's infidelities, and she stays with him even though sex with husbands is wives' greatest risk of exposure to HIV/AIDS. In his dying days, she continues to gamble with her own health, not just to comfort him but to appear to others as a good wife. Because she is beautiful, she is already suspect, thought to be corruptible, to be susceptible to negotiating her beauty and sexual favors for money and goods. She lives in the city while her husband, a university lecturer, travels, and she doesn't sit at home every night. None of those who have kept watch on her behavior come out and say that she is unfaithful to her husband. But in popular thought, women are held to be vessels of contagion; could he have gotten the virus from her, rather than one of his girlfriends?

Besides indicating what a good wife does, Chipo's story is also one against which we can measure the changes that some women want to see in their marriages, which I will take up later in the book. Women who wish to have modern, companionate marriages seek men who can put family first, who see their wives as partners, and who want mutuality in their relationships. For most women, it is too much to hope for that men will be faithful—that is against men's nature, they say—but many wives would appreciate greater interdependence in the marriage and tenderness in the lovemaking.

This historical study alights in Zimbabwe at several crucial moments. The narrative of *Women and Power in Zimbabwe: Promises of Feminism* begins at the end of the colonial period, when black women aspiring to "a better life" entered homemaking classes taught by white women aiming to maintain colonial hegemony.[2] Few scholars see the Homecraft movement as feminist, but I argue that it had several unintended consequences: it encouraged women to move beyond the confines of their homes, to join in common cause with non-kin, and to name their desires. To the extent that women's attitudes and orientation toward themselves as women and as community members changed because of their participation in Homecraft clubs, I consider it proto-feminist. On the one hand, Homecraft gave women a respectable reason to venture from their homes; it began to whittle away at women's fear of the evil deeds and ill will of strangers, and it built women's appetites for new things and new experiences. On the other hand, learning the explicit lessons of cooking, cleaning, and child care buttressed Zimbabwean conventional beliefs about women, especially linking their prestige to their status as wives and measuring their degree of respectability by their own conduct as well as that of their children and female relatives. From this beginning, I consider different paths that women take, specifically four types of women in Zimbabwe: female combatants, feminist activists, beauty and modeling contestants, and working wives and mothers.

As countries across the African continent gained freedom from colonial rule, from 1966 to 1979 blacks fought Rhodesian forces for independence. Women who joined the anticolonial struggle and the socialist movement imagined a land of freedom and were inspired by the promise of women's emancipation. The experiences of women at war varied greatly: a few rose up in the ranks, some distinguished themselves in battle, others qualified for training overseas, but most did not see battle, reward, or travel. They suffered the hardships of ill-equipped military camps with their male comrades, or they were left in desolate mothers' camps with other pregnant and nursing women. After the success of the anticolonial movement, socialism did not take root, despite the support of communist countries (prompted by Cold War politics). And despite gains in the recognition of women as adults capable of being guardians of their children and owning property, gender equity is still a dream. This book examines the experiences of women who went to war against colonialism, for the dignity and prosperity of black men and women and for women's emancipation.

After the war, the Women's League of the ruling political party monopolized women's public expressions. This disproportionately affected women in rural areas, whose disappointment with the ruling party was not voiced. Rural women were most engaged in the war effort, most hopeful for women's emancipation, and most let down by the fact that it did not accompany the country's independence. In the cities, women writers, academics, and activists spoke out against government policies and formed NGOs of and for women, often taking their message to the rural areas. Many city women used the term "feminist" to describe themselves, but what they meant by that term and how they translated feminism into action varied. Zimbabwean feminists, unlike many women across the African continent, are not silenced by the accusation that feminism is Western or an effect of Western (un-African) influence. Since many of the factors that contributed to the country's gaining independence came from elsewhere, including arms and ideas from the then–Soviet Union and the People's Republic of China and money and publicity from supporters in the West, Zimbabwean feminists are aware of the hybridity at the foundation of their country. They choose from a variety of feminist approaches to address problems of sexism and gender inequality that are rooted in local and global ideologies of difference and disparities in power and resources.

One crucial moment in Zimbabwe's postcolonial history occurred in 1999–2000, when the ruling party lost a constitutional referendum, a strong opposition party emerged, and the country began a precipitous economic decline. During that time, several women's NGOs formed a Women's Coalition to contribute to constitutional reform; for a while that coalition spearheaded a women's movement in Zimbabwe. Over time that coalition became just one of a number of women's NGOs. Groups of women, in and outside the Women's Coalition of Zimbabwe, still gather to protest their treatment by the government and to demand recognition of their human rights. In this work, I give close attention to one feminist NGO, which I worked with off and on over the course of two decades. The group, like many, had to balance internal needs and external donor requirement; it also made accommodations to the political regime and struggled to stay on its feet during the turbulence of constitutional reform, economic decline, and increasing violence.

Though in Zimbabwe as elsewhere, there are many kinds of feminisms, some women I discuss in this book would never use the term "feminist" to identify themselves or their hoped-for future. I study two groups of women who fall into the category "not a feminist": working wives and mothers, and teenagers who participate in beauty contests and fashion or modeling contests. Though working wives and mothers feel the brunt of gender inequality at work and say so, they also recognize and honor gender difference at home. Among these women, and their sisters and daughters, are some who deploy more conventional notions of feminine power: cultivating beauty, using sexuality, making themselves indispensable to the running of the home, and unleashing the moral superiority of the good wife and self-sacrificing mother. Beauty queens and modeling contest winners do not assert power and autonomy as feminists but rather use their beauty and ability to animate different ways of being, through costumes and cosmetics, to nourish a sense of themselves as competent and successful and to gain power in their interpersonal relations.

Feminism can be seen as an example of what Lauren Berlant calls "cruel optimism": an attachment to an object, an idea, or a way of life that betokens a satisfying change—the good life—but that history shows to be fraught, unstable, fragile, or costly (2011, 1–2). Her examples of good-life fantasies include "upward mobility, job security, political and social equality, and lively, durable intimacy" (3). Berlant created this concept, in part, to explain the emotional costs of living in the American political economy, where capital determines value. I am drawn to it because of the weight it places on promise, the feelings generated by living a life in close proximity to what one desires but never reaching it, where the present seems interminable and the satisfying future never comes. Emotional responses to this situation, living with the object of desire just out of reach, vary widely: one can rationally apportion behavior to reach the goal, become obsessive about the steps toward the satisfying goal, maintain the desire but live passively as though one's actions don't matter, or comfort oneself with what is nearby, leaving the desired object beyond the horizon. In short, a primary interpretation of cruel optimism is that it entails hoping for a positive future change in spite of history or a sociopolitical environment that impedes it. For some women in Zimbabwe, feminism is an object of desire, a potentially satisfying way of life that draws them into real and imagined relations with the world. For others, feminism pushes them to both challenge and reaffirm their conventional beliefs and practices.

Conventional feminine goals—a happy and healthy family, a stable marriage, and the respect of peers—are also not so easily met, and the hopes of reaching them may turn into cruel optimism, especially when women's own conduct and attitudes interfere with their achieving their goals. Berlant's corollary statements on cruel optimism suggest that optimism may turn cruel when the very acts that a person performs to reach a positive future goal may prevent progress toward that goal or when holding onto a position or behavior creates an impasse, making the goal more distant. Berlant cites the film *What's the Matter with Kansas?*, in which individuals, swayed by hot-button issues such as abortion, vote against their own economic well-being, as an example of how emotional attachment to particular ideas or ways of being can work against achieving the good life.[3] One may also be thwarted in achieving the good life by wearing oneself out in the process, as in working too hard or too long at a job in order to secure a happy family in a nice home. As Berlant puts it, "The conditions of ordinary life in the contemporary world even of relative wealth, as in the United States, are conditions of the attrition or the wearing out of the subject, and the irony that the labor of reproducing life in the contemporary world is also the activity of being worn out by it has specific implications for thinking about the ordinariness of suffering, the violence of normativity, and the 'technologies of patience' that enable the concept of later to suspend questions about the cruelty of the now" (2011, 28). In *Women and Power in Zimbabwe*, I reflect on how women's attachment to seeing themselves as morally superior lets men off the hook, permitting them to be bad and irresponsible and at the same time denying women the reciprocal relations in marriage that many desire. Because women see the health and safety of their children at stake when they take a risk to be more like men or to hold men to women's higher standards, this situation could be called an impasse: "a holding station that doesn't hold securely but opens out to anxiety" (Berlant 2011, 199). This is a form of cruel optimism.

In contrast to Berlant's notion of cruel optimism, Ann Cvetkovich's work invites us to study how people who feel despair, shame, or depression try to make themselves feel better both in everyday life and in organized collectivities and politics, suggesting that negative affective responses are vital resources for political action (2012, 24–25). Cvetkovich describes this as the drive to escape "political depression": "the necessity of finding ways to survive disappointments and to remind ourselves of the persistence of radical visions and ways of living.... Survival also involves developing a higher tolerance for the conflicts that political life invariably produces ... [tolerance] in the sense of being receptive to [conflict or difference] and being willing to risk vulnerability" (2012, 6–7).

While Berlant asks what bad can happen when we hope, Cvetkovich asks what good can happen when we despair. I look at both under the heading of cruel optimism, because feminism, whether it is inspired by hope or provoked by despair, stands against a continuation of the present situation, where the present seems infinite (Berlant 2011, 42). *Women and Power in Zimbabwe: Promises of Feminism* shows the play of femininity and feminism in the lives of black Zimbabwean women, from the cruel optimism of ex–freedom fighters, to the opportunistic feminism of gender activists, the mix of feminine powers and feminist desires in working wives, and mothers and teenagers whose despair leaves them thirsting for freedom. In many different ways, some of the promises of feminism have been realized in Zimbabwe, but feminism calls forth a contradictory assemblage of feelings and politics, which I touch on in this book.

Fieldwork

I conducted research in Zimbabwe over a thirty-year period, during four stays in the country: two brief visits in 1982 and 2003 and stays of one year or longer in 1983–84 and 1999–2001. When I was at the University of Zimbabwe as a Fulbright Fellow in 1983–84, I worked with an organization that sought to empower women to have their voices heard by the government and in the national arena. At that time, I interviewed recently demobilized female ex-combatants and started a newspaper archive that I picked up again in my next stay in the country. During my last long-term stay, 1999–2001, I again worked with the same women's NGO in addition to studying two others. I attended meetings and training sessions for secretaries and interviewed working women in Harare during that time. It was also in that period that I attended fashion shows and beauty contests and spoke to their participants and organizers. Finally, living in university housing gave me a chance to enter the lives of many residents and workers in the area.

I use participant observation, interviews, archival research, and published fiction to tell the story of urban women's responses to the promises of feminism in Zimbabwe. The first three scholarly activities are standard for a historically minded anthropologist; I will take a moment to explain why fiction is also important to my approach. Though ethnographers and historians are ever alert to discordance, history and ethnography often elaborate shared values and commonalities of experience. Fiction writers differ from these scholars in that they find their best stories in the unique and also delve into the psyches of individuals. But the unique is seldom isolated. Just as historians and ethnographers do, fiction writers must provide background and context for their singular creations. Fiction is a cultural production, a thing made under the constraint and impetus of particular orientations and discourses. Works of fiction portray a sustained world of signs that can reveal narratives of self and society as well as the deep cultural structures that ethnographers look for. Novelists draw from, work against, and imaginatively mold social conventions and historical possibilities.

How I Came to Zimbabwe

Zimbabwe's liberation struggle took place during the crest of the second wave of feminism in the United States. When I first traveled to Zimbabwe in 1982, I went looking for the women of the revolutionary cadre, the type of new African woman who carried a gun to achieve her political ideals. Leftists and pro-socialists in the West had supported the Zimbabwean liberation struggle. We knew the names of Robert Mugabe and Joshua Nkomo and those of other leaders of both parties. Influenced by Cold War politics, we knew that the black majority was supported by the Soviet Union and China, and that South Africa, widely understood to be an ally of the United States in the war against communism, was the main backer of their enemy, the Rhodesian Front government. The struggle for Zimbabwe was for democracy, black majority rule—one person, one vote. And those fighting for independence vowed to treat women as full citizens. In 1978, the Women's League of the liberation party, Zimbabwe African National Union (ZANU), had declared, "For the revolution to triumph in its totality there must be emancipation of women."[4]

In the years since then, I have been saddened by the turn of events in Zimbabwe. Mugabe was supposed to be what Nelson Mandela was: a compassionate, intellectual, politically astute statesman who led his country to independence and had faith in the institutions established such that he could step aside and let others lead. Instead, Mugabe ordered the massacre of citizens, supported the destructive invasion of viable farms and businesses, drove the economy into a ditch, engineered massive election fraud, and fomented violence.

When I was looking for women revolutionaries in 1982, daily newspapers carried stories about female ex-combatants' struggles to find men willing to marry them. One ex-combatant I talked to was bitter about not finding a place in the military, while another told no stories of her experiences and only would speak about the beaded purse she had purchased in China. One woman talked to me about her sense of being excluded from the company of other women because she was divorced. These women, whose ambition for public power was thwarted or who desired a return to domestic normality, pushed me to investigate women's changing dispositions in a society that only grudgingly accommodates their aspirations.

But I also met women who fit into quite different categories. One young woman told me that the United Nations (UN) embargo against trade with the renegade state of Rhodesia (1965–79) had not interrupted the broadcast of her favorite prime-time soap opera, the thing that "makes life worth living." Another had developed her notion of beauty through her work with the Miss Zimbabwe contest. A third asked me in halting English, "Is it better to marry the person who loves you or the one you love?" This last question still intrigues me, and more than anything else prompted this book. I don't know if there is a right answer to the question she posed, but the question of whether to be the lover or the beloved led me to think of the different sources of women's power: had I overlooked some of these sources in my search for women's empowerment? What do Zimbabwean women think of and do with beauty, sex, and love?

I am interested in gender equity and how feminism has become a part of Zimbabwean ideas and practices, and I want to understand how women in Zimbabwe apprehend and confront feminism. But I have added to those interests a concern with what women see as distinctly feminine: the power of beauty, the rewards of maternal responsibility, and the dangers of wifely obedience to their health and well-being. This book traverses a broad terrain that women inhabit in Zimbabwe: balancing career and family, seeking pleasure and enjoying power, remaking themselves as homemakers, coming of age under patriarchy, accommodating and participating in the liberation struggle, feeling the nation in their bodies through beauty and violence, and organizing against the postcolonial government.

CHAPTER 1

Sticks and Scones

The Homecraft Movement in Colonial Zimbabwe

> Our home would answer well to being cheered up by such lively flowers. Bright and cheery, they had been planted for joy. What a strange idea that was. It was a liberation, the first of many that followed from my transition to the mission.
>
> Tsitsi Dangarembga, *Nervous Conditions*

Homecraft clubs, where women learned cooking, housekeeping, and childcare skills, may seem an odd place to begin a study of the promises of feminism. I hope to show that rather than the subjects of the classes they took, it was women's ability to leave home to attend classes, the common cause they found with women beyond their place of kin, and the new set of desires instilled by these popular and easily accessible classes that laid the foundation for later feminist consciousness and activism. Feminism is based on women becoming aware of their common interests as women, on their recognition of discrimination against women and girls, and on their taking a stand against sexism. The white women who started Homecraft clubs for black women were not feminists. Their prime interest was in maintaining white rule in this part of central Africa; they knew that women did not have the same rights and privileges as men, but they profited from their gender, race, and class positions in colonial society and were interested not in change for themselves but in maintaining the status quo.

The growth of feminism in Zimbabwe is, in part, a result of the rupture of relations between people and of relations between humans and land that colonialism wrought. Colonialist-subject and master-servant relations were established between blacks and whites as colonialists claimed the land and labor of indigenous Africans. Through settlers displacing black families from their land, colonial officers' codification of tribal law, surveillance and discipline of indigenous populations, elevation and collaboration of chiefs and headmen, conscripted and forced labor, urbanization and proletarianization of portions of the population, and separation of employed and unemployed family members, relations among blacks also changed. Under colonialism African women, educated in schools and attending churches, went beyond their safety zones and came together with non-kin. The very act of traveling from their home base and interacting with non-kin gave them a sense of agency. They gained new desires, not just for the consumer goods that colonialism introduced, but also for freedom of association and of choice. Black women who gathered around radios to hear broadcast classes or attended demonstration classes in township and rural centers challenged the sureties of colonialism and of their domestic lives and began to want a better life. Optimistically, they looked to a brighter future—adopting, rejecting, and reinterpreting colonialists' goals.

Homecraft groups were not the first organized associations of black women in colonial Zimbabwe. But with membership open to married and single women throughout the country, they were the most popular secular group. Groups, such as mothers' unions and women's prayer meeting, were sponsored by missionaries, affiliated with churches, and primarily for married women. On their own, black women living in townships initially formed groups to help newcomers, to maintain high moral standards, and eventually to fight colonial laws and to organize women laborers. Colonialism forced women into new configurations and they used their newfound relationships to build networks and to fight the powers that be.

Under colonialism, women in Zimbabwe also became aware of practices and customs from ethnic groups in neighboring countries. Women from Zambia and Malawi brought the Kitchen Tea, comparable to a raucous bachelorette party, to the townships of Zimbabwe. Unlike groups that persist over time, the Kitchen Tea is an ephemeral experience that incorporates generative principles of Shona culture, especially the tendency to activate latent social networks as needed, rather than relying on well-established groups for particular purposes, and the simultaneous recognition of hierarchy and communality among women. I turn to the Kitchen Tea to demonstrate the continuity and modernization of women's beliefs about what it means to be a good wife and mother and to set this in contrast to what black women were taught in women's groups organized by white women. The illustrative Kitchen Tea studied here took place about a decade ago, but much of this chapter is focused on an earlier times, from the end of World War II and the disbanding of the British colonial empire, to the period the Central African Federation when whites offered partnership with blacks, to the Zimbabwean liberation struggle and the eclipsing of white power.

Though in this chapter I describe a Kitchen Tea and survey independent black women's groups, at the heart of the chapter is a moment in Zimbabwean history, 1953–63, when black and white women cooperated in the spirit of progress, when the reshaping of selves was a mission undertaken by white women's social groups in the interest of the state. As members of the Federation of Women's Institutes of Southern Rhodesia (FWI), colonial white women turned to political activism with the founding of Homecraft Clubs for black women, and both black and white women were changed by their participation in them.[1] Tens of thousands of black women joined Homecraft clubs, where, in addition to homemaking skills, they learned to organize meetings and to work in concert with other black women across differences of age, kinship, and marital status. Participation in Homecraft clubs declined as the racial partnership of the short-lived Central African Federation ended, was followed by a unilateral declaration of independence (UDI) from Britain on the part of the white minority government of Rhodesia, and then by the violent liberation struggle that led to the founding of Zimbabwe. Disobeying wartime emergency orders that outlawed public assembly, women in some Homecraft clubs continued to meet. As two liberation armies struggled to increase nationalist sentiment in rural areas, women were valued for the cooking stick, used to stir large pots of *sadza* (cornmeal porridge, the staple food) that fueled the freedom fighters, and for baking scones, an iconic and prestigious British dish, similar to baking-powder biscuits in the United States. Homecraft women were not called "sellouts" because of their association with white women, but many found themselves protected because of one of the very skills that they had learned from white women, baking scones.

Through a study of the history of the FWI and the black organizations, Homecraft and its successor, Jekesa Pfungwa/Vilingqondo (JP/V), I argue that as white women taught domesticity and community service to black women, black women formed new attachments to one another, to new ways of being in the world, and to new things—for example, soap, shoes, diapers, lotions, tea, and jam. While learning domesticity, they began to assert themselves in the public sphere.

The Job of Domesticity

The extent to which Shona women were confined to a domestic or private domain before the coming of colonialism is debatable. If we take the view that the vital economic activities of women—farming, trading, cooking, pottery making, beer brewing, and to a lesser extent managing herds and flocks—fundamentally support the society as a whole, then women's activities have a public component and cannot be ascribed to a narrow domestic domain. When we look at the "public" through a strictly political lens, however, few women come into view. Here I would like to give a brief historical summary of the public/political roles and statuses available to Shona women, in order to address historians' contention that Homecraft took women away from community-wide service and concerns. Historically, women occupied few high-level positions and had no concerted public voice as women.

Great Zimbabwe, where kings amassed wealth through international trade and gold mining, represents the height of hierarchal elaboration in Shona society, with clear distinctions in material wealth and standing between royalty and commoners. This UNESCO World Heritage site, a city of unmortared stone edifices in southeastern Zimbabwe (the largest of many such ruins), was occupied between the eleventh and fifteenth centuries of the current era and was home to ancestors of members of the Shona ethnic group.[2] Though myths in the West suggest that this was the home of the biblical Queen of Sheba, a combination of archaeological, historical, and ethnographic evidence indicates that the rulers were kings and that there is no tradition of a female ruler: the king's senior sister had high status, and his senior wife was queen (Beach 1998). After the demise of the great kingdoms, dispersed chiefdoms predominated. Women could become chiefs and subordinate headmen under them, but they rarely achieved these roles. Elizabeth Schmidt's history of Shona peoples makes women visible in fields of knowledge and power, but she starts by admitting, "Although most power and authority in Shona society was concentrated in the hands of older men, women helped perpetuate this male dominated society" (1992a, 16). The summary below is based primarily on Schmidt's study of colonial records from the period 1870–1939 (1992a, 1992b).

Among these mixed horticulturalists and pastoralists, the rainmaker, the spirit medium, and the chief all presided over public rituals believed to ensure the continuity of life. Though it was not unheard of for women to occupy each of these roles, more women became spirit mediums for family or clan ancestors than became chiefs or rainmakers. Rainmakers probably had the widest dominion; ancestral spirits of the district, which joined together several localized kin groups, demarcated a narrower realm for the spirit medium. With few exceptions, women were not active at the highest levels of rainmakers and chiefs. An exception is Ambuya Nehanda, a regional-level spirit medium credited with rallying rebellion in the first war against colonial oppression, the first

Chimurenga, in 1896–97, and inspiring fighters during the anticolonial war, the second Chimurenga, 1965–79.

Specialized ritual knowledge gave women power and authority as midwives, grandmothers, mothers-in-law, and fathers' sisters. Postmenopausal women, whose dry, infertile bodies brought them closer to the ancestors, educated children, helped with birth, assisted in medical diagnosis and treatment, and adjudicated disputes within the family. The gifts of the spirit medium, the person through whom the ancestor spirit speaks, were used for physical and social healing as well as for focusing the energies and attention of the group in particular directions. The *n'anga* (medicine man, prophet, witch doctor, or traditional healer) determined the causes of misfortune, from physical ailments to failing grades, and supplied remedies. The converse of the healers was witches, people believed to use spiritual or supernatural powers for private rather than the community's benefit. Although people accused of witchcraft, especially in causing the death of another or in bringing about serious misfortune, could be severely punished, some women scared others by letting it be known that they had such powers and thereby were able to assert their will.

On the whole, women's greatest power lay in their informal influence as intimates of their husbands, respected members of their brothers' families, mothers-in-law to their sons' wives, and watchful and judgmental neighbors to their resident kin and affines. A woman's power was based on her moral virtue, her management of household resources, the behavior of those for whom she was responsible (children, sisters, and nieces), and the wealth and prestige of her male relatives. Women's power was extremely individualized: wives negotiated control of labor and resources with husbands. Shona individuals rarely interacted with men or women outside their kin group; women made few long-lasting ties outside particular kin relations, and women's interventions into public discourse were not based on their identity as women.[3]

Given the small degree of public sway that Shona women's positions and knowledge allowed them, it is hard to argue that their public standing decreased due to colonialism. It is easier to make that argument in West and East Africa, where women organized as age mates, market women, wives, sisters, devotees to gods, councils for deciding on disputes regarding women and marriage, and members of cults for the healing of the nation; they lost considerable power under colonialism. Certainly, a significant decline in women's status under colonialism generally occurred in decentralized societies and in those with dual-sex organizations, where women and men had parallel hierarchies, typically joined at the top by a king or overarching men's council (see Hafkin and Bay 1976). As power became centralized in the hands of colonialists and the

African kings, chiefs, and headmen through whom they ruled (and thereby removed from diverse men's and women's institutions and positions), women were marginalized, lost visibility, and lacked authority. Something like that did happen among the Shona: although Shona women had little to lose, colonialism tended erode that little. Women's public positions, such as spirit medium and traditional healer, fell outside formal political processes and were undermined as colonialists supported men in positions of chief and headmen. My argument is that, in terms of their public voice and exercise of power in community-wide matters, women had little to lose under colonialism; rather to the contrary, they gained a foothold in public discourse.

In arguing that Homecraft clubs increased women's presence in the public domain, my analysis departs from that of scholars who assert that because of colonial female domesticity programs, such as Homecraft clubs, women withdrew from their public, community-wide activities and turned toward being good housewives (Barnes 1999; Schmidt 1992a, 1992b; West 2002). According to this line of reasoning, women reimagined their roles as "incorporated" wives among the elite and, more generally, as household managers, rather than community members.[4] As Schmidt puts it, "They [women] were educated not to exercise authority in the public sphere, but for obedience and domesticity" (1992a, 148). In fact, women spent more time away from home because of their club activities, and to the extent that they joined with other women, they had broader community influence.

In his work on the black Zimbabwean middle class, Michael West similarly surveys Homecraft courses for African women and concludes that the clubs did not require or expect students to "to perform community service, its sole objective being to 'fit them to be better homemakers'" (2002, 72). My study of the FWI and Homecraft clubs indicates that community service was indeed a contentious issue—white women promoted it, but they found little interest in it among black women: under the yoke of colonial labor exploitation, many black women were more interested in making ends meet in their families than in helping unrelated others.

Yet on their own, black women did indeed form groups to benefit women and the community. Most popular was the Helping Hand club in Harare, which assisted newcomers to the city and looked after children of working women. The Federation of African Women's Clubs (now the AWC) was the most prestigious. In a 1954 Christmas message published in the magazine *African Parade*, the founder of the AWC pointed to women's role in shaping the nation: "Women of today have a great contribution to make towards the building of a great African race in Central Africa. You can do this by building up happy and ideal homes, help to improve the living conditions of the people around you, in the urban areas, in the mines, compounds and even on the farms, and so bring healthy families, prepared and educated to face the future under the British flag" (Barnes and Win 1992, 159). In addition to women working through the home to change society, women also "involved themselves in organized struggles for justice against the racist Rhodesian system" (154). These are all types of community service—helping women adjust to the city, building happy homes to promote racial uplift, and protesting against colonial injustice. These forms of community service were not about working together with whites. They did not meet the FWI goal of encouraging community service "to make partnership a living thing" (*Home and Country* 9 [1] [1962]).

White women in the FWI were not partners in welcoming black women's residence in cities and certainly not in political protest against the colonial regime. In fact, white women in the FWI were ambivalent toward black women settling in urban townships—on the one hand, they argued, having their wives in town could mollify male servants, but on the other, more African women in town could lead to more prostitution.

The Homecraft movement introduced new technologies in the care of self and family—innovations that were adapted and reimagined within a context of traditional practices. Traditional women's concerns with good behavior, marriage, long life, and healthy children made them interested in what white women had to offer on these subjects. Before colonialism and capitalism, before the FWI, women were concerned with their hygiene, appearance, and educating children. Women paid special attention to themselves and their bodies; they wanted to be clean as well as supple and shiny, presenting bodies that signified life, wet and fertile, using oils and ointments to convey attractiveness and readiness (see Burke 1996; Gelfand 1979). Long before missionaries and colonialists saw African women as a market for English gingham, unmarried women decorated their bodies with rows of necklaces and bracelets and hung beaded belts over their skirts of cured animal skins. Married women had to forego some of the decorations as they went through their household duties, which in child rearing mostly consisted of teaching children the proper ways of eating, talking, sitting, and greeting elders. Older girls were taught how to smear floors so that they would shine and to sweep the dusty ground outside the house in recognizable patterns. In addition to gathering firewood and hauling water from rivers and streams, they were also taught to grind grains and peanuts, to butcher small animals for meals, and to cook the staple porridge and relishes. While deviations were not punished except in the case of willful disobedience, young people were taught that there were right and proper ways of doing things, of interacting with people, and of presenting themselves to the world. Engaging in proper domestic behaviors and transmitting them to younger generations were the very stuff of everyday life. It was that life that colonialism disrupted, that white colonial women wanted to shape in their own image, and that African women, making their way under conditions of oppression and opportunity, reimagined.

Instead of domestic clubs drawing African women away from their community-wide interests, I suggest that the clubs tapped into women's personal and domestic concerns and through that interest pulled women out of the home and into new communities. The self/other and housewife/community binaries that fueled earlier arguments obscure the complexity of the situation: through the development of self and the cultivation of home, some women gained a public voice. Homecraft goals for the individual woman—to enhance her hygiene, appearance, and confidence—were congruent with those of many African women, even including the FWI's stance against polygamy.[5] Moreover, similar to other colonial enterprises that attempt to maintain racial segregation and police sexual boundaries, the clubs' overarching social goal was to improve health care and sanitation (see Stoler 2002). This was to be accomplished through white and black women working together, by white women doing their civic duty and embracing the narrative of progress.

The FWI's ideal relationship between domesticity and nation was foreshadowed in the title of its journal, *Home and Country*. From the FWI's point of view, the home reproduces, maintains, and validates social and labor relations in the wider world. To the FWI, the nuclear family home is not separate and isolated from the larger social sphere, but constitutes the social machinery that produces material signs by which a man demonstrates his status outside the home and, in some respects, is a measure of the value of his labor. But the public, the community, in this instance, is not just economic but also political. As the British Empire began to crumble and African states gained independence, white women in colonial Zimbabwe felt themselves called upon to work for the maintenance of the colony. In one sense, the domestic was a tool of the political, a form of governmentality, used to change the habits of daily life and thereby African attachment to the colonial powers. Moreover, the discourse of federation required that the public face of the majority black population show not only labor market viability but also domestic tranquility and progress.

But Shona peoples had different ideas of community and its relationship to home. For them, the home was always a part of a larger whole—physically, economically, politically, and spiritually. In English, "village" was the term used to describe the compound where a patrilineal extended family lived—usually elderly parents, their married sons with their wives and children, and their unmarried daughters and sons. Descendants of remote male ancestors might live near one another and would come together to celebrate weddings and funerals, to communicate with the ancestors, and to settle disputes. Though people could not trace genealogical ties to others who shared the same totem—for example, birds, crocodile, elephant—this symbolic association grouped individuals across geographic divides. Land was often a common good and allocated by chiefs to male heads of household. Land tied men together, but women would typically leave their homes at marriage. They were outsiders in their husbands' villages until they became mothers of sons. Physical and spiritual well-being as well as the exercise of the rights and responsibilities of place and person derived from kin and ancestral connections to land.

By bringing adult women together in groups that cut across family and kin lines, in groups not directly related to their totems and ancestral connection to the land, and in groups whose explicit agenda was their activities as women, Homecraft broadcasts and classes disrupted traditional patterns. African women in Homecraft clubs learned homemaking skills that they displayed in formal and informal competition, but they also gained mobility, could leave their homes to meet with other women, and shared their grievances as women and as colonial subjects. The oral history *To Live a Better Life* (Barnes and Win 1992), which covers the lives of fifty-two women who lived in Harare from as far back as 1920, details women's sense of accomplishment in simply being able to leave the company of kin to go to the meetings. Before the colonial period, respectable women were homebound; women who moved around were often called "prostitutes." Just being able to leave their homes to meet with other respectable women created a feeling of new possibility and extended a sense of community (Barnes and Win 1992, 153–68). For those in Homecraft clubs, domesticity was a way of making community.

Community also had to be constructed among whites in the colony. Not all whites were equally welcomed or accepted in Southern Rhodesia (see Mlambo 2002; Schwartz 2011). Class and ethnic differences were there at the beginning when settlers from South Africa, led by Cecil Rhodes and the British South Africa Company, attacked and tricked Africans into ceding land to them for mines and farms. British and Afrikaners, who had been enemies in two wars in South Africa, were in the pioneer column of colonialists and were joined by Portuguese and Greek immigrants among others, but Rhodesia became a British colony where British culture and institutions predominated. Nonetheless, differences based on country of origin and ethnicity threatened the unity of the white community.

The imagined community of Rhodesian nationalism was spurred by female novelists, for example, Gertrude Page (1907) and Cynthia Stockley (1903, 1911, 1923), whose search for identity in the new territory began to articulate a Rhodesian identity separate from South Africa, Britain, and the British South Africa Company. Important in this identity-making process was the search for mastery over the land and people. White pretensions of mastery over blacks helped to bring whites together and also blinded them to the existence of people living on the land. From the women's point of view the land was empty and full of possibility—to them, black people were "de-created": the writers de-peopled the land to realize the nationalist visions that depend on childbearing and nurturing colonial women (Chennells 1982). Not all white women shared in this ideal of white freedom to create a new Eden in a depopulated Africa; missionaries and women associated with the church engaged African women in prayer and mothers' clubs in the church for generations. But a major task for ordinary white women was building community among themselves, not reaching out to blacks. In Rhodesia, women protected their prestige on "islands of white" that they helped construct and whose rules of exclusion they enforced (see Kennedy 1987).

The incursion into the public domain through Homecraft marked a new direction for the FWI, a social club turned to civic responsibility. Middle-class British women extended their sense of community to include African women in subordinate positions. Homecraft opened a space for white women, as women, to make major contributions to Rhodesian nationalism through community service. With the beginning of Homecraft, white women in the FWI defined home as an area of scientific knowledge, finely articulating the steps in sweeping, washing, and rinsing clothes, putting into words their understanding of child care, and teaching how to organize and run meetings. The domestic skills that many white women may have taken for granted—they certainly were not used every day, since most white women had one or more domestic servants—now amounted to knowledge that could help build a hegemonic consensus about how "to live a better life."

Within the secular domain, colonial exercise of power over the persons and homes of African women led to the systematization of domestic knowledge for white settler women. The detailed African domestic syllabus bears the mark of substantial analysis of household labor, and the rigor of the syllabus contributed to a sense of professionalism for the white women who wrote the curriculum. They saw themselves as providing a community service, and at the same time, they must have seen themselves as able representatives of what, only upon analysis, proved to be intricate and specialized knowledge. This knowledge was generated, or, at the very least, made explicit, as part of the mobilization of colonial power to ameliorate native life and bolster the civilizing claim of the European settlers, while holding African nationalism on the brink.

African Women and the Homecraft Movement

Joining women's organizations marked an innovation for the majority of African women from Shona ethnic groups, who historically had participated only in ad hoc groups, not ones that were named or perdurable. The FWI Homecraft Clubs were not the first African women's organization in colonial Zimbabwe, but they were the most widespread and the most popular. Homecraft more fully articulated the new standards of order, cleanliness, and propriety that had already been insinuated by church groups, schools, and government outreach. African women became attached to these new ways of being and "were active agents in forging new conceptions of gender roles" through the church and other clubs (West 2002, 73).

As African women gathered in groups to be taught their latest lesson, they also learned how to work with one another and to use their voices to speak for women. Shona women did not historically form groups of women for women, though women's friendships and networks of kin and neighbors provided opportunities for shared labor, empathy, and emotional catharsis.[6] Contrast this to the men's *dare*, a place set aside in each homestead for men to socialize as well as a meeting to hear and adjudicate disputes. Women who lived near one another might gather in the kitchen of a senior woman and might jokingly call their meeting the women's *dare*, but they and the men knew of the limited authority and reach of their actions (see Mano 2004). Being organized in groups does not necessarily mean that women will exercise power in their society, just as not having groups does not mean that they are powerless. The existence of groups could mean that women's opinions, so labeled, could be more decisively dismissed (see Steady 2006, 8). What we do know about women in organized groups in other parts of Africa is that such groups allow women to build cohesiveness, acquire specialized knowledge, and express their will. Women in age-grades and secret societies function as organic intellectuals in the conscious organization of and reproduction of social life.[7]

The first formal women's groups in Zimbabwe came with the introduction of Christianity, when, in addition to prayer groups, women gathered in groups centered on home management, nutrition, child care, hygiene, and needlework (see Muchena [1980] 1984). West's *Rise of an African Middle Class: Colonial Zimbabwe 1898–1963* is a prime source for my discussion here of pre–World War II women's groups (2002). The Manyano-Ruwadzano movement was initiated by African women as the Women's Prayer Union of the Wesleyan Methodist Church around 1925. In it, women read the Bible, prayed, shared recipes, and traded tips on child care, home remedies, and sewing; they also preached the gospel and kept the missions alive (Ranger 1995, 42; Hinfelaar 2001). Manyano-Ruwadzano groups were exclusive to church members and restricted to married women.[8] When these groups spread to other churches and across the country, missionaries placed white women, wives of leaders, at the head of the groups. To the extent that church groups were comprised of women who had accepted Christian standards but still felt obligations to kin, they provided support and solace for those who, "between a rock and a hard place and in desperation, turned to each other for help" (West 2002, 74). West concludes that the colonial state invested in a domesticity-building program in the 1920s to thwart the rise of an urban African middle class and to encourage a rural version of the bourgeois domestic ideal (71). In Homecraft, we see a similar investment coming from civil society to halt the rise of independence movements as Britain ceased to be a colonial power. Outside churches, African women also organized groups on their own; members tended to be educated urban women married to important men—chiefs and other functionaries in the colonial administration. Savings associations where women took turns receiving the pot of members' contributions or could withdraw savings for funerals and other special occasions were among the first secular women's clubs. A segregated Girl Scouts program came to colonial Zimbabwe in 1926 in the form of Wayfarers and Sunbeams instead of Scouts and Brownies; in 1935, there were six hundred Wayfarers and three hundred Sunbeams (West, 71).

African women in towns organized community support groups as well as political groups. Women, who had to fight colonial restrictions on their movement from rural areas to cities, formed groups that extended a helping hand to those suffering from a broken society: abandoned and illegitimate children, children of working mothers, and visiting women (rural wives and relatives of urban workers who periodically joined their loved ones in town, often breaking the law to do so) (Barnes 1999). With a glaring absence of women in labor unions, women organized the Harari Employed African Women's League and eventually did enter the men's labor and trade unions and join with them in labor strikes, bus boycotts, and township rights movements.

In a study of women's groups in Zimbabwe's capital city during the period 1930–56, the following goals of the groups were identified: "first, to support the transfer of formal political power from white male to black male hands; second, to support the improvement of working conditions and salaries for

Figure 1. Women in church uniforms, Harare, around 2005. Photo by Nubra Floyd.

waged women; third, to improve the ability to display ever more finely honed domestic skills" (Barnes 1999, 161). The Women's Leagues of political parties meet the first goal and the women's labor unions, the second. Homecraft clubs fall into the third category, but in their case I would rephrase the goal. Women in these groups wanted to enhance their reputations as respectable women through the display of domestic skills, but also to improve their families' well-being, support other women, and boost the standing of African women in the colonial context.

The Homecraft movement, which spread across the three countries of the Central African Federation, marketed commodities (especially soaps, detergents, and skin creams), introduced women to new skills, developed new dispositions and sensibilities, and brought women together in new groups.[9] Radio Homecraft Clubs flourished throughout British central Africa in the 1950s. African women gathered together to listen to these programs, which were produced in cooperation with the government's Native Affairs Department. Even into the early 1970s, an estimated 10 percent of the total female adult population belonged to Homecraft clubs (Ranchod-Nilsson 1992, 196). Radio Homecraft Clubs were very often made up of only black women, but white teachers/demonstrators sometimes made presentations to the clubs in community centers. With the success of the clubs, black women became teacher/demonstrators. The impulse "to live a better life," to capture the rewards of civilization, was a sentiment shared by upwardly mobile black men and women who saw themselves as above the untutored masses.[10] Members of this class included educated men and women, especially teachers, nurses, and office workers, as well as wealthy farmers, merchants, and traders. Those with the highest education were the most esteemed.

For black women, Homecraft demonstrated that higher education was not necessary for upward mobility; an improved standard of living was possible for all willing individuals. To the dismay of the FWI, some black women used their newfound skills in income-generating projects, in an effort to provide for their children and families and to improve their standing in communities. But many black women in the Homecraft movement used their knowledge to demonstrate that they were responsible and respectable women (see Hinfelaar 2001). I like to compare African women's acceptance of the tenets of the Homecraft syllabus to emergent middle-class men's desire to be recognized and respected over and above the "raw native," as "civilized men."[11] Competency in domestic arts might have revealed the imprint of colonial hegemony, but it also made them respectable, civilized women.

Domesticity, of the sort that included tea, flowers, hand-knitted sweaters, well-scrubbed children, and salaried husbands, was a satisfying goal sought by a wide swath of African women, not just the educated and well married. Through its radio program and its traveling demonstration classes, Homecraft was available to the masses, not the exclusive purview of a rural or urban middle class. The lure of domesticity caught women, playing on their desire to see themselves as attractive, respectable wives and mothers. But the desire for a better life pulled women out of their homes into classes and clubs where they bonded with others and began to voice their interests in social as well as political issues.

Colonialism placed black women in many kinds of publics. Most overwhelming was the public universe of the money economy, waged employment, labor migration, and commodity consumption. But crosscutting ties formed in mission churches and schools, in a community of believers or a community of acquiescence, were also important. Before colonialism, Shona individuals seldom interacted with men and women outside their kin group, and women sustained few relationships beyond kin. In interviews with women NGO officers at the turn of the twenty-first century, I found that many women still harbor suspicion of non-kin. Several NGO officers spoke of the problems of organizing women into groups for self-help or community development. That people were afraid of witchcraft, more explicitly of the harmful effects of jealousy and envy, was high on their list of the problems they faced organizing in rural areas. Few women trusted working with others to whom they were not related. In the NGO Associated Women of Zimbabwe (AWZ), the subject of chapter 3, the officers I talked to did not find witchcraft beliefs to be a major problem but complained of the breach between married and single women: some married women would not participate in workshops with single women or unmarried mothers. To me, this suggests that there was little cultural foundation for getting unrelated women together in a cooperative endeavor. In a study of social life among farmworkers on a Zimbabwean commercial farm, Blair Rutherford (2004) discusses the near collapse of a literacy program that brought together married women and single women, some of them mothers—the married women refused to sit in a classroom with the single women, whom they called whores and prostitutes. In later chapters, I further discuss the enmity between married and single women.

Here I would like to ponder for a moment the pervasiveness of the fear of witchcraft, in order to examine what women had to overcome to work with strangers. Witchcraft accusations are a kind of boundary maintenance—establishing who is a member in good standing of a community and who is outside—and a leveling mechanism, targeting the people in extreme positions of power and wealth. Witchcraft requires no acts; its medium is jealousy and envy. Finding a witch is similar to a scapegoating process in which one person is made to bear the burden of the community's grief or despair. Generally, the person pointed out as a witch stands at one or the other ends of society: the high and mighty or the down and out. Though women who are outsiders in their husbands' homesteads are more likely to be called witches than are men, both men and women can be accused of being witches. Such was the case in Zimbabwe. Sometimes a person might go to a *n'anga* for protection against witchcraft, but generally the best protection is to avoid strangers, to try to blend in as much as possible, to not bring attention to yourself because of your accomplishments or your poverty.

The strength of witchcraft beliefs today as well as in the past leads me to speculate that despite having positions available to them outside the kin groups, Shona women, from fear of either harm or loss of social standing, preferred to have little truck with unrelated women and consequently had much to overcome

Figure 2. A *n'anga*, member of the National Traditional Healers Association, at Chapunga Sculpture Garden, a popular tourist destination in Harare, 2000. Photo by author.

in joining with others. The Homecraft movement, instead of deepening the isolation of individual women in their households, brought women together in ways that broke habitual patterns and opened the way to their forming groups of women and for women.

The Kitchen Tea

I am arguing not that it is necessary to have named groups or long-lasting organizations in order for women to come together, but that such groups can be effective in establishing solidarity among women, particularly when fear of unrelated people thwarts contact outside one's own kin group. At this point, I would like to turn the tables on the position I have been taking up until this moment—studying the forces that led women to join named and enduring groups—to examine an event of passing significance. I argue that this event, the Kitchen Tea, mobilizes women's cultural knowledge about who should participate with whom on which occasions in order to bring women together for a celebratory event in honor of a bride. Congregations of people, whether brought together for weddings, funerals, work parties, or communication with the ancestors, have recognizable forms, and particular people or types of people are expected to participate. In other words, the ideology and practices in Shona areas lead to discourses that identify types of subjects for different kinds of activities. What this meant for Shona girls and women is that they intersected with other girls and women as their daily tasks coincided, such as going to the river at around the same time, in contingent work parties, on ritual occasions, and in activities keyed to the agricultural or weather seasons. One type of occasion that brings women together to celebrate their common interest is the Kitchen Tea, an amalgam of British and central African customs in celebration of a bride-to-be. I'll take a moment to discuss this event and its informal grouping of women because the Kitchen Tea is one of those moments when women are taught how to be good, modern wives and homemakers.

A cross between a bachelorette bash and a tea party, the Kitchen Tea is a modern hybrid invention brought to Zimbabwe by immigrants from neighboring Malawi and Zambia, probably in the 1950s. The place-names connote the independence of women in matrilineal society and the mobility of women who have left their natal countries. Unlike at a bachelorette party, attendees at the Kitchen Tea should be married women, though that rule is not enforced at all parties. Kitchen Teas began in urban townships and spread throughout the country, though the parties occur more often in cities than in rural areas. Little African customary ritual remains in this raucous women's gathering, though I assume that forty years ago this was not the case. I write here about the feeling of freedom women have in these gatherings, their degree of suspicion of others, and the nature of the advice given to the bride-to-be, especially as it relates to the Homecraft goals for the individual: improved hygiene, appearance, and confidence.

When the daughter of my housekeeper was getting married, I was asked to host a Kitchen Tea for her in the University of Zimbabwe apartment that I shared with my husband; he was away at the time of the party. I agreed to host the party before I knew much about what it entailed. Once I said yes, I immediately started asking others about what I was letting myself in for. I talked with two secretaries at the university, two women administrators, one businesswoman in middle management at a large firm, and one woman reporter. I was told that women drink to excess and drink to get drunk, and I heard rumors (no one admitted to actually seeing this) that women stripped and danced naked. The businesswoman reassured me that things would go well if I started the evening with a prayer. A university administrator said that some prayers are dangerous: she heard one that went: "Dear Lord, thank you for *umm umm* [sex, sex organs].... That's good." Another woman said that everything would be fine if the bride's mother-in-law was at the party: neither the bride's friends nor her mother's friends would do anything to jeopardize that relationship. The problem lay in having strangers at the party; then things could get out of hand. I asked a neighbor who is a university lecturer and the mother of teen-aged girls to say the opening prayer and hoped for the best.

The Kitchen Tea started out with a ritual presentation of the bride, who was covered in a sheet and led from the bedroom by a senior cousin from her mother's side, as the mother-in-law-to-be and assembled guests looked on. After she was unveiled, a sedate prayer followed and then the gift giving. Each gift was to be wrapped in a dish towel—if not, then the giver must pay a small fine in cash. The dish towel designates the wife, who drapes a dish towel over her left shoulder before she kneels in front of her husband with a basin of water for him to wash his hands before a meal. The bride was given each towel-wrapped gift in turn and asked to guess what it was. This was a test of the bride's and the guests' modernity—she was supposed to know how to outfit a modern kitchen and to be embarrassed to show ignorance (Mate 2002). When she did not guess correctly, she had to take a drink of wine or beer and do a little dance. As the evening progressed, the bride's drinks were more than sips, and her dancing less controlled. The next morning, a dignified bride led her very pleased mother-in-law through a survey of the gifts.

After the gifts were opened, one by one the assembled married women gave advice to the bride. The advice concentrated on her relationship to her in-laws: "Treat all aunties the same" (paternal aunts on both sides are powerful), "give water to your husband's relatives" (take care of them), "be happy at home with your mother-in-law" (both get along with her and do not complain about being left alone with her while your husband is out). From a study of Christian women's groups, Rekopantswe Mate (2002) found that brides were told to obey their husbands when the husbands pursue a godly path, omitting blanket advice to always cater to the husband's wishes. Here the bride was advised to manage her time well, not try to keep up with the neighbors, and "don't ask your husband where he is going." Much of the advice was about sexuality. The minister who had offered the opening prayer urged the bride to insist on her own sexual satisfaction: "Men are like light switches [quickly on and off]; women like irons [slow heating]." Other women seconded the notion that women deserve sexual pleasure in marriage. One well-dressed middle-aged woman, one of the last to speak, advised the bride to "look as good as the mistress." She should be meticulous in her hygiene, take care of her hair, and dress as well as her husband's girlfriend.

After the advice came the dancing. By the end of the night, women were drunk and dancing with sensual abandon. Word had gotten out about the Kitchen Tea, and a couple of women whom the family did not know had come; the guests that I had invited also did not know who they were. These women set the stage for a rowdier event than any of us had anticipated. Fortunately for the bride, her in-laws had left before the most shocking acts were committed. This involved dancing, not a striptease, but carried away with the sensuality of the moment, I ended up almost lying on the floor (in a contorted position that surprised even me) with my dance partner gyrating just inches above my body. Later the bride's younger sister, one of the few unmarried women at the party, wondered why I had videotaped the gift giving and advice portion of the evening and not the dancing. "That was the best part," she said.

In the gift giving, in the advice to the bride, and in the sensual abandon that can only come when women are alone, patriarchy was alive and well at this Kitchen Tea. Comparing notes with a university administrator who had attended the Kitchen Tea at my invitation, I was told that her daughter's Kitchen Tea had been more "modern"—fewer admonitions about proper conduct toward the husband's relatives and more advice to be her own person. Office workers I interviewed in the city said that they enjoyed the Kitchen Teas and the Kitchen Top-Up (similar to a housewarming party, these are held to furnish a modern kitchen). These wild parties were not considered antithetical to proper Christian behavior; a couple of women mentioned them along with baby showers (these also include drinking and dancing) as treasured outings. An example of a cooperative innovation in Kitchen Teas comes from a secretary I interviewed who is a member of a Zimbabwean apostolic church and goes to services with her husband and children three times a week. She belongs to a ladies' circle: "Like a social club whereby we form a club, say four or five people, then we buy some kitchen equipment or gadgets for every one of us. We take turns to buy. Everybody chooses what she wants; then we buy for her." The party where they give the gifts includes beer and music: "I invited all the ladies from my workplace, my friends from church. We had a nice time. They gave me presents for the kitchen, for the whole house, anything. And we had drinks and beer. There was music and dancing. It was quite nice."

A 1992 article in the government-funded *Herald* about a Kitchen Tea among women richer and better placed than those I hosted or interviewed describes the event as an "excuse to eat, drink heavily and be merry, a time to show their true colours, doing things their husbands would shudder to imagine." With the party going from two in the afternoon until six, when the women go home to have dinner with their husbands, women came in their prim business suits and changed to skimpy party dresses and, for one company manager, into a "clinging mini-skirt, lace stockings and high-heeled shoes." As in the party I described, women gave presents, advised the bride, and danced: "The only form of dance allowed at kitchen parties is that from the waist down, pelvis wriggling and suggestive [of] sexual acts."[12]

A popular talk-radio program hosted by an outspoken woman broadcaster compared the Kitchen Tea favorably to men's bachelor parties: Kitchen Teas are educational; at Teas women talk about what marriage is really like; they assist in preparing the bride for marriage; and they have fun. The radio broadcaster also warned that women should not take advice from drunks at a Kitchen Tea, just as men should not follow the advice of drinking buddies at a bachelor party. Overwhelmingly, women callers said that they wanted a night out because men do not take their wives out. The Kitchen Tea, baby showers, and the Kitchen Top-Up are the only times that women can have fun (as men do at nightclubs, with alcoholic beverages, music, and dancing, situations where wives typically are excluded). Some men and women callers complained that Kitchen Teas "bring out frustrations and contribute to the breakup of marriages" because they allow women to give voice to their complaints, compare themselves to others, or let others "stick their noses where they don't belong."

Though the advice given at Kitchen Teas is more explicitly sexual than the lessons of Homecraft in earlier generations, examining this advice points to a convergence of interests of black and white women in the Homecraft movement in contributing to the success of their husbands: women should pay attention to their appearance and hygiene, they should not detract from their husbands' endeavors, and they should take care of the family. The Kitchen Tea is a party, a coming together of people, this time women in supposed relationship to the bride-to-be. It is an ephemeral event, like the work parties where women gossip and tell their stories, and here the emotion and excitement of the moment intensify the homemakers' lessons.

The Kitchen Tea, a recurring transitory event, is an excellent example of the discourses, ideas, and practices that motivate Shona dispositions. Shona women's quotidian routines, rather than leading them to create perdurable groups, instead institutionalize the disposition to gather as needed, and to collect individuals from predictable social categories, for the occasions and problems that shape Shona conditions of existence. My thesis, derived from Bourdieu's explication of habitus as generative principles that organize practice, is that Shona women were disposed to seek hierarchy in the midst of sameness, to distrust others even while honoring them, and to suffer their liminal status in the families into which they married.[13] In the Kitchen Tea, the superordinate mother-in-law's presence or absence shapes the kind of language and behavior deemed acceptable among women; guests are invited and treated well, but the stranger poses a threat to the bride's dignity, and the bride and her family are constantly reminded that they are outsiders to the husband's family. While disposing women to think of the social world as open to many possible aggregations of people, Shona generative principles also closed down possibilities, excluded participants, and separated status groups as women displayed respect and deference to superordinates, asserted privilege and exercised power over subordinates, and were on the lookout for witches and other indications of harmful occult powers.

Outside organized groups, events like the Kitchen Tea, a colonial innovation, shaped new sensibilities in Shona women while maintaining some old ones. A similar process was at work in Homecraft and other women's groups. Women who gathered in groups experienced consciousness-raising as they learned that what they had thought were personal problems were felt by other women. As one leader put it, she started Homecraft "because getting together made [women] ask questions without fear." She explained, "Those who couldn't speak English would say, 'I have such and such a problem.' It was very helpful. That's how we started clubs. I started the Radio Homecraft Club in 1952 because of some things we didn't like. We said, 'Let's get together'" (Barnes and Win 1992, 155). They wanted to learn organizational skills, to be group leaders; they wanted adult education; they wanted to earn incomes. I argue that as women learned domesticity, they also learned to articulate their desires, to organize, and to act in concert across internal lines of differentiation. Old and young, married and unmarried, employed and unemployed, nurses and street vendors, women from chiefly lineages and peasants came together to learn and to speak.

The FWI and African Women

Zimbabwe is like other settler colonies in Africa in that when white women began arriving in large numbers, one of their first tasks was to bring "civilization" to white men. White women as a whole strengthened the color bar, established dress codes, created home as refuge and status symbol, and forced interracial sexual liaisons and their products into hiding. As individuals, Southern Rhodesian white women found themselves isolated on large tracts of farming or ranching land. To ensure companionship and for the betterment of their community, British women began a chapter of the International Federated Women's Institutes in 1927. The Women's Institutes Movement, at that time popular in the United Kingdom and Canada, was brought to Southern Rhodesia by the wife of the colony's prime minister and retained an association with elite or aristocratic white women.[14] FWI aims were broad: "to create happiness, contentment and interest for its members"; to make "better homes, housewives and mothers"; to engage "public questions, world affairs, and national problems"; and to satisfy women's "desire for art, music, and literature" (*Home and Country* 1 [1952]: 4). Much of the content of their members' journal, *Home and Country*, concerns branch meetings throughout the colony and the activities of affiliated groups in other parts of the British Commonwealth, as well as book reviews, recipes, personal profiles, and articles for and about children. One of their major achievements, a history of Southern Rhodesia in embroidery, was still on display throughout several rooms in the Zimbabwe National Museum in Bulawayo two decades after independence.

White women, who shared white supremacist ideologies with colonial men, did not always see black women as potential allies. In its earliest journals, 1936–40, the FWI actively engaged the "native question," though in most instances the "native" in question was the African male domestic servant. Commentary in the journal ran a familiar circuit from expressions of the duty of whites to educate the natives to the fear that European culture ruins Africans to renderings of Africans as a "child race," with no sense of dignity or joy in work.[15] Concern with African men working in white homes surfaced in the 1930s. A report of the Native Interest Committee in 1938 raised alarm about venereal disease appearing in little white girls "from servants taking liberty with them" and about small white boys learning masturbation from natives (*Rhodesia Home and Country* 1 [1938]: 3). In order to protect themselves, the FWI took the advice of the East African Women's League, which laid down the following guidelines for white women in the presence of African male servants: be fully clothed, curtail conversation when servants are at table, make no pictures of nude European women available to servants, never leave European children in the unrestricted care of natives, and master the native language (*Rhodesia Home and Country* 1 [1938]: 3).

The FWI journal in the 1930s carried debates on the merits of black women versus black men as servants and found black men far better: black men might represent a peril to the persons of white women (white panic about the fear of rape by black men is referred to as "the black peril"), but black women represented a greater danger to the home.[16] White women were more threatened by the sexuality of African women than that of African men: this fear is sometimes called the "yellow peril," referring to the children of white men and black women, or the "white peril," referring to the white men themselves. Rather than protecting their purity from African men, white women wanted to keep African women away from their husbands.[17] The FWI, in the 1930s, shared white men's views of African women's sexuality: "Their passions were stronger. They have more of the animal about them in sexual matters" (Schmidt 1992b, 234). In their efforts to keep African women away from their husbands, FWI members considered importing European servants and investing in labor-saving devices (McCulloch 2000, 104–6). A decade earlier, white women in Southern Rhodesia had already been defeated in trying to criminalized cohabitation between white men and "native women." Now members of the FWI seriously deliberated whether to promote the hiring of African women as domestic workers. Some thought that black women were cleaner, more conscientious, and more tractable than black men, but most white women did not want African women as domestic servants.[18]

Issues of the *Home and Country* journal reveal FWI members' ambivalence about the relationship between black and white women. Up until 1947, the major intervention in government policy that unarguably can be credited to this group had been an attempt to stanch the flow of black women to the cities, by pushing for the 1936 amendment of the Natives Registration Act requiring African women to petition their parents or guardians and those guardians to obtain authorization of a chief or senior colonial administrator before African women or girls would be permitted to go to towns to stay (Schmidt 1992b, 229–30). The law, an effort to limit the African population in towns, is widely cited as a prime example of the collaboration of black and white patriarchy under colonialism: male African elders colluded with colonialists to maintain their control over women and girls, while colonial officials wanted to make sure that Africans did not make stable homes in the urban areas.[19] Black women risked arrest and being sent back home if they were caught in townships without the proper consent forms. They had to be married and visiting or employed to legally reside in the city. Protesting against this policy was among women's first political acts.[20]

A 1939 report of the FWI Standing Committee on Native Interests came out against employing African women in domestic service, concluding that they would benefit little from social uplift and European contact, that they could not adjust to men's new ways of being—keeping a schedule, mastering new appliances and utensils, presenting a docile demeanor, and speaking English—and that permitting more native women in urban areas would increase prostitution (*Rhodesia Home and Country* 1 [1939]: 4). A year later, the Native Interest Committee exhorted FWI members to "honestly face their obligation to African women" and address the need for "further education of African women, for their own people, for the Europeans" (*Rhodesia Home and Country* 1 [1940]: 5). This obligation was referenced in the pages of the journal through articles on agricultural outreach, the increasing enrollment in Wayfarers (black Girl Scouts), hostels for mixed-race girls, and women's clubs for African women. The FWI had existed for about twenty years before it began working directly with African women.

Federation and White Rhodesian Nationalism

In 1947, the Federated Women's Institute of Southern Rhodesia created Homecraft clubs to co-opt African women, as a pathway to social stability and colonial hegemony. The British South Africa Company had come to this territory in 1888; it became the self-governing British colony of Rhodesia in 1923, and the FWI was established in 1927. Why were they particularly interested in African women in 1947? What political situation prompted this move? I argue that the discourse of progress and partnership that marked what historian Terrence Ranger called the "golden age of participation" during the Federation prompted white women to cooperate with government in reaching out to black women. Southern Rhodesia, with little change in its restrictive laws regarding treatment of the native population, needed to showcase black progress in the face of African independence movements to the north.[21] Especially onerous were the land policies that, in an effort to get landless men into the labor force, restricted cattle ownership and grazing and tried to switch land allocation from common usufruct to private deed. In response to a backlash against these policies, the colonial government concentrated efforts on development of rural areas (see Schmidt 1992a). The Homecraft movement and government community-development programs dovetailed in trying to shape the sensibilities and dispositions of the emergent middle class. This kind of governmentality, founded on the creation of a consensus about right livelihood and moral rectitude through which the Africans would discipline themselves, was aided by white women in the FWI's systematization of knowledge about home economics concomitant with their heightened sense of Rhodesian nationalism.[22]

To study the impact of the Federation and the changed environment of colonial Zimbabwe is to study the influence of an idea, one that was promulgated by whites trying to hold on to power as independence was blowing in the wind across the British Empire. White settlers in Southern Rhodesia, the largest white population in the three central African territories, saw the Federation as a partnership that would allow them to manage the wealth of the Northern Rhodesian (Zambian) copper mines, expand their markets into neighboring territories, and industrialize Southern Rhodesia. In earlier times, whites needed to demonstrate their control over those on whom they were most dependent; under the Federation, they endeavored to conceal their mastery but to express it nonetheless. Blacks in all three countries, present-day Zambia, Zimbabwe, and Malawi, opposed federation.

To make the Federation palatable in the age of independence, Rhodesians preached that it would increase African participation in government by extending voting rights according to scale of income and property ownership. The Zimbabwe National Archives contain many documentary films made during this period that extol the colony's bustling economy and the advances and modernization of African daily life. Of the attention given to the jobs, modern conveniences, and social life in townships, most notable was one segment that focused on a flower garden fronting a home in a row of township houses. The camera lingered approvingly on the image of the clean and crisply dressed housewife who had planted the garden; no visits were made to the crowded interior or to the water faucet and toilets shared by a block of flats. Appropriate care of home and garden—paint, not traditional geometric designs; flowers, not dirt swept into patterns and certainly not vegetables for the family's consumption—showcased participation in the advantages of colonialism.

So powerful was the idea of progress and partnership that some influential educated African urbanites and upwardly mobile country folk in colonial Zimbabwe became captivated by it—but not for long.[23] During the early part of the Federation period, civil society was marked by integrationist organizations that brought emergent middle-class African men together with white allies and mentors. White members of groups such as the Interracial Association of Southern Rhodesia and the Capricorn African Society scandalized other white Southern Rhodesians by receiving Africans in their homes, sharing food and drink, and holding joint meetings with them (see Hughes 2003). At the same time, more-militant blacks criticized the middle-class black "tea drinkers" who participated in these social gatherings as "stooges" and "sellouts" (see Hancock 1984, 41; David Moore 1991, 484). In a novel set during the federation period, journalist Bill Saidi (1988) portrays township residents who oppose federation for its lies and its continuation of violent and humiliating racial politics. His study of township life presents only three wealthy and ambitious characters and a few distant, unnamed Africans who sought the partnership federation promised. Though the integrationist groups tried to put forward a social contract that would provide better residential areas for blacks, open all jobs to every race, improve education, protect individual rights, and provide for a single, nonracial electoral roll based on a qualified franchise, no office or officer of government signed on. The Central African Federation (CAF) ended after Malawi and Zambia both gained independence from Britain in 1964. The Federation spurred blacks to labor activism and anticolonial movements.

The white minority in Southern Rhodesia reacted to the collapse of the Federation by declaring unilateral independence from Britain (UDI) and calling itself Rhodesia in 1965. While other countries around them achieved black majority rule, Ian Smith, prime minister of Rhodesia, insisted there would never be black majority rule in his lifetime, and "Never in a thousand years" became a rallying cry of his party, the Rhodesian Front. Internationally, this government was not recognized, and the United Nations imposed economic sanctions on the country. Internal resistance to white minority rule heated up in 1966, and two armies, roughly but not totally associated with the two African ethnic groups and allied with the Soviet Union and the Peoples' Republic of China during this Cold War period, fought to establish Zimbabwe as an independent black-ruled country. In an effort to reach a compromise, the white minority offered a power-sharing government called Zimbabwe-Rhodesia; it lasted less than the one calendar year of 1979. When apartheid South Africa stopped supporting Rhodesia, especially cutting off the land-locked country's access to South African roads, railways, and ports, Rhodesia accepted a cease-fire, and all the warring parties went to the negotiating table in December 1979. At Lancaster House in London, they hammered out the constitution of Zimbabwe, and Britain took control of the country in order to hand it over to the Zimbabwe African National Union (ZANU), which had achieved overwhelming success in the first election that allowed blacks equal vote. After years of mayhem, in 1987 the party later absorbed its archrival, the Zimbabwe African People's Union (ZAPU), and became known as ZANU (PF). From its inception, Robert Gabriel Mugabe has run Zimbabwe, first as prime minister and then as executive president.

Homecraft in War: Sticks and Scones

Zimbabweans fought for their liberation against the renegade regime led by Ian Smith and the Rhodesian Front. Returning to the story of black and white women working today, I take up what happened during the liberation war to black women who had been associated with groups run by white women.

I have been trying to show that the progressive rhetoric of the Federation period pushed African and European women in colonial Zimbabwe together: white women discovered homemaking as a base for civic participation; black women joined in to learn skills to help them live a better life and left with a greater sense of themselves as colonial subjects and as women. Black women did not become more isolated or withdrawn from the public with Homecraft training but rather found one more avenue for entering into wider civil society. This coming together in named women's groups marked a change in Shona habits of mind and practice. The very openness of Shona social life had disposed women to practices that exclude, close down, and separate them from other women. Black women who came together in Homecraft Clubs learned homemaking and organizational skills in bettering their homes and working lives and in maintaining their prestige as women of value. Homecraft groups also addressed pressing political issues. Sita Ranchod-Nilsson (1992) reports that some clubs began advocating for liberation from colonialism even before formal political parties began consciousness-raising in their area.

Interview data that I collected suggest that women club members did not unambiguously support the liberation struggle in 1966–79. Liberation forces waged guerrilla warfare against government security forces and the civilian population. From bases in neighboring countries, they made incursions into rural areas, attacking white farms and utilities and rallying black villagers. The balance of power in African villages was often upset by liberation forces: the armed force enlisted the help of young men and women, in combat, as lookouts and scouts, and as porters of food and other material. Turning the patrilineal gerontocracy on its head, the comrades in arms often advanced the case of youth, who had less to lose, against the older men who conventionally controlled the labor and movement of young men and women.[24] Similarly, men lost out to women who cooked food and carried loads, as the freedom fighters needed women's skills and resources more than that of the male heads of households.

In a show of the power of the revolutionary regime, comrades not only gave preference to women and the young, but rich and influential men were subjected to beatings by the liberation forces and/or the villagers.[25] Like many other villagers, JP/V fieldworkers, from the successor group of Homecraft, felt caught in the middle of competing armies, two nationalist armies and the government forces.[26] Some of the black women's groups voluntarily joined the liberation struggle, acting as the village committee that organized labor and resources for the liberation forces. Some were forced to cooperate, and others, as I will show, found their Homecraft skills useful in keeping them out of the fray.

Though the government had outlawed public assemblies, Homecraft club members continued to meet at bus stops, one of the few remaining places where members of the public could congregate, where they would exchange knitting instructions and patterns. When the liberation forces tried to stop gatherings other than their own, the women continued to meet. One woman I interviewed

Figure 3. Jekesa Pfungwa/Vilingqondo (JP/V) member, interviewed in its Harare headquarters, 2001. Photo by author.

put it this way: "ZANU was jealous and said that [we] should join them. They wouldn't let [us] meet. Women there were not happy or operating well because they were afraid, but we tried other means to do our work. Those who were still doing skills [would] cut out articles [from the Homecraft magazine and other sources] and carry them home [from the bus stops]. So we didn't have to spend the whole day [traveling and meeting]."

I asked a group of JP/V field-workers if their previous association with an organization run by white women had put them in jeopardy during the liberation struggle. In reply, they spoke of frequent visits to their areas by government and liberation forces, as have many rural women (see Staunton 1990; Kriger 1992; Kaler 1997; Nhongo-Simbanegavi 2000). When members of the liberation armies—commonly known as "the boys" or "comrades"—swept through their villages, these women were protected because of their skills and resources. Another JP/V fieldworker remembers it this way:

> I also gave credit to Homecraft because most of the clubs, we used to call them Homecraft Clubs, they didn't suffer much. If the comrades or if "the boys," as they called them, would get to a place where they would identify that there were Homecraft people or there were Homecraft women, they would not really be very harsh, but instead they would ask for scones or they would ask for children to bring them scones to the bush. So I think Homecraft played a part in the war, in a way. But in most cases it wasn't easy; it was very dangerous. You never know which group has come and for what. So it was very difficult. You wouldn't know

who to please. And in most cases there would be a group that would pass there. And then after that group, [another group would ask for food], if you give them food, after they have eaten, you would take a broom and sweep so that the next group wouldn't know what happened.

Homecraft members had ovens—three-legged, covered clay pots with charcoal placed on top, buried underground—in which they baked scones. A third JP/V fieldworker recalls, "At other areas they defended themselves by making scones, because those boys they liked scones too much. So those who were jealous they told those comrades that these people are given flour by Smith [the Rhodesian government].... So that time it was very, very difficult, it was. But we managed together to do what we wanted to do." Fresh baked goods caused suspicion; they caused some women to be beaten, but they also saved lives.

Why scones? It is my guess that scones as a prestige food represented part of what the battle was for, especially to the extent that nationalist sentiments began with members of the emergent middle-class who felt the brunt of racial discrimination as they acquired the trappings of Western civilization. "Forward with the cooking stick" was a slogan that ZANU liberation forces used to praise women's contributions to the liberation struggle (Nhongo-Simbanegavi 2000, 19). Most definitely the cooking stick, used to stir the thick cornmeal porridge that was the staple of the Zimbabwean diet, represented the greatest contribution of noncombatant women to the liberation struggle. And often the cooking stick must have prevented women from bearing the violence of the forces that tramped through their homesteads. But scones sometimes trumped the cooking stick, as women in Homecraft were singled out, not because they were sellouts, but because they could use the skills learned in Homecraft for the particular pleasure of the liberation forces.[27]

Nongovernmental, and especially nonnationalist, organizations came under attack toward the end of the war and after independence when the Women's League of the ruling party asserted its right to a monopoly on women's voices. About this period, the official history of JP/V states, "In the later years of the war, the ZANU Clubs (Women's League) were formed and the Women's Institute Homecraft members were forced, at local level, to join them and prohibited from continuing with their own clubs" (*Jekesa Pfungwa/Vilingqondo Newsletter*, special ed. [2]: 7).

The nationalists wanted to claim their voice, the government wanted to shut them down, but still they met. The JP/V fieldworkers faced imprisonment and worse by gathering at bus stops to share Homecraft materials. In one sense, they risked their lives for patterns, but in another, these were patterns of new lives.

The End of Homecraft

I became interested in the association between black women and white women in formal organizations in 1984, when, after I was interviewed on the radio in Harare about my work with a newly formed NGO (for which I am using the pseudonym Associated Women of Zimbabwe [AWZ]), I received an angry letter from a white woman proclaiming that our international, multiracial collaboration of women in AWZ was nothing new; white women had taught black women domestic skills in Associated Women's Clubs in Southern Rhodesia long before independence.[28] I was insulted that AWZ, which had taken a principled stand against the government's roundup and detention of women, was being compared to a domestic skills club. And I was angry that our mode of cooperation was likened to a teacher-student relationship. But I was intrigued by the history this correspondent pointed to and wanted to know more about the historical relationship between black and white women. It was not until I returned to Zimbabwe in 1999 that I completed a study on this subject, poring over the FWI journal in the National Archives and interviewing members and leaders of the FWI, JP/V, and the AWC. By that time, there was very little public association between black and white women's formal organizations. New white immigrants had come into the country with different political and economic agendas, and the aging FWI membership had drastically dwindled.

Even before Rhodesia became Zimbabwe, the FWI was on the decline. By 1966, the journal had lost its glossy pages and appeared in newsletter format, with the words "Contents Passed by Censor" stamped on the cover. The 1974–79 issues lament the loss of members as many women left the country, and one writer quips, "We need a liberation movement to liberate us from all of today's liberators" (*Home and Country*, 1974–79), a call for white solidarity as many were leaving the country. Book reviews, recipes, personal profiles, and articles for and about children still filled the pages, but items about security, petrol shortages, and news from members who had emigrated competed with them for space. As the liberation struggle lingered, a compromise Zimbabwe-Rhodesia was tried, and a successful cease-fire was negotiated. Through these changes, the Homecraft movement was still alive—the 1974–79 volumes report three new Land Rovers (British four-wheel-drive off-road utility vehicles) for Homecraft and donor support from the Dutch, Swedish, Canadian, and American embassies as well as from churches in the Netherlands and England. After independence, desktop publishing replaced mimeographed copies, and the topics covered were much less political and more social.

The FWI and Homecraft split into two unequal parts—Homecraft became JP/V, the present-day donor-funded agency that supports African women's income-generating projects—and the FWI was less a civic organization and more a social club. The name of Homecraft's successor organization, Jekesa Pfungwa/Vilingqondo ("Open your mind" in chiShona/siNedebele), came from a Homecraft slogan, emblazoned on the side of the group's Land Rovers. I heard quite different reports about the split from black and white women, and I am trying to understand the two ways that they see it. When I interviewed JP/V leaders, I left with the impression that the black women felt the split was not amicable. From their point of view, the white women felt betrayed, believing that black women had left when resources for white groups dried up and only blacks had the opportunity for more funds. Black women felt they had been reproached by the white women; blacks were ungrateful daughters. The president of the FWI said no such thing. According to her, the FWI realized that after independence few resources would come to their organization because of their white membership, and they encouraged Homecraft to breakaway, to become independent.

The president of the FWI recounted a final meeting in which one black woman after another came to the microphone, in tears, saying that the FWI was her mother and she did not want to leave, but the FWI said that the split was for the best. The kinship metaphor is significant in both versions: In the first, JP/V is the daughter, asserting independence and claiming agency. In the second, the FWI is the mother, claiming moral superiority in her sacrifice of self for her children. A tension that was a part of the Homecraft movement from the beginning is retold in the story of the split. From the beginning, white women worried that black women were using Homecraft not for community service and racial uplift but for personal profit and increased income. In fact, JP/V has become an organization that supports women who gather in self-generated groups to develop income-producing projects. Their staff helps with feasibility studies and organizational management and awards start-up monies from grants funded by international donor agencies. This is a different version of home and country than the FWI had promulgated, and one more in keeping with goals of women who feel the effects of the loss of social services, increases in unemployment, and insecurity of political and economic institutions. JP/V's model of home and country fits best with the women-in-development model that sees investment in women as one of the best ways to make sure that resources will be used to increase the viability of families and communities.

There was another solution to the problem of few resources going to women's groups with white leadership in a black country. Why not fold the FWI into Homecraft and make Homecraft the mother organization, with black leadership? As far as I can tell, this was not considered. Doing so would mean that the FWI would lose its affiliation with other Women's Institutes in British

Commonwealth countries. To do so would mean the reversal of colonial hegemonic relations. Some women's groups in Zimbabwe, without such a long colonial history, have incorporated white women into their membership and middle-management; even JP/V had a white woman in the central office in 1999–2000. But the women of the FWI are not active with JP/V; most left Zimbabwe even before its economic crash at the beginning of the twenty-first century.

Cruel Optimism

Was the Federation, the golden age of participation, rife with cruel optimism? No doubt about it. I don't think that whites believed their own propaganda about progressive change. Apartheid South Africa, for many the epitome of an independent white-minority-ruled country, kept Rhodesia going. Ian Smith, the leader of the Rhodesian Front, called South Africa's closing of its transport lines to land-locked Zimbabwe and its reneging on pledged financial support "the great betrayal" (1997). What colonialists were optimistic about was staving off African nationalism and the loss of the colony. The compromises they made whetted Africans' appetites for greater freedom and independence, but don't get me wrong: even without the golden age of participation, the end of colonialism was coming to central Africa. Like the flowers that grow around the doorways of houses in overcrowded African townships, the Federation was a showy promise of partnership that could not mask the states' injustices and deep inequalities.

Did Homecraft amount to cruel optimism? Was the way of life this movement seemed to offer black women impossible because of the racist capitalism of the colonial regime? Giving the benefit of the doubt to scholars who conclude that Homecraft created isolated housewives where there had been none, let's ponder whether the conditions of colonialism prevented black women in Zimbabwe from achieving the goal of homemaker and thereby prioritized their identities as wives, mothers, and housekeepers. Answering that query, I note that capitalism is notorious for exploiting women's unpaid labor in providing care and comfort to generations of workers. Any number of family arrangements can support capitalism: family members may be shared across households as in some Caribbean and African American areas; husband and wife may live separately as was the case in my early research in Kenya; and a nuclear family may be domiciled and sustained in one place, among other arrangements. The particular brand of racist capitalism found in Zimbabwe, a form of apartheid, reserved some jobs for whites only, segregated schools and residences, and paid low wages to African men because they supposedly had homes, farms, and family in the rural areas. By this reasoning, blacks were temporary workers in cities, mines, and industries and were sustained by their property in tribal areas. Colonialists subscribed to a program of separate development for the races, based on the idea of limited potential for black progress. But the economy of white Rhodesia, the very survival of the colony, was absolutely dependent on black labor, land, and markets. Separate development was a lie; it was a way of denying the privileges and resources of citizenship to blacks. This is the contradictory system in which black women tried to become homemakers in a new mold. Was their optimism misplaced?

The answer differs, in part, with a family's income level and the number of workers it includes. Many women whose husbands earned low wages knew right away that they needed to secure additional income. Women needed funds to pay school fees for their children's education; they needed to buy food, since village farms suffered from lack of labor and resources; and they wanted to buy kerosene lamps, among other new commodities, to provide light at night for children doing homework. For all these reasons, black women turned their cooking, dressmaking, and knitting skills into income-generating projects, upsetting FWI plans early on. Women in need also sought full-time employment in factories and in white households as domestic workers. They claimed some of the benefits of Homecraft in their attitudes toward home, but the work of supporting their families prevented the realization of the happy home life they sought. Lauren Berlant (2011) pictures cruel optimism as working toward the goal of a good life and wearing yourself out in the process, as well as striving for a satisfying goal when history and social conditions collude against you. Racism and capitalism insidiously permit many kinds of families and attainment of intermediate goals, but it can wear you out in trying to reach the ultimate goal of the good life, here considered as a happy marriage, healthy children, a well-appointed home, and long life. For many women, Homecraft brought cruel optimism.

Women at higher income levels, who were married to teachers or other salaried men or who were themselves teachers or nurses or earned a good salary, had greater leeway to achieve the good life. These well-provided-for women who sought respectability, refinement of taste, and new domestic skills could gain them through the Homecraft movement. The working wives hired and trained domestic workers, and as I will show in chapter 4, they also cooked and cleaned to show that they too were good women. On the face of it, for them Homecraft did not represent cruel optimism; they could rationally and reasonably expect to be seen as women of good repute and to attain a version of the good life.

So it seems that some women can attain the good life proffered by the Homecraft movement, while that life eludes many because their work to provide for families takes them away from the home and family they are attempting to nurture. Women with better financial resources and household help come closest to the satisfied-homemaker ideal. But that analysis is based on the premise that Homecraft was primarily about learning homemaking skills.

Now I would like to turn to what I think was really going on in Homecraft and pose the question: Did Homecraft as a break in Shona women's social habits amount to cruel optimism? In this chapter, I have argued that learning homemaking skills in Homecraft not only allowed women to achieve a better home life but also opened them up to engage and evaluate the world around them by traveling from home, meeting non-kin, and voicing their own desires. In other words, I have argued that the medium is the message. How women learned mattered as much as what they learned. In going to community centers and gathering around someone else's radio, women asserted themselves as mobile, as willing to join with others, and as desiring subjects. These were unintended consequences of the domesticity movement. Now I ask, was Homecraft as conceptualized as a rupture of Shona women's conventional orientations cruel optimism? Because I see the new attachments and orientations that women developed in Homecraft as a precursor to feminism, perhaps my answer will depend on whether I find the promise of feminism in Zimbabwe to be cruel optimism. Women were optimistic when they gained mobility, trust in others, and public voice. This optimism led to changes in the way they lived and what they wanted and brought along with it new opportunities as well as new insecurities. I am sure that the freedom, autonomy, and sociality fostered by Homecraft led at some moments to political depression—the feeling of despair, when things don't turn out right—as we will see in the following chapter. But on the whole, I believe that women were justifiably optimistic that things could and would get better.

CHAPTER 2

Flame, Nyaradzo, and Pretty

Black Women and Girls in Harare with Reason to Hope

> I don't know what people mean by a loose woman—sometimes she is someone who walks the streets, sometimes she is an educated woman, sometimes she is a successful man's daughter or she is simply beautiful. Loose or decent, I don't know.
>
> Tsitsi Dangarembga, *Nervous Conditions*

Zimbabwe is a relatively small country, occupying an area the size of the combined states of Kansas and Nebraska in the United States, with a population density of thirty-three people per square mile, similar to that of Kansas. The population, around thirteen million people in 2011, fluctuates with decreases caused by the AIDS pandemic (at its peak at the end of the twentieth century, it was estimated that one in five Zimbabweans between the ages of fifteen and fifty-four were infected; in recent surveys that number is down to 15 percent) and mass departure caused by economic decline (with one of the world's highest rates of inflation, deindustrialization, and collapse of agricultural production and markets, many people left for neighboring South Africa and farther afield).[1] Zimbabwe also saw two great influxes of people: in the 1980s after independence and after the formation of the 2009 unity government that promised an end to economic austerity and political violence. Due to a concentration of wealth at the top fostered by use of government connections and low wages and lack of employment at the bottom, overall inequality in the country has increased. For Americans living and working in the country as expatriates, though, there are few rungs in Zimbabwe's social ladder—fewer than six degrees of separation between people at the top and the bottom. For instance, I met a

Figure 4. A university graduate and her friends, Harare, 1984. Photo by Carol Bradshaw.

former vice president at a dinner party, shook hands with President Mugabe at the Book Fair, had a minister of state at my house for drinks, and took doctors, lawyers, professors, teachers, secretaries, gardeners, and housekeepers out to lunch. This chapter showcases some of the types of women in Zimbabwe's capital city that I got to know during my years in the country. In chapter 1, I discussed the rise of middle-class attachments, habits, and feelings among black women; those I introduce in this chapter—the war veteran, the working wife and mother, the feminist activist, and the beauty queen/model—can be their daughters; they are city women who come mostly from the middle class of Zimbabwean society.

A popular report on the Zimbabwean people at turn of the millennium, 1999–2000, based on a survey of five thousand people throughout the country conducted by a news magazine, identifies seven categories or classes in Zimbabwe, according to education, income, residence, occupation, ownership of property, and attitudes toward family and social change. People in the bottom two levels, 1 and 2, live in rural areas; have primary school education; are farmers; own farm animals, radios, and plows; and are wary of social change. The top two groups, 6 and 7, have completed secondary school, some have specialized training, and about a quarter have university degrees. Members of these two classes own cars, color televisions, satellite dishes, vacuum cleaners, and washing machines and have internet connections. They spend the least amount of time with family, go to church the least, welcome change, and "fewer men think they should have the final say."[2] The remaining three groups constitute the vast middle class—this is the group to which most of the women I discuss in this chapter belong. They have typically completed high school and live and work in cities; a large percentage of women in these groups who have graduated from high school have found employment in service sectors as cooks, housekeepers, child-care workers, retail clerks, and waitresses, or in government as nurses and teachers. Those in this grouping who are street vendors or market women or job seekers are not covered in my study. The range of income, from occupations in service, government, or industry, in this middle group is great, with individuals at its high end making a hundred times more than those at the low end. They own, at the low end, black-and-white televisions and hot plates, and at the high end, stoves, refrigerators, CD players, and video recorders; some have access to the internet. Most travel by bus or commuter omnibus; a quarter of them own cars. Both men and women in this mid-class group believe that "the man is boss" or "the man should run the family."

Women in the middle groups identified here predominate in my study of the promises of feminism in Zimbabwe. At the time of my field research in 1999–2001, they lived in the capital city in middle-class suburbs or in single-family homes in urban high-density suburbs. Typically they had completed the first level of high school or were in high school.[3] The adult women were gainfully employed, and most of the married women had children. Feminist activist professors and NGO directors whom I present in this chapter typically come from the highest echelons covered in the survey, though some feminist activists are deeply ensconced in the middle classes. (The chapter immediately following this one goes into greater detail on one feminist NGO.) Female war veterans come from all the levels: the women who gathered for adult education after the liberation war came from rural backgrounds, groups 1 and 2, but with training moved into the capital city's middle classes. Two of the women heroes of the liberation struggle are in the highest groups; one is vice president of Zimbabwe and the other, a former member of parliament (MP). On the whole, the beauty queens and models I discuss come from the vast middle class, from the two major cities, Harare and Bulawayo, though the father of one of these women is a managing director of the local headquarters of a multinational corporation and the other's father is a gardener.

The chapter covers three of the four types of women that are central to my study—female ex-combatants, feminist activists, and beauty queens and models.

I tell the story of the working wives and mothers in chapter 4; they epitomize middle-class lifestyles, virtues, and contradictions. Most of them make good salaries, live in single-family homes in low-density housing (former white or coloured suburbs), in apartments in the city center, or in outlying high-density suburbs (former African townships). To have been chosen to attend the National Secretaries Convention, where I got their names, suggests that they were recognized and distinguished at work. In interviews with them, I tried to grapple with their everyday lives at home and at work as well as their sense of themselves as women. I discuss them in passing in this chapter and take them up as a group in chapter 4. I call women who fall into this category "Mercy" or "Nyasha," the most popular female name in Zimbabwe. The name refers to the mercy or grace of God, who has delivered a healthy child; it also refers to moral qualities hoped for as the girl matures: compassion, forgiveness, and self-effacement. At work, she is not expected to aspire to the same professional status as men. If she does, she is immediately branded as unrespectable. Mercy here represents the working wife and mother who must negotiate between assertiveness and respect, containing herself so as not to be labeled ambitious or a prostitute.

In Zimbabwe, at the turn of the twenty-first century, most women represented in this chapter had reason to hope for a better future. I organize this discussion around three of four types based on popular names for women in Zimbabwe. The name "Flame" falls outside this norm of popular names; it is a nom de guerre taken by a female combatant in a Zimbabwean feature film of the same title. This "Flame" represents the women warriors, combatants in the liberation struggle who broke with tradition and who suffered for it, tripping on the contradictions between men as warriors and women as nurturers. After independence, some of them kept on fighting for equality, but others gave up. The second name, Nyaradzo, means consolation. Here I use it in the general sense of comfort and support and in the particular sense of the comfort received after a disappointment—a girl baby is the consolation prize for the boy her parents would have preferred. My choice of the name "Nyaradzo" suggests that the girl knows that she is second best, a consciousness that spurs the women discussed under this heading to fight on for women's emancipation. Finally, I have chosen "Pretty" to represent the expectation that girls and women be pleasing to the eye. Under this heading, I discuss Shona ambivalence toward female beauty and the celebration of physical beauty in pageants and fashion shows.

Feminists, those who called themselves feminists and those who acted on feminist principles without the label, were among the most vocal in articulating women's possibilities and the potential of approaching gender equality.

For others, gender equality was not the goal; some called for gender sensitivity (consciousness of rights and interests of women), and others used femininity (a combination of attractiveness, grace, and responsibility) to make a way for themselves in the world. In this chapter I discuss academics and activists whose broad vision for change continues to have effect in the present day. But I also engage women and girls with smaller ambitions, not concerned about the state of the nation, but more viscerally confronted with husbands, boyfriends, children, clothes, appearance, and livelihood.

I draw on a range of literary, scholarly, personal, and journalistic works that show how Zimbabwean women write about their own lives, analyze their situation, imagine the future, reconstruct the past, and trouble the present. Young women combatants in the anticolonial liberation struggle write of what pushed them into the struggle, the joy of comradeship, and their experiences of the continued struggle. Historians give context and amplification to the voices of women ex-combatants. Women and girls whom I interviewed speak of their everyday lives, their problems, their dreams, and their attitudes toward women's liberation. Feminist scholars and activists publish articles and speak out on the social condition of women and on the women's movement in Zimbabwe. The words and ideas of activists who do not publish position papers appear in newspaper and magazine articles. In addition to commentary on women's struggle for social justice, papers and magazines carry stories on beauty, fashion, brides, and weddings. The news magazine *Parade* prints photos of entrants in the annual Miss Parade contest. The Miss Zimbabwe contest, the Face of Africa contest, and advertisements also keep beautiful women in the public eye. Across the country, women's clubs and NGOs deal with women's access to land, health, education, and inheritance, and with violence against women, among other issues. This varied assemblage of sources contributes to the insights I share in this chapter.

Flame

In Zimbabwe's fourth decade, it is obvious that women combatants—freedom fighters—from the liberation war who expected to lead the way to a just and equitable society did not do so. These are the women I call "Flame." Many went to war as girls, returned as single mothers, and were reviled by families and friends who they thought would embrace them.[4] In the last decade, scholars have reevaluated the roles of women combatants in the liberation war and revealed the great extent of sexual abuse to which many guerilla girls were subjected and the small degree to which they participated in actual combat.[5] When I examine the hopes and aspirations of a group of women freedom fighters in this chapter, I do so knowing that their comments reflect what they believed when everyone was optimistic, when Zimbabwe was young. Perhaps their greatest accomplishment is that they once inspired other women to believe "that we can create something and build the future" (Bond-Stewart and Mudimu 1984, 64). Their own stories are filled with desperation and hardship; they are fighting despair to find hope.

During the liberation struggle, official propaganda held that women and men were treated equally. In 1979 Robert Mugabe, as the commander of the Zimbabwe African National Liberation Army (ZANLA), said that women fighters "have demonstrated beyond all doubt that they are as capable as men and deserve equal treatment, both in regard to training and appointments" (Lyons 2004, 188). In training camps of the armies of both liberation parties, ZANLA of the Zimbabwe African National Union (ZANU) and the Zimbabwe People's Revolutionary Army (ZIPRA) of the Zimbabwe People's Union (ZAPU), men and women were brought together under the rhetoric of comradeship. A ZIPRA female war veteran remembers the leveling of the sexes this way:

> Initially we were told that we are comrades. And the word *comrade* was an umbrella word, which meant you are my pal, you are my brother, sister, you are everything to me—*except sexually motivating*. . . . So that we all wore combats, trousers and a shirt, and a cap, which was military gear, and boots. You could not identify that that was a woman and that was a man from a distance. . . . We would undertake similar training. . . . If someone collapsed, collapsing could be either a man or a woman. Anybody would collapse. (Lyons 2004, 190, emphasis in the original)

Zimbabwe was not alone in having young women as active combatants in the liberation war and in trying to inculcate a sense of equality among the sexes. Eritrea, in its thirty-year war for independence from the much larger Ethiopia (1961–91), ranks near the top for its successful incorporation of women into the military. Though the participation of women in combat and their equality within the ranks were exaggerated for propaganda purposes (as it was in Zimbabwe), in Eritrea women were generally not confined to support roles; many fought at the front, and their participation was extensive and significant (Hedru 2003, 439). Eritrea did step ahead in recognizing sexuality and marriage as an ongoing element in the co-ed army. Its rules for sexual relations and revised laws for marriage in the field overturned many customary practices: "Marriage laws basically barred the 'feudal marriage norm based on the supremacy of men over women,' the coercive aspect of marriage, child marriage, unilateral divorce by men, polygamy, concubinage, and the dowry. The laws went even further and presented marriage as a partnership, mentioned the importance of love, and equalized the economics of the union" (Hale 2001, 160). Even though few of the laws and policies enacted for soldiers during the war were maintained postindependence, women combatants in Eritrea were more broadly trained than those in Zimbabwe, less often sexually abused, and less often stigmatized as sexually active women.

In Zimbabwe, Josephine Nhongo-Simbanegavi's (2000) history of the women in the ZANLA army during the anticolonial war challenges official orthodoxy that a gender revolution occurred as a part of the liberation struggle and that a generation of liberated women emerged from the struggle. Archival and firsthand reports on women's activities during the anticolonial liberation war show gender discrimination in the assignment of duties: women were generally porters, cooks, cleaners, and teachers. Norma Kriger found that "only 5 percent of cadres sent for special courses by ZANU were women; all ZANU representatives abroad were men; leadership selection was based in favor of men even though women did more of the work" (1995, 193). ZANLA documents and women's own testimonies also reveal that there was a definite failure of comradeship as the brother-sister ethos transmuted into one in which women sought protection from men by attaching themselves to one, women gained resources through sexual alliances, and women were harassed, molested, and raped by men of higher rank and by their comrades (see Lyons 2004).

This scholarship joins with others to explode the myth that the freedom fighters "conscientized" the masses, that is, that the liberation struggle brought about a critical understanding of the sources of oppression and a willingness to engage in the anticolonial battle. Instead, the view of the liberation war that emerges is of a movement spearheaded by ambitious, educated, urban men who fought against the color bar and for self-determination, and of rural communities that joined the battle for a promise of land beyond subsistence. The liberation armies used intimidation and physical violence to subdue local populations and displaced patriarchal male authority with spirit mediums, women, and youth. The Rhodesian troops, which included black men, burned villages, tortured men and women, raped women, and used the power of the state to divert resources and corral the population. In the liberation armies' story of their victory over Rhodesian forces, all black women are potential winners. Those women who did not go to war but provisioned the freedom fighters have proclaimed their contribution to the victory after the war. So too have the young boys who served as messengers and lookouts and the girls who cooked in the villages for the combatants.[6] After the government's second payout to the war veterans (which started the precipitous downward slide of the Zimbabwean economy), spokespeople for villagers who had supported the freedom fighters pressed the government for compensation, to no effect. Zimbabwe did not live up to its promise to take care of the people or to reward those who fought for independence. Nonetheless, we cannot let the failures of the Mugabe government erase the memory of the euphoria of independence. Children born around that time were named Independence, Freedom, Fortune, Prosperity, and Moreblessing (see Vera 2002, 48). Although the Zimbabwean liberation struggle was not a popular uprising, the promise of freedom spurred many young people to join the armies and to anticipate the fruits of victory.

Young Women in the Liberation Struggle: Stories and Poems from Zimbabwe, edited by Kathy Bond-Stewart and Leocardia Mudimu and published not long after independence in 1984, beautifully presents a group of guerilla girls, portraying who they are, what they did during the war, and what they want from independent Zimbabwe. The contributors to the book were students in an adult education class after the war; all of them had left primary or secondary school to join the liberation struggle,

Flame, the freedom fighter, probably joined the struggle as an adolescent girl after "the boys"—as the male freedom fighters were called—had visited her village to hold an all-night "conscientizing" meeting. Photographs in the booklet show the women combatants in costumes for a guerilla theater piece, teaching villagers about the nature of their oppression by white colonialists: "politicizing the masses" is how they spoke of it. The first chapter of Dangarembga's second novel, *The Book of Not*, portrays another kind of conscientizing meeting: Babamakuru, the head of the Sigauke lineage and the proud and demanding headmaster from *Nervous Conditions*, is called back to his village, where he is denounced as a sellout and beaten in front of neighbors and relatives, including his sister-in-law, who seeks satisfaction in his downfall; she blames him for the death of her son and for taking her daughter away from her by sending her to school (2006, 3–20). In telling that story, Dangarembga does a good job of showing the collusion between the freedom fighters and village women and in making clear that old grudges, especially against those who benefited from the colonial regime, may be settled in new wars. The eponymous *Flame*, the film from which I took the title of this section, contains a moment of reprisal when Flame, while in a battle near her home village, decides to burn the shop of a man who had humiliated her father.

Some girls were abducted or hoodwinked into going with "the boys." Others ran to them and away from childhood poverty and hardships caused by colonialism, sexism, and parental authority. Poems by contributors to the 1984 anthology about their lives before the war include the following lines: "My past was a place in the desert / as tormenting as the devil's home. / My past was a seed / sown in the thorns" (Bond-Stewart and Mudimu 1984, 3). But while they fled difficulty at home, their journey away was also hazardous, emotionally and physically. Once they decided to leave the past behind in order to join the liberation struggle, the young women had to walk miles with few provisions, hard by wild animals, over mountains, across rivers, and near Rhodesian troops. Sometimes they came under enemy fire from airplanes and troops on the ground. Life in the army encampments was difficult for both men and women—clothing and food were scarce, disease endemic, aerial attacks frequent, and death abundant. These are not stories of heroism; they speak of survival. When women freedom fighters write about their best experiences, they mention learning to operate a gun, witnessing equality of the sexes in Cuba or China, where some went for special training, and teaching or "politicizing the masses." One captures the oft-remarked-upon development of self-esteem in the combatants: "My best experience in the struggle was to see that a human being is very precious. Before I went to the struggle I didn't know that. I learnt a lot how to talk to people, and how to behave myself. Now if I go somewhere I never feel inferior when I meet new people" (14).

In interpreting their experiences, women ex-combatants emphasize the power to think for themselves and to act decisively that they gained from the war. At independence, many believed that their struggle for freedom and equality as women still continued. They believe that the courage, strength, and analytical clarity they had used to free Zimbabwe could be used to free themselves. Education, a good job, and a good steady income that would allow them to provide for their children and families are the primary goals they seek in their feminist vision.

When the war was successfully concluded, the women returned home to find parents and family members dead, villages ravaged by further impoverishment, little or no remunerative employment, and a cool reception by friends and neighbors. Their writing about this is suffused with metaphors of birth and pain: "I'm a new born baby," "My present life is hard," "I wish I hadn't been born," and "Life has not been all that smooth" (Bond-Stewart and Mudimu 1984, 52–53). This sense of desperation was shared by many of their male colleagues, but men were more often incorporated into the national army, and they received reparation during the demobilization exercise when ex-combatants were officially released from liberation armies and given stipends for their transition. Many of the women ex-combatants were treated as refugees, not soldiers, and were given no stipend or training. Some NGOs started programs for high school completion and specialized training for both male and female ex-combatants. The contributors to this booklet were fortunate enough to be in such a program. Two years after independence, these female ex-combatants maintained their desire to fight for women's liberation. Accompanying their statements about the hardships of the present is their resolve to continue the battle: "I can help women all over the country who may face problems similar to mine, and encourage them not to give up" (53). The young woman who wished that she had not been born keeps up her spirits by saying, "The important thing to remember is resistance" (53).

In writing about what is important in their then-present lives and in conceptualizing the "new Zimbabwean woman," the contributors emphasize women's independence and development of their potential, equality of rights and property between men and women, and proving "to the nation as a whole that women are not inferior" (Bond-Stewart and Mudimu 1984, 53). This new ideal of womanhood is legitimated by the women's experiences as combatants, by their active role in transformation of the nation, and by the changed relations between men and women that the war brought about. I don't mean to belabor the idea that some women freedom fighters emerged from the war with an increased sense of agency, but I want to present it in opposition to a contrary finding: "Although African men were empowered by their role as combatants, African women revolutionaries were at risk of being disproportionately disempowered by their participation in anticolonial wars. Firsthand accounts of anticolonial African women combatants suggest that military life often undermined their sense of agency as a result of increased vulnerability to gender-specific human rights abuses perpetrated by enemy troops as well as their own comrades" (A. M. White 2007, 868). In the Zimbabwe case, women who joined the liberation war did not leave homes where they felt empowered; the act of leaving itself gave them a sense of agency, and surviving the walk to the camps gave them a sense of their own power. Many escaped what they felt was gender and age abuse at home. They suffered in war and survived.

Some women were silenced by their experiences during the war, and others found strength to carry on. One of the final poems in the booklet rallies women with these words:

> Women of Zimbabwe
> Why do we sit on top of our hands?
> The time has come
> to show how clever we are.
> We are not yes-women
> We can stand on our own.

We'll teach our men
about equal rights.
We'll show them
That we are strong.
That we can create something and build the future.

Women ex-combatants' pride of accomplishment was counterbalanced (pride is never the sole feeling of any combatant after a war) by the treatment they received on returning home. "Female ex-combatants faced additional problems associated with conservative traditional customary beliefs about the social and marital position of women in Shona society," historian Muchapara Musemwa has argued (1995, 38). In many ways, the ex-combatants whose works appear in this booklet are among the lucky ones. Some joined the regular army, and others were trained for government or business jobs. Two ex-combatants I talked to three years after independence represent both female freedom fighters' aspirations and their reluctance to claim the limelight for themselves. One, a noted leader during the war, educated and highly skilled, could not find appropriate government employment and was bitterly resigned to working for a British charitable agency. Another did not want to speak of the war or her experiences. When I met her at a wedding reception, she carried a beaded clutch purse that she had gotten in China, but she would say nothing more about her experience there. She was a wife and mother and presented those as her major achievements.

The greatest silence in *Young Women in the Liberation Struggle: Stories and Poems from Zimbabwe* is about the fathers of the babies that so many ex-combatants are pictured with in the booklet, about their husbands, and about their relations with men during the war and since. Rumors circulated around the capital city that women ex-combatants couldn't find husbands and that they were deserted by the men whom they married without bridewealth during the war. In his study of the rehabilitation of ex-combatants, Musemwa reports, "Some men were of the opinion that female ex-combatants were too haughty to be married, in spite of the fact that 'even among civilian women there are these who are born tough'" (1995, 50). In a 1981 interview, the most prominent female ex-combatant, Joice Mujuru, known then by her nom de guerre, Teurai Ropa (Spill Blood), the first minister of community development and women's affairs and later vice president of Zimbabwe, defended her comrades against the accusation that they could not find husbands:

> No, this is very, very distorting. For instance, when newspapers could come up saying women can't get husbands or ex-combatants can't be married because

men are afraid of marrying them. It is an inferiority complex which is found among some of the men who were not fighters; because they think freedom fighters who are women can easily challenge [them]. But that [ex-combatants cannot find husbands] is not the case; most freedom fighters who are women are married. They are marrying even today. And some of them have even married those ones who were not even in the armed struggle. Yes, I know of several, for instance, myself. I'm married. I'm an ex-combatant. I married (the late General Solomon Nhongo) who was an ex-combatant. But I know of other ex-combatants who married girls who were not in the armed struggle. And of men who were not in the armed struggle who married ex-combatants. So it is a question of time or a question of timing.[7]

Mujuru's statement directly addresses the fear that female freedom fighters are not proper, self-effacing, non-assertive Shona women. After the war, women bore the brunt of Zimbabweans' ambivalence about the conduct of the liberation struggle: women were not treated as heroines but were called prostitutes and murderers. They did not benefit from the warrior discourse that embraced men as defenders, even creators of the nation. In response, many ex-combatants, like one of my interviewees, "chose to silence their own voices and history" (Lyons 2004, 291). Tanya Lyons suggests that women's military roles are reinscribed into domestic roles as mothers, which denies them the benefits of political independence and the benefits granted to (male) citizens based on their military and political/nationalist contributions (2004, 213).

In the more than thirty years since independence, most women ex-combatants have faded back into the fabric of women's everyday lives and struggle. But a few have continued on to make public contributions to the country. As a member of the ruling party, Joice Mujuru transitioned from "Spill Blood" to minister of women's affairs (who endorsed the first roundup of unescorted urban women out alone after curfew in 1983) to vice president (with policies of urban removal and rural intimidation in 2005). Over the years Mujuru has proved herself to be loyal to the party: she was a poster girl for women freedom fighters, though she never fought in combat in Zimbabwe; as minister of information, she blocked the licensing of a viable telecommunications company so that her husband and a nephew of the president could have a monopoly, and in 2013, she became acting president while Mugabe was out of the country.[8] Mujuru is widely rumored to be the leader of one faction that expects to rule after Mugabe's death.

Margaret Dongo also transitioned from liberation fighter to public figure, though along a politically divergent path. Having joined the liberation army in 1975, when she was fifteen years old, she is still fighting for democracy and women's rights. When asked why she became a combatant in the liberation struggle, Dongo pointed to her township family as being politically involved, and said that she wanted to help end discrimination and racial imbalances in education and wealth. After independence, she learned to type, worked in then prime minister Robert Mugabe's Central Intelligence Organization, and was instrumental in founding the National Liberation War Veterans' Association. With the help of the war vets, Dongo was elected and served five years as a member of parliament for the ruling party, ZANU (PF).[9] But she soon grew disillusioned with the one-party state, corruption in the ruling party, and its administration of government. When she spoke publicly about this, she was drummed out of the party. She then ran as an independent but lost a gerrymandered district in a corrupt election. Charging election fraud, she took her case to the high court and won the right to a new election, which she campaigned for and won. In parliament, she continued to speak out against Mugabe, to expose corruption, and to express outrage when her war veterans invaded and took over white-owned farms. She was the first to release the names of government officials who acquired farms through the takeovers. As an opposition politician, she was vilified, threatened, attacked, and her children traumatized.

Dongo seems to live up to novelist Yvonne Vera's depiction of women veterans at the end of the war: "These women are the freest women on earth with no pretense, just joy coursing through their veins. They have no desire to be owned, hedged in, claimed, but to be appreciated, to be loved till an entire sun sets" (2002, 48). In some circles, Dongo was "appreciated" and maybe "loved." But love did not come easily to women who upset normative gender expectations, and many did want to be claimed, eventually to be married.

Changing society's expectations of women and inculcating gender equality were a part of the liberation platform. When freedom fighters went into villages to raise consciousness about colonial oppression, they turned gender relations topsy-turvy, marginalizing the men and forming alliances with women and children who gave them shelter, provided food, served as couriers of ammunition and information, and worked as lookouts for government troops. But many of "the boys," as they were referred to at the time, also exploited patriarchal privilege—girls who brought food to them were taken as sex partners, and women and girls who joined the revolutionary forces were abused and raped. After the war, these women who expected to be appreciated and loved were shunned as sexually loose, dealers in death, and unwomanly.

Margaret Dongo represents that continuing struggle: she went to war to fight for equality and was raped by a comrade; she spoke truth to power, was batted down, fought back, and won. She married and had children, fought and won the right to be able to secure travel documents for her children when only fathers had been allowed to do so. Dongo continues to live in the capital city of Zimbabwe and is a noted human rights activist and social commentator. No longer in the government, she continues to speak out. Turning her attention ever more to women, she speaks for women who are chased away from their marital homes when their husbands die, who are denied access to land because they are single, and who must strive to protect themselves in families that should provide security but instead threaten their safety.

Women in this category joined the war but were seldom legible as warriors, protectors, or creators of the nation; instead they were labeled prostitutes. To the extent that they were seen as warriors, their credibility as wives was questioned. Facing disparagement by their families and neighbors, some women sought solace in conventional roles, but others fought back. Margaret Dongo is one example of the obstinate optimism of the promise of feminism.

Nyaradzo

"I am a feminist (without even the slightest whiff of an apology for naming myself thus). I am an activist and a fearless fighter," said Thoko Matshe, chair of the Zimbabwe National Constitutional Assembly (2001, 61). Civic leader Matshe is among the women I have grouped under "Nyaradzo," the sign of consolation. These women are alike only to the extent that they actively and nonviolently work to change their society, to eliminate sexism, to increase women's access to resources, and to end gender discrimination. They may be in NGOs that deal with domestic violence, the welfare and safety of the girl child, women and HIV/AIDS, the stigma of childless married women, women's access to and ownership of land, or women and human rights. Their organizations may be grassroots, community-based, national, regional, or international. Nyaradzo also stands for Zimbabwean women who write in feminist journals, who speak out as feminists, and who are members of the women's movement. I start with a discussion of feminism at the university and in intellectual circles and end with a look at one women's NGO. These categories are not necessarily distinct: a glance at the curriculum vita of one of the country's leading feminists, Amy Tsanga, shows that while holding a position in the law faculty at the University of Zimbabwe (UZ), she has served as a consultant for national or international agencies about once a year for the past fifteen years.[10] Tsanga and Patricia McFadden, a long-term resident of Zimbabwe who was born in Swaziland, are particularly adamant about a need for a theory that will connect women throughout the country, spur them to action, and influence policy.

When I was in Zimbabwe in 1983–84, I was cajoled into presenting the pro argument in a debate on the proposition "Feminism is the progressive force for change in the world today." The debate was sponsored by a women's NGO after its success in extracting an apology from the Mugabe government concerning the conduct of a cleanup program that was supposed to rid the capital city of prostitutes. The NGO thought it would be forever branded as "Western" if one of its white members were to speak for feminism and was wary of stigmatizing one of the black Zimbabweans by asking her to take this role. As a black American, I was a good compromise. Joining me on the pro side was a white male medical doctor. On the con side were two black men: a lecturer in religion from UZ and an editor of a national newspaper. A young sociology lecturer, who later became one of the leading feminists in the country, presided over the debate. To prepare, I went to a less-publicized panel discussion that touched on women's changing roles. Olivia Muchena, an outspoken lecturer at UZ and a consultant for one of the first-ever reports on the situation of women in Zimbabwe, participated in the panel.[11] She was extremely matter-of-fact in her retort to men's claim that feminism was Western. She simply remarked that none of the men was wearing animal skins and loincloths, and that her guess was that Mercedes and not horse and buggies awaited them outside the building. She could have gone on to say that the ideology that most of them espoused was scientific socialism— another Western import.

Decades later, feminists still face the charge that feminism is un-African, that it goes against African culture. Throughout sub-Saharan Africa, arguments seesaw between opponents who say that feminism was imported and proponents who point to outstanding women ancestors who stood up to patriarchy and colonialism and could be claimed as early feminists (see Guy-Sheftall 2003). Feminism has been shaped through African interactions and global ones that are not solely Western. The first meeting of the African Feminist Forum in 2006 in Ghana came up with a charter of feminist principles that recognized that the struggle for women's rights is political, questioned the legitimacy of structures that subjugate women, and supported the use of varied tools for analysis, transformation, and action (Tripp et al. 2009). Following the third African Feminist Forum—in Dakar, Senegal, in 2010—a Zimbabwe Feminist Forum was held in 2011, where the goal was to "create a space for vibrant feminist thinking and critical dialogue towards movement building in Zimbabwe and South Africa."[12] The African women congregating at such events are not defensive about the use of the term "feminist," and many are willing to stand against African culture and traditions of gender discrimination in public and personal domains. The entryway to a Zimbabwean NGO's office attests to this. There, proudly displayed, is a poster of Nafis Sadik's famous challenge to reject arguments about culture and tradition that are used against feminists: "We must not bend under the weight of spurious arguments invoking culture and traditional values. No value worth the name supports the suppression and enslavement of women."[13] As is clear from the necessity of arguments against it, the "feminism is Western/feminism is not African" argument is tenacious, yet African feminists have not kept silent. In fact, they have proliferated. There would be no problem finding a black Zimbabwean feminist to debate today, though now she might question the discourse of progress, and she might have the same problem my side had with whether feminism is "the" force for positive change or "a" force for positive change. When I spoke in 1984, I used a socialist feminist approach that tied women's position in society to changes in political economy and critiqued patriarchy, capitalism, and the family. Some of my colleagues in the NGO were unhappy with the approach I took; because it criticized the centrality of motherhood and the family, they felt that it would turn off many African women.

The African Feminist Forum notwithstanding, no single African feminist standpoint exists, though following the pioneering work of Sierra Leonian anthropologist Filomina Chioma Steady (1981), a number of scholars have tried to identify concerns that distinguish African from Western feminism. The commonalities in African feminism usually include recognition of women's status as constructed through race, class, and gender; commitment to working with men against colonialism and foreign domination; high regard for motherhood and women's biological roles; prioritizing the realities of African women's everyday experiences; and critical assessment of African institutions—accepting some and rejecting others (see Steady 1981, 2006; Boyce Davies and Graves 1986; Ogundipe-Leslie 1994; Mikell 1997; Oyewumi 1997; Guy-Sheftall 2003; Tripp et al. 2009). On what African feminism is not, summarized later in this chapter, Molara Ogundipe-Leslie sizzles: African feminism is not parrotism of Western women's rhetoric, not opposed to African culture and heritage, not a choice between patriarchy and separatism, not about sexuality, not a cry for homosexuality, not reversal of gender roles, not oppositional to men, and not a separation of race and gender (1994, 219–22). Filomina Steady, a leader in the study of African women's groups, suggests that most women's groups do not merely react to gender discrimination and women's secondary position but are "shadow development agencies" that seek "empowerment that promotes a socio-centric agenda that aims to advance society and humanity as a whole" (2006, 9). Some African women who believe in gender equity are "reluctant to name and own a feminist ideology," preferring to call themselves "womanist," acknowledging their plight with African men in an international context and rejecting the perceived anti-male stance of Western feminism (Essof 2001, 124).

In Zimbabwe, leading scholars have embraced both the name and the ideologies of feminism. A brilliant and fearless sociologist whom I got to know during my Fulbright year at UZ, Rudo Gaidzanwa, is one such feminist; she is one of the most productive women scholars on the continent (Guy-Sheftall 2003, 33). As a public intellectual, Gaidzanwa built her career on rigorous disciplinary research, hard-hitting journalism, and active participation in civil society. Her theoretical approach is eclectic. Though I suspect a set of socialist feminist principles to be at the center of her thinking, her work effectively deploys intersectionalist—emphasizing the junctures of race, class, gender, ethnicity, and religion—and human rights discourses. Radical feminist Patricia McFadden, an anthropologist from Swaziland, was another outspoken feminist active in Zimbabwe. Her work contains unrelenting critiques of heterosexism, capitalism, neocolonialism, African patriarchy, and all African institutions that condone or support gender inequality. Based on a reading of her editorials in *Southern African Feminist Review* (*SAFERE*) and her organization of the journal, I gather that McFadden would like to see well-developed tactics for analyzing and undermining capitalist political economies, support for wide-ranging cultural politics, and self-critical sexual politics.[14]

Two major changes in African feminism in the past decades have emerged: acceptance, even celebration, of internationalism and openness to discussing sexuality. This has made room for African lesbians to come out, but coming out is not all or none. I met only a handful of out lesbians from Zimbabwe, and not all of them in Zimbabwe. The woman I got to know best was the partner of a white American student in the California State University education abroad program. That student complained about being teased and harassed on the UZ campus because she did not wear skirts or dresses. Her Zimbabwean partner was an athletic woman in her midtwenties with one child. When they started living together, they were careful not to go to shops together for fear of harassment. Still one shopkeeper put one and one together and treated the black lesbian miserably when she shopped alone. In conversation, she explained that lesbians have been subjected to what has been called "corrective rape" in rural areas and towns, where gangs of men rape suspected lesbians with the goal of turning them heterosexual.[15] A member of Gays and Lesbians of Zimbabwe (GALZ) with whom I spoke in the United States reported that there are few lesbians in the male-dominated gay rights organization. In newspapers, some letter writers specifically refute Mugabe's statement that homosexuality is un-African.[16] Some writers point out that Shona and Ndebele cultures identified effeminate men and tough women and allowed that they might have same-sex partners, but a "don't ask, don't tell" policy was in place. At home, lesbians and gays tended to stay in the closet—though "in the rafters," women's secret hiding places, may better fit traditional Zimbabwean houses. In cities and towns, they had to be careful, but there, at least, meeting others was a possibility. International ridicule of Mugabe's antihomosexual tirades and international discourses on homosexuality spurred GALZ to be even more visible and gave lesbians a language to discuss their desires. Nonetheless, in most of my discussions and interviews, no one brought up lesbianism as a topic of interest.

Today women (and men) in Zimbabwe winnow African and international feminist ideas, choosing what to keep. In Zimbabwe, some women are like liberal feminists, working to secure seats for women at the table where major decisions are made. Others want to resist the state in its many guises. Some combine cultural politics and sexual politics, deploying words and images to subvert the powers that be. A growing number of women take to the streets in nonviolent protests. "African women's movements have placed the state at the center of post-colonial activism," writes Shereen Essof—making the choice of strategy crucial, given that women can be co-opted into the structures implicated in their oppression (2001, 126). Is it most effective to work within the system or from the outside? Amy Tsanga, senior lecturer in the Faculty of Law at UZ, deputy director of the Southern and Eastern African Regional Center for Women's Law, and former director of the Women's Law Center, chose to work with the government to draft a constitution that guaranteed women's rights. When I asked her why she chose to work with the government instead of with its civil society rival, she replied, "Because I am pragmatic. Some people want to bring about change through resistance, but I believe in engagement."

A meeting held in 2000 at a popular hangout for intellectuals and opposition politicians, the Book Café in the Avenues district of Harare, sparked my conversation with Tsanga. The Zimbabwe Women's Resource Center and Network (ZWRCN), one of the leading women's NGOs, called the lunchtime meeting; the place was packed with local women plus a sizable number of men. For the ZWRCN, this was a continuation of its Gender and Development series, moved to a new location and with a larger audience: about sixty to seventy people attended. The room was filled with prosperous women in cosmopolitan African-style dresses and fancy head wraps, unlike the simpler dresses and head scarves most Zimbabwean women wear. Most of the women represented women's organizations. One of the women at my table was the founder of an organization for married childless women. Women who have not borne children or whose children do not survive infancy are among the most reviled in Africa. They are

Figure 5. Amy Tsanga speaking at a meeting on the women's movement in Zimbabwe at the Book Café, Harare, 2000. Photo by author.

often accused of witchcraft, of eating their unborn, and of killing other women's children, especially those of their co-wives. Among others represented were women working with AIDS organizations, women working against domestic violence, and an environmental organization working to empower local communities. Amy Tsanga was one of two presenters. She explained that the women's movement in Zimbabwe is diverse—with dialogues across race, class, and geographic differences—and is distinctly activist. The movement needs theories to inform coherent ideas about where to go, she said, and it needs to broaden its base. Bringing up issues that divided feminists in Zimbabwe, the other speaker, a woman from Zambia, emphasized that the women's movement needs to build a critical mass among the majority of women; women should not shun politics as dirty and corrupt but should participate within and outside party politics, and women should be where decisions are being made.

This session on the status of the women's movement in Zimbabwe brought out more dissatisfaction than celebration. What is the women's movement and who is in it? That question caused a stir. Even as the women's movement was described as diverse in race and class, and in urban and rural constituents, it was criticized as being out of touch with rural women and their survival issues. Some women see the women's movement as constituted by the wide-ranging civic organizations and NGOs that deal with women and gender issues. One woman reproached the organizers for calling a meeting to discuss the women's movement at the Book Café: poor women from outlying high-density suburbs could not afford the cost of transport to the center of the city. Two members of the audience wanted the women's movement to "bring us together" and to "spread the knowledge to the rural areas." A woman musician from a high-density suburb—the only person to begin her contribution in a local language—capped this moment in the discussion by complaining that there are many women's organizations in Zimbabwe, but they are for elites. "What are they doing for the average woman? Executives [of these women's organizations] are the beneficiaries," she said. Women's organizations should be for all, not dependent on political affiliation, and should not make money just for the organizers. This last point is an interesting echo from the past, discussed in chapter 1, when groups sponsored by white women were turned into an organization sponsoring income-generating projects.

What is the state of the women's movement in Zimbabwe, and where is it heading? The people attending this meeting argued over perennial problems, bringing out the tensions in Zimbabwean women's lives: the rural-urban divide, differences in class and economic opportunity, bias according to political affiliation, and the lack of an economic agenda. The invited speakers and others urged a mass women's movement through commitment to social justice for all. One woman praised the coalition of women's organizations in Zimbabwe for taking a stand against the government in the 2000 constitutional referendum. But others said that that stand was divisive. Whether voluntarily or through intimidation, they argued, rural women are members of the ruling party, even as they, and most people, do not want to engage in politics. With this rebuke, women who lived in middle-class neighborhoods were being reminded that the Women's Coalition's cagey strategy had not worked: it had advised women not to vote against the government but to "Vote Wisely." That slogan did not fool the government—the Women's Coalition did not say vote yes and therefore it implicitly encouraged women to vote against the government. Being on the wrong side of a political issue in Zimbabwe can lead to assault, rape, and death.

In the pages of Zimbabwe-based feminist journal *SAFERE*, the term "the women's movement" is sometimes used to refer to the Women's Coalition that grew out of the constitutional reform process of 2000—a process started by the National Constitutional Assembly (NCA) and almost co-opted by the government's Constitutional Commission. Priscilla Misihairabwi, one of the founders of the NCA, in an interview with *SAFERE* editor McFadden, explained that the women's coalition came about because women had difficulty being heard in the

NCA, the group from which grew the strong opposition party, Movement for Democratic Change (MDC). Once the Zimbabwe Women's Lawyers' Association joined the NCA, the Women's Coalition was launched to "define a woman's agenda and stick to it" (McFadden 2000, 47). It was even more important to define the women's agenda after women began to pull out of the NCA to work with the government in the Constitutional Commission: feminists such as Amy Tsanga and Rudo Gaidzanwa joined the government's effort to redraft the constitution. Then women from the ruling party joined with members of the opposition in the Women's Coalition. Tensions were high and disagreements rife, the agenda frayed and the politics nasty, but the coalition continued. Misihairabwi concludes, "We can sustain the Women's Movement because ... we have had the experience of taking a position, it's going to be much easier now to take positions on issues as women together. So you will see that the kinds of struggles we are going to have now, I think, will take a different turn. This is why I am sure that for quite some time we will be able to maintain the Coalition" (McFadden 2000, 47). A few years later, feminist Everjoice Win, once a leader of an important women's NGO, was not so certain of the longevity of the Women's Coalition: "A major blockage for the WC [Women's Coalition] is its lack of a clear position on its relationship with the State. Equally, the movement has been reluctant to confront the issue of the use and misuse of State power" (Win 2004, 25).[17]

The formation of the Women's Coalition in response to the constitutional reform movement exemplifies what is new in African women's movements. A comparative study by political scientists and activists examines what they call new women's movements since 1990 (Tripp et al. 2009). This refers to increased visibility of women as political actors and the adoption of national policies regarding women's rights. The central claim of the anthology is that "autonomous women's movements are one of the most important determinants of the new gender-based policies adopted after 1990 in much of Africa" (xiv). Earlier postcolonial women's movements "tended to be closely associated with the ruling party and state" (81) or based on welfare, domestic, and developmental agendas. But since the 1990s, or back as far as the 1980s in some cases, women's groups have increased pressure for political participation as well as constitutional, legislative, judiciary, and bureaucratic reform. On the whole, the rise of new women's movements both created democratic openings and benefited from opportunities arising after national crises. They are informed by the diffusion of international, regional, and transnational ideas and also influence those ideas and organizations. New communication technologies and resources, from membership fees and international donors, help sustain groups formed as a part of new African women's movements.

Whither the Women's Movement in Africa

A recent study of African women's movements (Tripp et al. 2009) suggests that there are several paradoxes in assessing the effectiveness of women's movements in changing policies in African countries. One is the absence-presence paradox: some countries (e.g., Mozambique) expand rights of women with a minimalist women's movement, while others have strong women's movements but little progress on women's legislation (Kenya, Cameroon, and Mali). Another is the democratization puzzle: "countries have exhibited the same level of readiness to pass women-friendly legislation regardless of their level of democratization" (220). Zimbabwe, with the passage in 2006 of a comprehensive domestic violence bill, falls into the category of a nondemocratizing country with strong women-friendly laws. How to explain these seeming contradictions? A women's movement or women organizing themselves in political pressure groups may be a necessary but not sufficient cause for legislative action. What is most relevant for expanding the rights of women is that women press for changes in legislation and social relations at a time when other social and political changes occur, in order to avoid deferring or deflecting their demands. After times of social upheaval or civil conflicts or war, when the society is restructuring itself, especially through constitutional reform, women are more likely to successfully present their case. Factors external to the country also matter. These include international discourses of development and human rights, changing global norms, international and regional pressures, and donor incentives. Countries with greater access to donor resources tended to incorporate women's rights, promotion of gender mainstreaming, and gender budgeting into their political process.

The 2000 Zimbabwean constitutional reform process garnered the widest voluntary participation of the populace of any governmental effort. Everywhere people were talking about, and planning for, change. Yet the draft constitution itself was hastily written and did not contain many of the provisions that had spurred people to voice their opinions to civic organizations and to government. Working in civil society and government forums, members of the Women's Coalition successfully pushed to include legislation favorable to women in the draft constitution. The greatest tension in the coalition came when it was time to take a position—to vote "yes" or "no" on the draft constitution. Voting "no" meant standing against Mugabe; it was that sentiment that prevailed: the women's coalition contributed to the defeat of the draft constitution and Mugabe's first loss.

Because Mugabe was handed his first-ever political defeat, most women felt that they had done the right thing to vote against the draft constitution. Amy

Tsanga does not agree. In an interview with me, she said, "We threw away a good constitution [the draft constitution] in hopes of a perfect one. It's like saying I won't drive unless I drive a Mercedes, or I won't eat unless I eat rice. We have gone backwards, because we were looking for the perfect solution, in a perfecting world." A new constitutional reform process has begun in Zimbabwe under the power-sharing agreement that brought together Morgan Tsvangirai, the ostensible winner of the 2008 presidential election, and Robert Mugabe, who fostered electoral violence to keep himself in power. Once again women's groups were active in educating people about what a constitution is and why its provisions matter.

Repression—curbs on public speech and assembly, police and military brutality and torture, confiscation of private property—increased after the ruling party's loss of the first constitutional referendum and with each election since that date in February 2000. One women's organization, more than others, took to the streets to protest violence in Zimbabwe: Women of Zimbabwe Arise (WOZA; the acronym forms a siNdebele word meaning "come forward"). Started in Bulawayo in 2002 by a mixed-race woman, Jenni Williams, who refers to herself simply as "Zimbabwean," WOZA does not use the term "feminist" in its public pronouncements; instead its members protest as women for their families and for their country. "WOZA was formed to give voice to ordinary women and men and to demand social justice for all Zimbabweans. We did not set out to seek recognition beyond that of our own government respecting us as citizens and recognizing our concerns as legitimate. We are mothers of the nation, longing for the award of dignity, and a bright future for our children," Williams said on receipt of the Kennedy Human Rights Award in 2009.[18] In his speech at the presentation of the Kennedy Award, President Obama underscored the mother-centric message of these fearless freedom fighters: "WOZA's guiding principle is 'tough love'—the idea that political leaders in Zimbabwe could use a little discipline. And who better to provide that than the nation's mothers? Since its founding, the organization has grown from a handful of activists to a movement of 75,000 strong. There's even a men's branch, I understand—MOZA. And over the past seven years, they have conducted more than a hundred protests—maids and hairdressers, vegetable sellers and seamstresses, taking to the streets; singing and dancing; banging on pots empty of food and brandishing brooms to express their wish to sweep the government clean."[19] WOZA, with more than seventy thousand members, comes the closest to a mass movement for social justice in Zimbabwe. Its "theory" goes back to the mother-centric approach that feminist intellectuals, such as McFadden, had found inadequate to capture women's diversity. It just might be that what motivates the majority of women in Zimbabwe is their responsibility as mothers and that their critical analysis points to the state as the fount of their problems.

WOZA comes under the sign of "Nyaradzo" even though a fight against sexism is not central to its mission. WOZA members work as women, not just as undifferentiated citizens, to improve the lives of women and their families. Magodnga Mahlangu, a WOZA leader and corecipient of the Kennedy Award, put it this way in her acceptance speech: "Thousands of my colleagues have faced arrest, torture and abduction—their only crime, wanting a better life for themselves and their families."[20]

Women risk loss of respectability by speaking out in public. The audacity and lucidity that Nyaradzo accesses to bring about change in her society may put her at odds with local values and practices. Women in politics, activists, and feminist women, whether they work with or against the government, are called whores and prostitutes. The term "prostitute" is so pervasive in Zimbabwean public discourse that male and female politicians who "flip-flop"—change their stances on issues—and especially those who change political parties are called "prostitutes." However, this negative label has the greatest onus when applied to women and is often accompanied by the coup de grâce, "not African." Nyaradzo ignores these slurs. She knows that she began as a consolation prize, but she is changing the playing field and the prizes to be won.

Pretty

Beautiful women have a form of power in Zimbabwe, and that power is an essential part of gender politics. One secretary I interviewed told me that one of the distinctive features of women is that they are attractive: "We are very attractive as compared to men. That's why they easily lose their ideas when they see a beautiful lady." Picking up on attractiveness as sexuality, another secretary coyly pointed to this as an advantage that women have: "A woman can do whatever you want to with a man. Sometimes [men] go out of their way to please [women]." This reasoning was certainly an understanding of the power of beauty shared by Kiki Divaris, the white doyenne of the Miss Zimbabwe/Miss World Beauty Pageant. She was hesitant to talk to me: "Are you on my side?" and "Do you think you are better than our blacks?" she asked in a phone interview. When she started talking more freely, Divaris was anxious to let me know that the pageants celebrate women's power and lead the way for them to be successful in many endeavors (that one Miss Zimbabwe went to Harvard is often cited). Women have to learn to use their power, the patron of the Miss Zimbabwe contest told me. But beauty, no matter how it is defined, whether it is the sharp features, slim body, and long hair of the beauty queen or the full face, rounded body, and sensuous movements of the traditional dancer, also puts the woman in danger. In Shona traditional culture, the woman whose beauty was extreme was looked at suspiciously, as she could have some "dark spots" on her personality, endangering herself and others (Matereke and Mapara 2009, 206)

To the extent that power is relational, the power of women's beauty is realized in interaction with others. These others are not only male—a study of the beauty premium showed that women were more likely to reward beauty than men (Rosenblatt 2008)—but women's beauty is definitely an object of negotiations between men and women. Herein lies the problem: both men and women believe that in intimate relationships women bring bodily and emotional resources—beauty, comfort, vulnerability, and sexuality—and that men's resources draw primarily from the realm of things—money, houses, cars, food, travel, and gifts. Because beauty can be traded, because it is one of the ways that women can get power and things, a beautiful woman can be considered immoral or infinitely corruptible (Gaidzanwa 1985a, 12). In a study of Shona ethno-aesthetics, Kudzai Matereke and Jacob Mapara conclude, "Shona poetry ... is full of caution to the young boys to be careful of women, especially the beautiful ones. The woman was conceptualized in contradictory and ambivalent ways: as both the mother and the witch; the wife and the prostitute" (2009, 212). One such proverb is *Mukadzi munaku kukona kuba anoroya* (A beautiful woman who does not turn out to be a thief becomes a witch) (Matereke and Mapara 2009, 211). Beauty is immodest in a society that generally socializes women to be self-effacing and unassertive (Hungwe 2006, 42). Women and girls who participate in beauty contests and fashion shows do so in opposition to traditional values of modesty and self-effacement; they adopt cosmopolitan values by which they measure themselves against distant—and to them progressive—standards.

It is amazing that these cosmopolitan standards can still be thought of as progressive, given the images of women, especially from the West, that are displayed in some media. Toward the end of the twentieth century and into the current millennium, women's fashion magazines displayed sadomasochistic images that referenced dominatrices in leather, and heroin chic, featuring models with dark circles under their eyes, pale skin, and waifish figures. In contrast, magazines that originated in Africa, such as *Drum*, *Parade*, and *Mahogany*, featured photographs of women whose appearance reflected conventional Western standards, sometimes in bathing suits or wearing evening gowns, but more often in business or casual attire. The magazines published in Zimbabwe and South Africa aimed at the women's market contain articles on fashion, cooking, health, and beauty, plus stories on women overcoming odds to find their true love or meet their own goals, and, of course, the ever-popular horoscopes. I have often thought about the function of horoscopes in the lives of young African women, though I did not ask questions about astrology columns in interviews. It's my guess that astrology, a generator of mass identities, is an individuating force in Zimbabwe: it defines women as belonging to particular types—outgoing, emotional, straight shooter, mysterious—and with particular likes and dislikes, usually based on conjunctions or oppositions of planets, moons, and the sun. Women don't have to believe in the veracity of the horoscope to engage new ideas about themselves: they fashion an image of themselves and playfully orient choices according to that image. Through women's and fashion magazines women learn that their choices matter in shaping the kind of person that they are. Instead of imposing a predetermined sense of what will happen, magazine horoscopes open up new possibilities. The titillating images in Western magazines open new worlds to Zimbabwean women.

In a 1984 survey that I conducted in Harare at two high schools and at the University of Zimbabwe, young women indicated that soap operas were among their favorite shows on television. While the variety of television programming increased between that time and the turn of the century when I was back in Zimbabwe doing research, according to the *Parade* magazine's "Portraits of the People of Zimbabwe," soap operas, locally produced, South African, and American, are still widely watched. Their long-arc stories revolve around jealousy, greed, intrigue, and infidelity. In the midst of the AIDS pandemic, church and health-care literature trumpet the virtues of monogamy, fidelity, and honesty, but soap operas are filled with promiscuity and deceit. High school student fans of an American soap opera asked me if Americans are as loose as those portrayed in the show and wanted to talk about the black and white Americans who appear on sensational talk shows, such as *The Jerry Springer Show*: they "exercise no control" in the behavior that got them on the show (for instance, a mother having a sexual relationship with her daughter's boyfriend) and "no constraint" in their behavior on the program—cursing, throwing chairs, engaging in physical fights. Young people do not consciously imitate the behavior they see on soap operas or try to follow the bad eggs on the talk shows, but their moral universe has expanded as a result of exposure to both kinds of displays.

In Kenya, Rachel Spronk found that mediatization of love and sex (magazines, radio, and television) greatly influenced unmarried women's perceptions of love as a source of self-fulfillment as well as their willingness to use makeup and clothes to appear desirable. Another influence in Zimbabwe is the romance novel: in gothic bodice-rippers and modern-day dramas, women soften as they find their man and often end up having a strong sense of achievement and a loving relationship. I happened upon a used-book store in the Avondale shopping area in suburban Harare and was surprised to find almost half the store devoted to romance novels. Striking up a friendship with the white octogenarian bookseller, I spent several hours in the shop over a period of weeks, talking with the bookseller and customers. Not many whites turned up at the shop; most of the books on history, science, travel, and biography were ignored. Young women came in wanting the next in a series of romance novels or anything by a particular author. "Escape" and "delight" were the phrases I heard most often to describe what they got out of the novels, but I think that it is also worth considering the findings of an anthropologist who studied romance novels. Brackette Williams in an unpublished essay suggests that romance novels underscore the independent spirit of the female protagonist: she is alone, orphaned, in the care of distant relatives. Whether her personality is outgoing or shy, she must find her way to love on her own. And when she finds love, it is always fraught. Both she and the love interest have to overcome obstacles to be together—their love is an accomplishment not totally in her hands, but dependent on her self-positioning, her creation of a particular kind of self. The crafting of a new self is what I think is a deep-seated effect of women's reading romance novels. I agree with the conclusions Spronk reached in her Kenyan study: the consumption of media on love and sex leads women to use cosmetics and fashion to increase their desirability and to believe that finding love is self-fulfillment. But in Zimbabwe, I think, something even more basic is happening. Women are constructing themselves as modern liberal individuals who have a right to choose, whose choices matter, who admit to their own desires, and who rejoice in being objects of desire. As I noted in chapter 1, women in Zimbabwe wanted to appear attractive, desirable, and fecund, before colonialism, capitalism, and globalization brought them many more products by which to do so. Media expand their options or sometimes cruelly hold out alternative ways of being.

A workshop on makeup at the National Secretaries Convention in 2000 afforded me the opportunity to see many women's reaction to the lure of cosmetics, lotions, creams, and perfumes. On the banks of Lake Chivero, a former colonial resort, at the outskirts of Zimbabwe's capital city, I sat in the workshop with over a hundred other women. The session was a part of the Fourth Annual National Secretaries Convention held in September 2000. An attractive young black woman in fashionable athletic wear and a body by Nautilus explained that as summer approached we should use a lighter-weight moisturizing cream and should shave our arms as well as armpits to wear sleeveless tops. Her presentation was sponsored by a local cosmetics company, whose products were prominently displayed behind her.

At the convention the following year, I interviewed secretaries, mostly married women between twenty-five and thirty-seven years of age (discussed in chapter 4). I expected to find women who invested in their appearance and had included several questions on grooming and clothing. What I found surprised me. Women expended very little time on a daily beauty routine, and cosmetics and perfumes were low or nonexistent items in their budgets. Those who did not dismiss the question out of hand said that they did not spend any money on cosmetics, just on their hair. Only a couple of interviewees wore foundation makeup or had shaped their eyebrows through plucking, razor, or waxing: lipstick and a little powder were the primary beauty enhancements.

The first time I walked down the sidewalks in the city center, what struck me was that most of the young women were wearing synthetic hair extensions—down to the middle of their backs, long pony tails, or short braids in black, brown, red, and blonde. There were quite a few wigs and weaves (strips of straight natural or synthetic hair sewn onto their own hair, which has been tightly braided close to their heads). Some had their hair chemically straightened and curled or wore "freezes" of tight plastered waves. But extensions ruled the day. As I discuss in chapter 4, I later came to think of thick, lustrous hair as a sign of health in a country ravaged by the wasting disease—one of the ways that HIV/AIDS was referred to because of its effects on the body mass and hair. To show their health, city women who can afford it might be comfortable increasing their body weight: a "strong" or big body is a sign of respectability in a married woman and wealth in families. In cartoons and comic strips, a comely or shapely woman is usually represented by long hair and a big butt; the cartoonist might draw a dotted line from the man's eye to a woman's well-developed buttocks. Generally, I did not find women concerned about their body image except for a worry about being too thin. At a cultural festival where men and women present dances of their ethnic groups, I overheard a man remark that thin women can't compete with the big women in dances that focus on the butt—he said that he felt sorry for them. To achieve a healthy, slim, sculpted body takes time and money, diet and nutrition, but hair can be bought at a relatively low price.

The value attached to long hair in Zimbabwe is probably overdetermined. Popular magazines, television shows, and movies feature actresses and models with long, flowing locks. The black female model with a bald head or a short afro might be occasionally popular, but long hair is a standard of beauty. The Miss Zimbabwe contest of 2000 was cosponsored by a synthetic hair company, and all the contestants wore fake hair. I interviewed Miss Zimbabwe of 1998, Annette Kambarami, who, unlike most Miss Zimbabwe contestants, was not a veteran of beauty pageants. She did not add extensions to her hair, which fell to her upper back. Her natural hair, chemically straightened, was very long by Zimbabwe standards. The major complaint she had about the Miss World contest was that in that environment, her hair was considered short. Other contestants commented on it, and she was told over and over again that it was a drawback.

Annette Kambarami is a dark-skinned beauty, with narrow nose, oval face, and big eyes. She is tall, poised, confident, and intelligent. Scouts for the Miss Zimbabwe contest found her on her university campus in the highland city of Mutare and convinced her and her parents that she had the body and face to compete well at the Miss World contest. The Miss Zimbabwe beauty contest is not unlike other contests around the world in seeking contestants who will win by international criteria as opposed to local ones. Recent Mr. and Ms. Zimbabwe bodybuilders attest to increasing cosmopolitan tastes. Local standards are changing: both men and women might appreciate the rhythmic pulsing of the voluptuous buttocks of the traditional dancers, who often perform with their backs to the audience, but a segment of the population desires the minimal curves of the fashion model.

Statistics on the weight and height of the Miss Zimbabwe contestants were not printed in the program nor was their race. Without the statistics, I cannot definitively say how the Zimbabweans measure up to beauty contestants in other countries. Of late, the Miss Zimbabwe Trust has instituted minimum height (5'7") and maximum weight (132 lbs.) requirements as well as maximum hip measurements (39 inches). There was a considerable range in height, and the winner in 2000 was among the shorter contestants, but all girls appeared to be slender. This appearance held true for the contestants in other beauty pageants in the country and the region, including the Face of Africa and Miss Parade (hosted by the publishers of the popular news magazine *Parade*). One major difference was that both the Face of Africa and the Miss Parade contests included a variety of white and mixed-race contestants, while the Miss Zimbabwe pageant had no white contestants. The "coloured," or mixed-race, contestant in the 2000 Miss Zimbabwe pageant was booed when she took the stage.[21] Overall, the audience at the pageant was not particularly attentive—the dull roar of voices crescendoed when speeches were given or sponsors' messages were aired. At one point, the mistress of ceremonies, Kiki Divaris, said to the audience, "I won't talk until you quiet down"; in response, the audience sent up a wall of noise. The participation of the young coloured woman, who worked at a radio station, had riled some black nationalists, and letters to the editor in newspapers had argued that she had unfairly used her connections to get into the contest. Some wondered if a coloured woman should represent

Zimbabwe; black and coloured women had not been chosen for the all-white Miss Rhodesia contest during the colonial and the Rhodesian separatist periods. Regional preferences were also audible at the Miss Zimbabwe contest, with the Bulawayo contingent determined to make the most noise when their contestant appeared. The winner of the Miss Zimbabwe contest was a caramel/brown-skinned woman from the provincial town of Kwekwe. A coloured woman, Corrine Crewe, won the Miss Parade contest. The international contest, the Face of Africa, was won by a black woman from Namibia (Zimbabwe's entrant was of mixed race), and a white South African woman was one of the five finalists.

The Miss Zimbabwe contest did not undergo a smooth transition from the all-white Miss Rhodesia contest. A year after independence, Joice Mujuru, then known by her nom de guerre, Teurai Ropa Nhongo, minister of community development and women's affairs, rejected the Miss Zimbabwe winner as a representative of Zimbabwe "but [accepted her] as plain Miss Beauty on behalf of those who wish to commercialize her physical assets" (Lyons 2004, 216). Questioning the criteria by which a Miss Zimbabwe was chosen, Mujuru asserted, "Our real Miss Zimbabwe is the special breed of woman who works hard and who sweats to improve her life and the lives of her community and her nation. . . . A woman's contribution to the improvement of the standard of life of her society is the yardstick to measure the crowning of Miss Zimbabwe" (Lyons 2004, 216). A similar critique of the Miss Zimbabwe contest was launched about thirty years after Zimbabwe's independence. A former Miss Zimbabwe Princess (2005) argued against naming a beauty queen as Miss Zimbabwe: "The new Miss Zimbabwe is the woman who manages to succeed against all odds, the woman who gets up at 3am to go and order vegetables so she can resell and put her children through school. She is the young woman launching mind blowing ideas in the boardroom and yet maintaining humility, grace and poise. She is the 70 year old taking care of HIV orphans and the woman who has gathered the strength to walk away from abuse. For me this is the New Miss Zimbabwe, a far cry from the figure eight who wants world peace but can't even spell it."[22] The differences in the two critiques show the changing social and political landscape for women in Zimbabwe. Just after independence, Mujuru concentrated on women's contributions to development of the new nation. The more recent Web site posting noted women's individual successes in overcoming hardships, indicating the continuing problems for women in the country. Others questioned the ethics of representing Zimbabwe on the world stage as the state grew more dictatorial and brutal. To a certain extent, the continuation of the contest clothes the regime in a cloak of normalcy, and the state gains legitimacy by its association with the Miss Zimbabwe competition.

The Miss Zimbabwe contest has not only faced political and ideological opposition, but over the years it has had trouble finding sponsors. On my brief visit to Zimbabwe in 1982, one of the first young women I met, the fiancée of a university lecturer, worked on the Miss Zimbabwe contest in the offices of Procter & Gamble, then a major sponsor of the contest. Though Procter & Gamble products could still be found on the shelves of stores in Zimbabwe at the turn of the century, they no longer appeared on the list of sponsors for the contest. Sponsors were local businesses—banks, boutiques, jewelry and beauty shops, travel and hospitality industry agencies, and "the Hellenic community," the last in honor of the Greek heritage of Kiki Divaris, whose determination kept the contests going. No office building provided space for the contest. The meetings concerning the national contest were held at Divaris's home, and the management of the city contests was decentralized.[23] The one constant has been Kiki Divaris herself, who has groomed scores of beauty queens in Rhodesia and Zimbabwe.

Divaris, who is close to the age of Zimbabwe's president, Robert Mugabe (he was born in 1924), compares herself to him, noting that despite their age, they both have energy and a passion for the nation.[24] But Mugabe has held on to his position, while Divaris has been displaced as head of the Miss Zimbabwe Trust. The new director, a former beauty queen and top model, has taken the contest in a different direction. Disappointed with the lax standards at the provincial level, she now conducts the contest through auditions for models, and the entire search is set to become a reality television show.[25]

Clothing Miss Zimbabwe, in some ways, has been easy. Zimbabwe does not have an official national dress or even a popular style that is recognized as modern Shona or Ndebele. The dance costumes, dance steps, and drumbeats of Shona groups—Zezeru, Ndau, Manikyia, Korekore, and others—are distinctive. In national ethnic dance competitions, men are often bare chested and wear skins, bark cloth, or raffia skirts. Women may wear similar skirts, with shorts underneath, and a bandeau or halter top. Many women will wear dresses with a collar and buttoned bodice and a gathered skirt in bright colors with contrasting scarves tied around the buttocks, and men can appear in shorts and shirts. Newspapers occasionally carry stories about the need for a national dress or show potential examples. The most common style features a toga with one shoulder bare, similar to the way the leader of the 1896–97 Chimurenga (anticolonial war), Mbuya Nehanda, wore her blanket. The Miss World contest does not require that the contestants wear authentic national costumes, but does require that the women represent something of their countries in the presentation of the nations. Using the works of leading fashion designers, Miss

Figure 6. Traditional dance performance, Harare, 2000. Photo by author.

Zimbabwe has evoked, among other things, the fauna of the country through an elaborate porcupine-quill costume and its flora through a colorful bird-of-paradise gown. At the pageants and on official occasions, Miss Zimbabwe dresses elegantly in modest, rather conventional Western-style clothing.

More trendy and playful clothing and more provocative attitudes were evident on the runways in the capital city's many fashion shows. I am not sure when black Zimbabweans began participating in fashion shows, but the Homecraft club movement's journals depict black women in a fashion show in the mid-twentieth century. At the turn of the twenty-first century, high schools held fashion shows as fund-raisers, well-known designers from the region put on fashion shows in convention centers, and neighborhoods held them as community builders. When willowy Britta Masalethulini was Miss Zimbabwe 1999, newspaper articles compared her looks to Naomi Campbell, a black British top model. Other black models from Africa and the United States were also seen as exemplars, but of an edgier style than that of the beauty queen. Walking the runway is about presenting oneself to others with imperiousness in a country where women are taught to be modest and unassuming. In fact, many displays of fashion are called "modeling contests" rather than fashion shows. In modeling contests, clothing was important, but it took second place to "attitude."

One of the teenagers whom I knew well won the Miss Travel Expo modeling contest and placed highly in her high school's Summer Breeze contest. I accompanied her to the Miss Funky Town modeling contest and got a bit of a backstage look as she scrambled to pull together costumes for an "ethnic" look and opted out of the evening wear because she had not brought a gown. Backstage,

Figure 7. Miss Summer Breeze and her mother pose for a photo, Harare, 2000. Photo by author.

I encouraged her to smile, but she adamantly kept the haughty look of the high-fashion model. I spent most of my time in the audience at Miss Funky Town; once again, the audience was rowdy, mostly youths and drunken men. My field notes record that "not one of the parental generation was there." Since the crowd could not be quieted, the event ended before the announcement of the winner. The crowning of the queen was held the next day in another venue. Miss Zimbabwe 1998, Annette Kambarami, was very critical of modeling, implying that beauty contestants were a higher class of people. To her the "catwalk" invited coarse behavior, but "the ramp" served "beauty with a purpose," the motto of Miss World.

From the catwalk to the sidewalk, Zimbabwean streets and public places do not burst forth with the blazing colors seen in other parts of the continent. Most women seen on the city streets wear skirts and jackets of matching fabric— typically solid, light-colored, polyester—or they wear pleated or straight skirts with contrasting overblouses. In thinking about fashion in Zimbabwe, I say to myself, isn't this the fashion sense that would come from being colonized by middle-class British people in their "solid shoes and sensible cloth" and by Afrikaners in homespun and desert boots? Well, not exactly. Look at Nigeria. They were colonized by the British and have vibrant clothing traditions. One difference between Zimbabwe and Nigeria is that Nigerians had been weaving and making cloth long before the British came. Another difference is that Nigeria was not a settler colony. The interaction of blacks and whites in Zimbabwe set up an intricate pattern of mimicry and alterity, of the use of clothes to mark exclusions and to warrant inclusions. Moreover, as I discussed in chapter 1, in the height of the colonial period, women colonialists consciously tried to bind African women to them by teaching them child and home care as well as hygiene and fashion. A booklet on how to build a wardrobe written by white women for African women, forty years ago, could represent the guiding principles behind today's fashions.

Clothing and morality are intertwined. The miniskirt is the lightning rod of the storm over cultural values: those against it see it as indecent and un-African, while proponents argue that it provides more coverage than the pubic apron and bare breasts of traditional garb. Women have been assaulted and stripped naked for wearing miniskirts.[26] One such incident happened years ago on the university campus but was still much talked about at the turn of the twenty-first century. A white woman whom I met in a suburban bookstore complained of being harassed at a commuter minivan terminus when she wore a dress with a high side slit. I experienced firsthand the fear women have of wearing the wrong thing in the wrong place when I took five teenaged girls from the suburbs to a movie in the city center. When we reached the central terminus, a crowd of men was pushing toward a van. The girls, most of them wearing jeans, immediately thought that someone was getting her clothes ripped off. They would have been comfortable in their jeans in the suburbs, but here in the city center they were clearly afraid. I abandoned the attempt to take them by van, and we took a private taxi home. We never found out what was going on at the terminus.

American university students in Zimbabwe told me that young women in upscale nightclubs dress "barely legal"—in low-cut and form-fitting clothes. In this way, educated, well-to-do young women play with the cultural contradictions between respectful and loose, between wife and prostitute. As Spronk writes of young professional women she studied, "Images of 'prostitutes' are a frame of reference through which young professional women are sometimes judged or through which they define themselves" (2003, 6). They are not prostitutes, but they ambivalently negotiate a pattern of nonconformity that stands in opposition to gerontocratic authority while still presenting themselves as eligible to be wives. Some of these young women are not unlike Third Wave feminists in the West: on the one hand, they value femininity, sexual expression, and the power they have over men. On the other hand, they are liberal feminists, demanding choice and self-determination, wanting equality in the workplace and at home, and needing the protection of human rights.

Feminism and Optimism

Flame, Nyaradzo, and Pretty represent different kinds of women living in cities in Zimbabwe. The types are not as distinct as I present them here. Each wants more from her society, all are eclectic in their principles and goals, and at one time, they each had reason to hope.

Flame—in the person of Joice Mujuru, Margaret Dongo, women in adult education classes, and women who have retreated to domestic silence—starts out with a critical assessment of society and government, especially of her experiences of age and gender discrimination, and learns to name the racist, capitalist colonial system as oppressive. She teaches this to others, but at the same time, her experience of oppression heats up. In military training camps, these women are shot at and bombed; their training is limited and upward mobility thwarted; they enter into voluntary and forced sexual relations; and they keep their children in camps with them or go home without glory. What is feminism to them? Certainly it was not what I learned from the propaganda spread by the ZANU information and publicity offices about strong women fighting side by side with men as equals; rather, it was the promise that their sacrifice in war would matter to women. Feminism, as freedom for women, was a partner of independence. Freedom Nyamubaya, a poet who participated in the Zimbabwe Feminist Forum, speaks of their estranged relationship: "Independence came / But Freedom was not there. / An old woman saw Freedom's shadow passing, / Walking through the crowd, / Freedom to the gate. / All the same, they celebrated for Independence."[27]

Individual women, better educated, well connected through marriage and family, with dogged determination, did benefit from their service in the liberation army. Joice Mujuru, who fought well and married well, has more successfully combined career and family than many women. She speaks for the maintenance of conventional values, and in her position in government, she acquiesced to curfews for women, the rounding up of single women in cities, forced removal of the urban population, suppression of speech, and other government excesses. A powerful Joice Mujuru is part of what makes working for feminism an experience of cruel optimism in Zimbabwe. Margaret Dongo, too, is a female ex-combatant who has a public career and a family. She has been on the other side from Mujuru on some issues, especially in regard to government corruption and vote rigging, and she continues to fight for women's rights within Zimbabwe. When there are openings in society that make change possible, she seizes them. When confronted with a brick wall, she chips away at it. She might be the best example of recovery from the malaise of one-defeat-after-another that Ann Cvetkovich (2012) discusses in her work on depression as a public feeling: after deep disappointment in her government and herself, Dongo regroups and keeps on going.

A document I found after I had completed research for this chapter amalgamates the feelings of the academic feminists. *Feminists (Re)Building Zimbabwe* is the report of the Zimbabwe Feminist Forum (ZFF) of 2011, where thirty or so feminists who came together for revitalization turned to poetry, theater (*The Vagina Monologues*), music, and dance to enhance their vibrancy and to keep attuned to their key question: What then?[28] After we take one step forward, what then? What happens after the Mugabe regime? What happens when all the right laws are on the books? Among the feminists gathered to discuss these questions were two represented in this book, Tsitsi Dangarembga and Amy Tsanga. The objectives of the ZFF, as listed in the report, include providing an alternative platform to engage critical discourses affecting women—personal, political, and economic—to build a feminist space, and to develop critical consciousness through feminist analysis and actions. The report describes many different kinds of actions that feminists are encouraged to undertake; it honors its local feminist foremothers and praises the work of WOZA, a group

I considered under the moniker Nyaradzo in this study. This feminism has a new feel—it recruits the mind, body, and spirit for the long run. Because these Zimbabwean feminists keep reenvisioning the future, the promise of feminism is not cruel optimism to them; rather it is found in sets of tools, analytical approaches, and coalitions of individuals and groups that can spread the word, inspire others, and force questions. These women display great resilience, the renowned resilience of African women. Visitors to the continent remark on it constantly, with the subtext of "those women with so little, how can they keep smiling?" I am trying to say something different about Zimbabwean feminists. They are not grinning and bearing it but rather refueling their cells with energy from home and the world, recalculating their tasks, and setting out strategies that call on a variety of resources.

Beauty queens and models, those women I've represented as "Pretty"—even as many have their sights elsewhere—are not immune to the deterioration of the Zimbabwean political economy and the rise of authoritarianism. Still these women and girls seek to use their beauty and their social graces to gain power, prestige, and resources. Most do not claim a feminist stance, and a few see feminism as an enemy, denying them the moral authority that comes with vulnerability, dependence, and submissiveness. Kiki Divaris, once the moral compass of the Miss Zimbabwe contest, wanted me to understand the power that a woman has when all heads turn as she walks into a room, as men and women gasp at her beauty. Such exquisite moments come to few of us, but such is the power of Helen of Troy, which, as Shakespeare showed us in *Troilus and Cressida*, is easily debased and turned against the woman and her protectors. I will not argue that women and girls turn to this form of power out of frustration with feminism. The power of the beautiful woman is conventional within Zimbabwean and international contexts, though in Zimbabwe, the beautiful princess and the wicked witch are combined and in Western cultures they are opposed. Modeling and beauty contests are about showing the range of possibilities of different lives, of different worlds.

When I started thinking about bringing Flame, Nyaradzo, Pretty, and Mercy together, I thought that this would be a time to include a look at women who were not interested in empowerment. But as it turned out, it seems that all women want power. They use different methods to get it, they want different degrees of power, and they want it for different purposes. Instead of power–not power, I found a mine field of oppositions that women traverse at their peril: African–not African, nurturer-warrior, respectful-assertive, wife-prostitute, mother-witch, Christian-sinner, and beautiful-corrupt. Though they are not all feminists, all these women resist the stasis of an overwhelming presentism that is an alternative to cruel optimism. Whether they are women who turned their backs on memories of their service in the war or women who profit from it, women who write papers against government policies or women who are arrested for their stance against those polices, or women who perfect their makeup and practice their walk, they refuse to let the present trample them; they refuse to be stuck in place.

CHAPTER 3

Women against Government
An NGO under Stress

> They've trapped us. They've trapped us. But I won't be trapped. I'm not a good girl. I won't be trapped.
>
> Tsitsi Dangarembga, *Nervous Conditions*

The feminist NGO Associated Women of Zimbabwe (AWZ), which I write about in this chapter, has a long history in Zimbabwe, having gotten started in 1983, only three years after independence. Unlike feminist groups in East and West Africa, which grew out of the collective action of sisters, wives, market women, or age mates, AWZ came into being because expatriate and local women living in the capital city were optimistic that they could influence the newly independent government to do the right thing. I was active in the group almost from the beginning, introducing feminist consensus-building processes, facilitating group discussions, participating in workshops, and writing reports. In this chapter's critical review of its functioning, I have chosen not to use the real names of the group or its director and to disguise some its earliest activities to avoid bringing harm to the group by revealing insider knowledge. Tsitsi Dangarembga, the Zimbabwean author whose works signpost this book, was also active in the group and I believe satirizes it under the fictional name "Women's Association for the Protection of Illegitimate Mothers (WAPIM)" in her play, *She No Longer Weeps* (1987). The beauty of pseudonyms is that the reader never knows exactly what group is being referred to. In the play, Dangarembga pokes fun at the moral superiority of society matrons who have formed WAPIM, a charity to redeem loose women. I turn to the NGO to show varieties of feminism and the influence of a political and economic crisis on a feminist organization in

Zimbabwe at the turn of the twenty-first century. The group still exists; though much has changed since its beginning and the pivotal historical moments I discuss, the NGO is still active under its original name, providing resources and services to women and girls in Zimbabwe.

My study of this feminist NGO further develops topics raised under the sign of Nyaradzo in the previous chapter—women who consciously organize to fight sexism in Zimbabwean society. This time I focus on the cosmopolitan nature of feminism in Zimbabwe and the relationship between a feminist NGO and the state—especially in relation to the politics of inclusion, state-sponsored violence, and economic decline. I ponder how an organization that once stood against government lost its edge, even as government became more oppressive, and I show what happens to an NGO dependent on international donors when the money stream begins to dry up.

In a study of African women's movements by academics and activists, Aili Tripp and her colleagues (2009) found that democracy does not necessarily promote strong women's movements or protect women's rights; rather, advances for women most often come during the period of flux and transition immediately following a crisis such as a civil war or, in this case, a liberation struggle. Moreover, instead of simply responding to the need for gender equity, countries adopt female-friendly policies for many reasons: recruiting women's political support, enlisting their service in the economy, complying with external donor objectives, and showing that the country is modernizing (Tripp et al. 2009, 13). Zimbabwe, therefore, is not alone as a nondemocratic country with a strong women's movement, representation of women in government, or laws guaranteeing women's rights. Tripp and her colleagues credit feminists in Zimbabwe for being able to hold demonstrations when the government ruthlessly suppressed others and to spearhead the passage of "some of the most progressive legislation regarding domestic violence anywhere in the world"—in a country they consider to be a semi-authoritarian state in serious economic and political turmoil (12). It is possible that this law, as well as treaties supporting women's and human rights, may never be implemented—especially in a country in which the president derides the rule of law as an infringement of its sovereignty. Yet these laws could not have been passed without women agitating for change. And once on the books, laws are available for use under different circumstances and for various purposes. Progressive laws may start off as show legislation, like the "show elections" that many countries hold to demonstrate democracy to the world rather than ensure it for their people, and yet they may eventually be implemented to accomplish genuine change.

Democracy is not a crucial variable in Lauren Berlant's study of the conditions that contribute to cruel optimism—striving for a goal that is impossible to reach under present circumstances or in the foreseeable future (2011). Berlant, it must be said, was writing not specifically about Zimbabwe or even about Africa, but about the United States' political economy and social landscape. And the culprits she goes after are neoliberalism (reduction of government spending and reliance on deregulated markets and privatization) and the penetration of the market into all aspects of life. But market principles do also affect the Zimbabwean political economy. Just as happened in many other developing countries in the late 1980s and early 1990s, Zimbabwe was counseled by the International Monetary Fund and the World Bank to cut back on government expenditures for social services, to let the free market regulate prices and services in an Economic Structural Adjustment Program. When that policy was adopted, out went the free education that the new regime had promised, and with it many citizens' hopes for upward mobility. Individuals and businesses saw reversals of fortune, and the citizens expressed their discontent through food riots, labor strikes, and student protests. This was countered by an increase of centralized power in an executive presidency along with heavy-handed use of force. Corruption grew with privatization, as government officials took advantage of their contacts and knowledge to make deals that benefited themselves. During this time and for decades afterward, NGOs began providing services that had once been the government's charge, especially in health, civic education, community development, and food security.

The group of urban women who organized AWZ—black, white, Asian, and coloured (mixed-race) women students, lecturers, activists, labor organizers, and development officers—were reasonably optimistic that they could effect change in the new country. Though women and men in rural areas around the country had gained little from the land redistribution programs, which along with women's emancipation had been major platforms in the liberation struggle, the government had offered hope through the appointment of a minister of community development and women's affairs. By directly petitioning the minister of women's affairs, the Ministry of Law and Justice, and the head of the ruling party and the government, Robert Mugabe, AWZ protested against a government cleanup program that mandated arrest and detention for black and coloured women out after curfew. AWZ won an apology from Mugabe and an end to the program that had spurred them into action. Following this success, the NGO gradually made accommodations to the government regime, which years later left it subject to charges of irrelevance and collusion. An examination of the options open to a director of AWZ at an economic and political crisis point in Zimbabwean history sheds light on this history, revealing the director's attempts to both subvert and stall the promises of feminism.

A Brief History of AWZ

This chapter contains several stories that capture the feel of the moment when Zimbabwe was poised on the brink of calamity, when optimism turned to fear, and when inflation ate away all sense of financial security. I place myself as a character in these stories and reflect on what I knew and what I did.

Across a crowded theater lobby at an event at the Harare International Festival of the Arts in 2000, the director of AWZ made a beeline for me. Reaching me, she embraced me with an open smile and a warm handshake. I had only recently joined the group's board of trustees, and she wanted me to know that she felt she had a friend in me. I tried to return her embrace with equal warmth, but I was stunned. Having reviewed her conduct of staff meetings and the annual reports that she generated, I was not happy with what I had seen: limited discussion of issues and an uninspired application of a business-outcome model—based on job demand, allocation of resources, and number of customers—to nonprofit work with women in rural areas. My disappointment with the director and the direction of the organization did not distinguish me from any of the other members of the board of trustees that year. A popular new opposition party and a constitutional reform movement coming from civil society had energized political life, leaving many people dissatisfied with the accommodations that individuals and organizations had made with the corrupt and authoritarian rule of President Robert Mugabe and his political party, ZANU (PF).[1] Not only did the AWZ board of trustees want to see a change, but the international donors, European and American aid agencies, were wary of the bloated operational costs and minimal outreach that not only AWZ but many well-established NGOs exemplified. Buoyed by the political changes, international donors used their purse strings to encourage greater grassroots participation and democratic reforms. This occurred around the time when the Zimbabwean economy was beginning one of the most spectacular declines of any nation in modern history: by 2008 the inflation rate was in the billions.

In this section, I trace two trajectories of AWZ's history. In the first, the group moves from protesting an action of government to lobbying effectively for new laws and culminates as a workshop-generating organization that complements government. The second trajectory covers the same time frame, but it might be described as a U-turn instead of a downward arc from protest to accommodation, if you will. In the beginning, as a collection of predominantly upper middle-class, highly educated professional women with ties to government through work or family, AWZ did not approach government officers as subaltern. Instead, its members had confidence that their peers in government would listen to them. Later, as the group became more representative of black women in Zimbabwe, it lost its leverage in local affairs but gained international recognition. At the time of this study, with a director in place who could trade on close ties to the government, AWZ was once again in a position to be listened to, but the message it conveyed was accommodation, not confrontation. At the end of the twentieth century, after decades of compromises with an increasingly authoritarian regime, the group's board of trustees wanted to ride the wave of democratic change in the country in hopes of bringing about positive change for women in Zimbabwe. And they wanted to keep the organization alive during the economic plummet that forced downsizing and restructuring. This put them at loggerheads with the director, who was not unhappy with the status quo.

BACKGROUND—WOMEN AGAINST GOVERNMENT

When AWZ got started in October 1983, our action was against the Mugabe regime's attack on women's freedom of movement and assembly. I had just arrived in Harare as a Fulbright Lecturer at the University of Zimbabwe (November 1983 to December 1984), and a note was pushed under my office door telling me about a meeting of concerned women in a church in the city center. I was curious about the purpose of the meeting, and it was made clear to me when I reached my home that same day. I had dawdled, looking at the trees and the flowers, talking to other walkers on my way home, and arrived there after 5:00 p.m. The woman I had recently hired as a housekeeper was in tears. She explained to me that she had missed the last bus that would get her home before curfew: if she were out after curfew, she was likely to be arrested. I didn't have a car to take her home, so I went knocking on doors in the university flats until I found a neighbor with one, who could get her safely home or to a place where she would be sure of getting home before curfew. That experience was enough to convince me that something rotten was happening in Harare and that the invitation to join in to help was one that I could not pass up.

As I recall, around fifty women were at the first AWZ meeting I attended. They were outraged that just three years after independence the new government, with its Ministry of Community Development and Women's Affairs, would ride roughshod over women, treating urban women like so much trash to be cleared away. The group sprang into action. The law students and lecturers among us took depositions from women who were released from jail or detention and visited others in their holding tanks, taking note of the conditions of the facilities. Members wrote letters to the editors of newspapers, were interviewed on radio, and eventually presented their case to the minister of community development and women's affairs. The cleanup program was called off, and Prime Minister Mugabe expressed regret about how the raids had been conducted. Even then Mugabe's statement had a hollow ring—he regretted *how* the sweep was conducted, not *that* his government had denied women freedom of movement and assembly. With this concession from the government, the group's members were energized and, with grant from an American aid agency, monetized, and they wanted to do more. That is when we held our first large workshop. AWZ was a pressure group, and from the start, members used their connections with government, legal knowledge, media, and lobbying to get its message across. Only after the success of its first campaign did the group turn to educational workshops.

When did workshops become a prime method of social change? How are they supposed to work? A fair amount of scholarly and activist writing has been devoted to analyzing participatory models and trying to assess them, but few people question the workshop model as a whole.[2] I think that workshops capture the sense of possibility because of the double imagery of the term: (1) the manual labor of putting something together—the woodshop or metal shop, the shop floor—and (2) the humanistic or intellectual process of drawing out creativity—the actors' workshop, the writers' workshop, where ideas, products, performances are shared, critiqued, and reformed. No matter their style and structure, whether taught by a master or led by peers, workshops call on our most creative, empathetic, and affiliative impulses. The problem with—or some would say the beauty of—the workshop as a form of social change is that all one needs to do to make a claim to making a difference is to hold a workshop. The work of the workshop, the hammering and the melding of ideas, the critiques of positions, the articulation of new subjectivities, and the building of support networks, instantiates social change. This leaves the system open to corruption. In 2001, a journalist told me about a friend of hers who started an NGO focused on gender and democracy. With the money donated to her NGO from an international aid agency, she was building a house in an exclusive suburb, she bought a big new car, and she sent her child to an expensive boarding school. As for doing what the donors gave her money to do—have a workshop, it's done! Write it up as successful. Of course, charlatans can abuse any system, but the belief in the power of individual change, coming from intellectual or emotional involvement and effecting change in social relations, makes the onetime workshop an especially attractive grifter's tool. Donor agencies are aware of this, and many have devised elaborate evaluation and assessment programs to judge the effectiveness of workshops. But I am getting ahead of myself with this digression.

AWZ had faith in consciousness-raising, inspired both by Paolo Freire's ([1973] 2003) revolutionary "conscientizing" and the women's movement's consciousness-raising sessions, which many of the group's older African and Western members had participated in and its younger members respected even though such groups were beyond their experience. Some members had been in Marxist groups whose mode of operation included group and self-criticism sessions called "criticism/self-criticism." A few members had helped organize labor unions, while others had taught men and women through agricultural extension programs. In offering its first workshop, the group wanted to bring urban and rural women together to recognize their common plight and come up with their own plans for addressing their problems. We embarked on this process with the highest hopes.

AWZ expected three hundred women at its first workshop, but over five hundred showed up. One thinly disguised motive for sweeping women off the street had been for then prime minister Mugabe to shore up his political base—rural women—who often complain that "prostitutes" in the city take their husbands' money, leaving wives and families bereft. Rural women's distrust of urban women was one obstacle in bringing them together. We faced another obstacle: the ruling party had a lock on women's voices. When AWZ members went into urban areas to spread the word about the workshop, some women refused to meet in groups without a ruling party representative present; they were afraid that they would be thought disloyal. At other times, meetings of four or more were broken up by party members because the party had not authorized the meetings. In rural areas, officers from the Ministry of Community Development and Women's Affairs accompanied the group's representatives; that ministry also provided transportation or money for transportation so that rural women from all over the country could come to the capital for the workshop. This early collaboration with the government is often overlooked in the story of AWZ's beginning. My study of the affiliations listed by attendees at the workshop reveals that most belonged to organized groups; income-producing cooperatives in rural and urban areas were the most common. Other affiliations included the ZANU (PF) Women's League and three labor unions.

Enabling rural and urban women to listen to each other and recognize their common plight was one of AWZ's goals. Using a randomized system to disperse women who had traveled together, all female participants were assigned into groups of about twelve or fifteen members. The few men in attendance were assigned to one group. Each group selected one of its members to serve as a reporter, responsible for summarizing the members' concerns and suggestions.

Unscripted workshop groups were the heart of the day's activities, but the day started much more predictably. Welcome speeches included rhetoric from the liberation struggle: following the speakers, women raised their fists, shouting "*Pamberi ya* [Forward with] . . ." and lowered their fists to shouts of "*Pasi ya* [Down with] . . . .": what we were for and against went by so fast that I never knew why I was raising and lowering my fist. The main business of the morning was a play, presented in hopes that by identifying with the characters, we could encourage conversation across differences. The Harare-based Workers' Theater Group created and performed in the play, which dealt with two sisters, one a rural wife with an absent husband and the other a pregnant teenager who leaves for the city in disgrace. From the laughter and the tears in the audience, it was clear that the play struck a chord. Women talked freely in the ensuing workshops, earnestly disclosing their needs and hopefully suggesting how government could meet them. One thing that most women wanted was for the government to take family allowances directly from their husbands' paychecks and send them to wives and families at home. Their belief in the power of government and its will to do

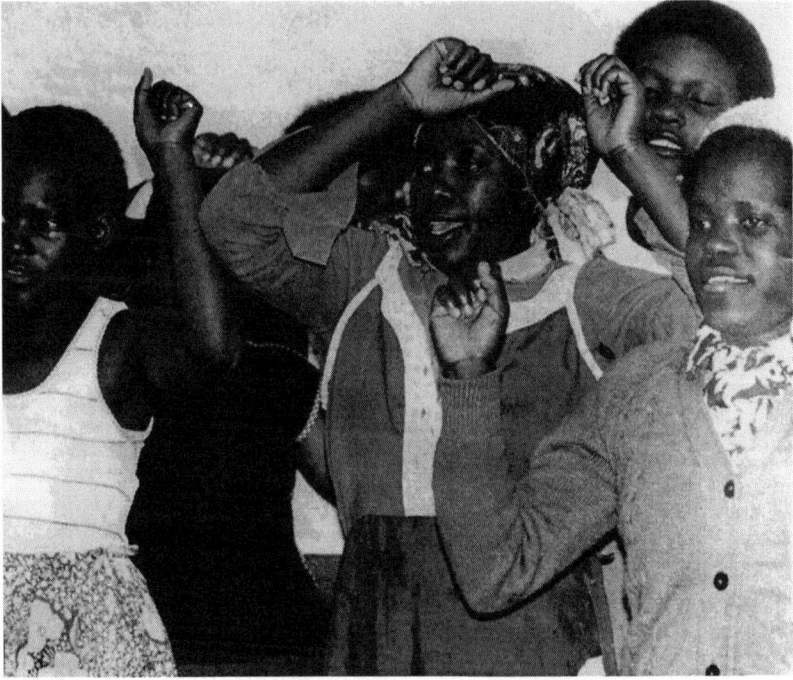

Figure 8. Sheila Chikoore and the Workers' Theater Group, Harare, 1985. Photo by Birgitta Lagerstrom.

good distinguishes the early stages of Zimbabwean independence, though this positive attitude was even then tempered by fear of government reprisals, for talking with NGOs, for instance. Government is the stern father from whom all blessings flow but whose arms are mighty and swift.

After the workshop and despite criticism from the ruling party, the fate of AWZ rested with a few individuals who were determined to act to improve the lives of women in Zimbabwe. The leading national newspaper ran a front-page story on the workshop, but with the criticism of "airing dirty linen in public" lodged at it by the Women's League of the ruling party. The league claimed that the party had already addressed the issues women raised—the need to enforce laws already on the books, for women to gain access to land and to get maintenance payments from husbands—as they saw it, nothing new was said. A history of AWZ written by one of its founders reports that during the group's early days government actively engaged in discrediting the group, though other organizations, including the Zimbabwe Women's Bureau, were making public women's complaints and insisting that "independence is not only for one sex."[3] Criticism of AWZ appeared on editorial pages and in letters to the editor: one op-ed piece, based on a reading of a magazine article about me, lambasted me as a Western woman trying to tell black Zimbabwean women how they should live. AWZ members flooded the two major English-language newspapers with letters supporting me and extolling the work of the group. Many of us thought that if the writer of the op-ed article had known that I was a black American, she would not have been so vituperative.

The workshop spawned other workshops, a newsletter, and later a magazine. Subsequent workshops took account of women's health issues, a topic that the group was not intrinsically drawn to but which grew from their listening to the concerns raised by women throughout the country. The newsletter morphed into the magazine, which was circulated to members and subscribers, including other women's organizations, and sold at newsstands.

In the early years, AWZ took up controversial issues, including "baby dumping," in which single mothers were represented in news media as demons and monsters.[4] In the mid-1980s, newspapers carried stories of newborn babies found in pit latrines and garbage dumps. The actual cases were fewer than a handful, but the penalties exacted were particularly harsh. A 1987 case of a rural woman who was given a sentence of nine years hard labor for murder when she was found guilty of killing her newborn galvanized many people into action. AWZ held a workshop and conducted a media campaign that included circulating its own newsletter. With support from many fronts, the sentence was appealed before a three-judge panel. While the judges did not all agree on what an appropriate sentence was, they all agreed that infanticide is less reprehensible than murder and that the law should reflect this. In 1990 the government instituted the Infanticide Act, by which if a mother—suffering from (1) stress due to effects of a birth; (2) a social, financial, or marital situation in which the child was born; (3) perceived difficulties in raising a child; and/or (4) psychological problems due to the birth or other causes—kills her own child within six months of its birth, she can be charged with infanticide rather than murder. Under these circumstances, a guilty mother is liable to be imprisoned for a period not exceeding five years. This law, which has been implemented, is one of the achievements of activists in AWZ.

CONFRONTING OR COMPLEMENTING GOVERNMENT: AWZ GROWS UP

Though it had much to its credit, AWZ was criticized for the racial makeup of its members—more white than black and a sizable proportion of expatriates. In the face of that criticism, we argued that we provided a platform for the voices of black Zimbabwean women to be heard, but the members who remained after the first few years knew that the group could not depend on expat and wealthy women as volunteers and that AWZ needed more black members to be considered authentically Zimbabwean. The core of the original group, who were professionals and activists, found the solution in establishing a board of trustees to manage assets for the organization and hire a director. Once this structure was in place, staff members for the programs and the magazine were hired, fieldworkers in each province were put in place, and a nominal membership fee was collected from its thousands of members throughout the country. This is the institutional structure the group had when it became a consultative agency for the United Nations, a position it continues to hold.

AWZ's mission statement, as it appears on the organization's current Web site, has changed little since the group's formation: "To promote, advocate, and defend women's civil, socio-cultural, and economic rights in Zimbabwe." Reflecting changes at home and abroad, earlier language in the organization's objectives that had set goals of promoting civil rights and contributing to national development has been dropped in favor of "promoting women's human and legal rights," "promoting gender-sensitive portrayals of women in media," and "supporting efforts to open broadcast media." Where once an objective of the group was "to advocate [for] women's participation and inclusion in decision-making processes and structures," it has been strengthened to "to promote women's leadership in decision-making processes." To advocate for access to basic health and to develop and implement programs that address HIV/AIDS remain foci. These objectives shaped the work of the three sections of the NGO: Legal, promoting legal literacy through its referrals to attorneys, broadcasts, and the magazine; Health, addressing a wide-range of women's health issues through the magazine, workshops, and broadcasts; and Editorial, publishing the quarterly magazine.

Over the years, as AWZ evolved from a volunteer organization to a professionally staffed, internationally funded NGO with a membership base of thousands, it also changed from an organization that stands against the government to one that works with government. In terms of their attitudes toward government, the group's founders were not too different from me. I had come to Zimbabwe after years of skirmishes in the United States, for civil rights, against war, and for women's liberation. I had come hoping to find a government that I could work with rather than against. During the early years of Zimbabwean independence, many African exiles returned and others came to the country, inspired by the liberation struggle, by the promise of socialism, and by the possibility of toppling neighboring apartheid South Africa. Some of AWZ's founders worked for the government: one was an agricultural development officer, and one had especially close ties to members of Mugabe's cabinet. Their belief in government, in the potential for government responsiveness to the plight of women, spurred them into action. Their early tactics—publicizing the events, taking depositions, petitioning the government, sending delegations to ministries, writing articles in newspapers and magazines—were politics of confrontation; speaking truth to power is one way of putting it.

AWZ was never like Women of Zimbabwe Arise (WOZA), winners of the Kennedy Human Rights Award in 2009 (see chapter 2). WOZA rallies its members to civil disobedience, to take to the streets to protest government policies and in opposition to draconian laws against public assembly. Its members use love as a weapon of social change: wielding valentines and carrying flowers, they hope that guerilla theater will melt the hearts of legislators and other government officials. AWZ's style of protest has much in common with the Zimbabwe Women's Writers' Project, an organization committed to increasing literacy among women and to helping women write their own stories. Tackling what it calls "unsafe issues" such as rape, abortion, and wife beating, the ZWWP holds forums and workshops and publishes books of short stories and poems. AWZ's work is more academic—operating in the scholarly and rhetorical realms of social science, legal studies, and journalism—but uses similar technologies. It brings women together to speak their truths and subsequently turns their experiences into statements that can be used in national, regional, and international forums on the status of women.

From the organization's beginning in 1983, AWZ's methods garnered media coverage and political attention. A report on its first workshop, containing rural and urban women's recommendations for changes, was written and distributed to government ministries. When I delivered a bundle of the booklets to the Ministry of Justice, I had in my mind movies that show a stream of newspapers hot off the press with headlines exposing corruption. And the next scene shows the culprit in handcuffs. It felt good to let the government know what women experienced and what they wanted. This sense of accomplishment led me to imagine scenes from other movies, where a judge rules and the innocent are set free. In reality, that bundle of booklets may well have been filed away and never opened. Or if they were read, the issues they raised could not have been seriously considered. But the group did not rely solely on one mode of communication. Newspapers were not so tightly controlled when the NGO got started; along with news magazines, women's magazines, radio, and television, they carried AWZ's message and stories about the group. We also were able to talk one-on-one with midrange and highly placed government officials. That is one of the beauties of a small country; in that first decade of Zimbabwe, university lecturers, members of parliament, and ministers of government showed up at the same cultural events and partied at each other's homes.

Over the years, differences in wealth, lifestyle, connections, and power increasingly divided these groups. Government officials began to speak a different language—a language of deals and angles, a language that justified their perks and denigrated activists and academics as naive idealists, at best, and antigovernment obstructionists, at worst. Activists who wanted to be taken seriously by government adopted some its attitudes and orientations. AWZ's willingness to confront government also changed during its first two decades. Some of this change involved new understandings of how government worked, especially in the 1990s with Structural Adjustment Programs that reduced government spending on health and education, and more sophisticated approaches to playing the angles in business and government for private gain. The group had some successes, especially in supporting court cases, such as the enacting the laws on infanticide, and in joining with other groups in Zimbabwe to lobby for changes in legislation to grant women the right to money from their husbands for maintenance of their households and the right to inherit marital property at their husbands' death. These successes, many won through negotiations, made it easy to think of the government as a machine that would run smoothly with the right handling. Maybe because of its accomplishments at home and its participation in international and regional forums, the group didn't notice the government's increasing authoritarianism or the tightening grip of its iron hand.

Zimbabwe's leader, Robert Mugabe, began his rule with an ostensible politics of inclusion. In a psychobiography of Mugabe, journalist Heidi Holland concludes that Mugabe's relationship to the last colonial governor showed "not only the real affection that existed between unlikely allies but what was possible for Mugabe when he was in an accepting, loving environment" (2008, 80). After independence had been won, Mugabe literally reached out to hold the hand of the leader of the white supremacist regime, Ian Smith. Smith remembers: "Well, I don't like holding hands. So I got my hand out of his hand and moved to the other end of the sofa" (1997, 87). Journalist Richard Dowden agrees with Holland that Mugabe wished to be accepted by the British, and that his anger at their rejection drives his pursuit of power. Dowden writes, "He is a complicated schizophrenic man, driven by respect for the Western mentality for logic and order and a passionate sense of injustice and rejection by whites. He has both a vision of wrongs to be righted, even revenged, [and] the lust for power" (2009, 145–46).

Mugabe's political rhetoric in Zimbabwe's first decade—mostly directed at whites, rural populations, workers, and the churches—emphasized "reconciliation and unity, development and nationalism" (Dorman 2003, 46). This hegemonic politics of inclusion was never complete: the people of Matabeleland, massacred in the Gukurahundi immediately following independence, were not included. And I would argue, the urban population, students, and women in the city were also beyond the embrace of the ruling party. This is not to say that individual speakers of siNdebele (the language spoken by the Matabele people), urban politicians, university graduates, professors, and women were not given high positions in government or allowed to enjoy the perks of office. Zimbabwean historian and activist Brian Ratopoulos captures the tension in a strategy that seeks social unity without exploration of the will of the people: "The nature of ZANU (PF)'s hegemonic position was characterized by a popular level of consent and a distinctive coercive strain, which sought to enforce a particular strategic unity."[5] NGO directors cooperated with the government in order to participate in national development, to advance their own agendas, to work effectively in the country, and to win in the local prestige game.

In a 1999 interview conducted by political scientist Sara Dorman, the director of the group spoke about the advantage of collaboration over confrontation:

> When we have our members' meeting, I always call for a government official to attend, to show we are not doing anything wrong. I always emphasize that as NGOs we complement the government. Strategies are important. . . . Lobbying depends on the issue we are dealing with, what level you should act on. . . . There are situations where confrontation doesn't help. If people agree to sit down with you then you can get somewhere. . . . You may seem to be weaker but you can make mileage that way, try not to make enemies. . . . If you are allowed to sit at the right table, that is where you can have influence. (Dorman 2001, 141)

This nonconfrontational strategy had worked for most of the decade under the leader who was the director when I joined the board of trustees.

Some members of the staff did not share the director's accommodationist views. The assistant director was an especially dynamic speaker and more willing to take a stand against government policies. The board of trustees could see a battle for power brewing between the two. Some definitely wanted the assistant director to win, but all were concerned about an orderly transition and about maintaining all the functions of the group. Another member of the director's staff confided in us that the director's pro-ZANU (PF) associations were hurting the group's image and led us to believe that a vehicle bearing AWZ's logo was used by ZANU (PF) candidates in the parliamentary election. That the director had associations with ZANU (PF) came as no surprise—her husband was a minister in Mugabe's cabinet. I was not around when she was hired, but my guess is that as feminists, the trustees would not judge a woman by her husband's position or his politics. Given the confidence that this implied, some of us were especially incensed about this use of the vehicle, as we had visions of our logo linked with preelection violence. We increased our scrutiny of the director's personnel and fiscal management and of her political activities.

As the director said in the quotation above, the group functioned to complement the government, not stand in counterpoint to it. After almost twenty years, AWZ had learned to work with the government. But in 1999–2000, with the potential for a change of government brought by the founding of the Movement for Democratic Change (MDC), the board of trustees wanted AWZ to put more-effective pressure on the regime; it wanted to speak out against violence leading up to the elections, and to disentangle itself from the ruling party.[6] Board members openly presented two concerns to the director about her behavior and her representation of the group. One entailed her membership on the Harare City Commission. The city commission had been put in place by the minister for local government when the capital city's elected mayor was removed from office—a shake-up rumored to have taken place at Mugabe's personal request. Our statement to the director about why she should resign her post reflects the board of trustees' own accommodation to the political regime and our ambivalence toward it. Although we had originally thought that the director's position on the city commission provided a good opportunity for her to represent AWZ and women's issues, trustees now questioned whether she had other political goals in serving on the commission. Our real concern was that the Harare City Commission had overstayed its welcome: civil-society activists and opposition politicians now forcefully argued that the city should be run by elected officials. The group could no longer justify its director's continued involvement in a city commission that usurped the role of democratic elections; the board advised her to resign. The director refused to resign her post on the commission, stating that she was there in a private capacity, not as director of AWZ, and that she did not take time away from her duties in the office to work there.

The second concern of the board of trustees was the violence in the run-up to the 2000 parliamentary elections—the first election contested by the MDC, the newly formed opposition political party, held just a few months after the ruling party's defeat in the constitutional referendum. Newspapers were filled with stories of violence: the government newspapers charged the MDC with thuggery, rioting, and illegal assembly, while the independent press ran pictures of the swollen and beaten faces of MDC candidates and supporters. What I learned from people traveling about the country was that the police, army, and war veterans had been enlisted in a campaign of violence. Friends of mine were injured in a peace march calling for an end to preelectoral violence. It is clear from the director's response that she thought that the violence was perpetrated by ZANU (PF), but she declined to send out a press release denouncing violence because doing so would align the group with the opposition party. AWZ's job, she maintained, was to stand for women, not against the government; the group's members came from both political parties.

Referendum and Crisis—Increased Democracy, No Money

The board of trustees' crisis of confidence in the director began in 2000. This period, after constitutional reform was defeated in what was essentially a referendum on the Mugabe government, ushered in many changes for Zimbabweans. In this section, I examine AWZ's role in the political process as it advocated for women and promoted women's civil rights in the context of increasing political competition, electoral violence, and a declining economy. A number of factors influenced Zimbabwe's economic decline. Chief among them was that the buying power of the once-strong Zimbabwe dollar began to fall after the government caved in to political pressure from war veterans and began printing more and more money. Around this time, Zimbabwe also joined other countries in a battle for territory and resources in the Democratic Republic of the Congo (formerly Zaire). In sum, "popular outrage about rising costs, deteriorating public services, corruption and the intervention in the war in the Democratic Republic of Congo (DRC) [cost] ZANU (PF) much of its former support in the urban areas," reported a human rights group examining the background to the 2000 elections (African Rights 2000, 1).

While the economy was declining, both pro- and antigovernment political activism was increasing. The 1990s had seen a rise in student activism and strikes by civil servants including doctors and nurses. In 1998, the National

Constitutional Assembly (NCA), a coalition of individual citizens and civic organizations including trade unions, student groups, women's groups, human rights organizations, and church groups came together to try to effect change through constitutional reform. Prominent on its list of concerns was the heightened concentration of power in the hands of the executive president, though that was not the NCA's sole agenda. The NCA was nonpartisan, but a number of its members had actively opposed the government in the 1990s. Spurred on by the possibility for change that the NCA represented, some of its members formed the MDC opposition political party. In 1999, both the NCA and the MDC were agitating for political change on behalf of a population whose buying power had decreased, a population that saw funds going to the DRC, not in national interests but for private gain, and a population that had been asked again and again to pay a special, one-time tax, called a "levy"—this time it was the AIDS Levy—only to have the funds disappear, never reaching the intended recipients. A journalist told me that she had learned from the minister of finance that the first $11 million of the AIDS Levy was used to cover Mugabe's travel abroad. This was not reported in the newspaper; journalists self-censor, I was told.

The constitutional reform campaign, which sparked political revolt in Zimbabwe, was a massive adult civic education exercise on the part of both the government and the NCA. Through television and radio broadcasts and in brochures, newspaper feature stories, advertisements, cartoons, and song, the people of Zimbabwe were told what a constitution does, informed about the history of and problems with the present constitution, and urged to exercise their responsibility to set things right. Forums on presidential powers, the structure of parliament and the judiciary, religion and the state, gender and social change were held primarily in the city by the NCA. When the government entered the arena, the Constitutional Commission (CC) took these issues and more to the rural areas as well. Government advertisements trumpeted that it was now time for the people of Zimbabwe to write a constitution for themselves and to get rid of the one thrashed out in Britain during the independence negotiations. This moment may have captured more of the aspirational sense of democracy than any before or since in Zimbabwe. The vote that established majority rule and Robert Mugabe as prime minister at the end of the liberation struggle certainly was full of hope, but it did come at the end of a long war in which "conscientizing" liberation armies demanded food, supplies, retribution, and collaboration, while the government forces doled out few rewards and much punishment. Constitutional reform gave people a chance to reflect on how their government should be structured and what the law of the land should be; they could create a homegrown constitution and inscribe it with the voice of the people.

Improving the status of women was among the many issues taken up in the constitutional reform movement.[7] Gender is a highly contested terrain. The ruling party, in power since independence in 1980 and violently trying to hold on to the reins of government, promotes women's issues in its newspapers and as signatories to important international conventions on the rights of women. The Zimbabwean government has also passed far-reaching legislation extending women's rights as legal adults, mothers, wives, and employees. Women within and outside the ruling party protested that there was not enough positive coverage of women in the media, that the laws promoting women's rights were not enforced, and that recent court rulings rolled back previous legislative gains. Also working against the reality of the emancipated woman in Zimbabwe is the existence of a bifurcate legal system of customary and civil law. Under customary law, women are not equal to men, and the "discriminatory nature of customary law is maintained and protected by the constitution" (Cawthorne 1999, 77).

Women's groups pursued these issues in the NCA. But once the government established the CC, they were divided about whether to join in the deliberation of that body. As the CC was associated with the ruling party and the NCA with the opposition, no one could be on both sides. The Women's Coalition grew out of this impasse. Dozens of women's NGOs working throughout the country came together to craft a platform that dealt with women's issues and that women working with the NCA and the CC could draw from. Women from civil society's NCA and the government's CC, who were members of the Women's Coalition, reached unanimity on the Women's Charter, a document that guided their advocacy efforts.[8] The question of accepting or rejecting government proposals did not find the coalition unanimous. A political analyst who worked with the Women's Coalition told me that in debates about whether to vote for or against the government's draft constitution, the director of AWZ was middle-of-the-road to pro ZANU (PF). While most members of the coalition stood for "Vote No," the director did not council members to vote "yes," the position of the ruling party, or to vote "no"—both the MDC's and the NCA's position—but to "vote wisely." Even this noncommittal-sounding exhortation came under criticism from ZANU (PF), and rural women, long the stronghold of the ruling party, feared reprisals if they did not toe the party line.

There were several controversial issues in the 2000 draft constitution, but the ruling party was most concerned with a land redistribution program that would allow the government to take over white-owned farms. At the last minute, Mugabe had added a clause to the draft constitution that would permit the state to compulsorily acquire agricultural land and to oblige the former colonial power to compensate displaced farmers for their loss (Dorman 2003). Before the vote, ZANU (PF) claimed that the MDC members were puppets of the whites and that white farmers and the MDC wanted to return the country to colonialism. Voters turned out in droves to defeat the draft constitution. Women were not specifically targeted in the violence in the run-up to the vote, when wearing T-shirts or using symbols of the opposition party brought blows and torture, but they were punished by beatings and destruction of property after the party's first loss.

Women's voices had been heard in the constitutional reform campaign: when state-owned media outlets refused to carry information about the opposition party, the media did print and broadcast stories about the women's coalition's deliberations. A consideration of the causes contributing to the defeat of the 2000 draft constitution leads one to ask: Is there a women's vote in Zimbabwe? Of course, this cannot be decided without an analysis of voting patterns that we don't have; researchers are unlikely to get access to the data, if they exist. The best speculation is, if there is a women's vote, it is most likely for the ruling party.

Most women live in the rural areas, though Zimbabwe's population is urbanizing, and the sex ratio in the city is not as unbalanced as it once was. Women in rural communal areas often depend on remittances from husbands and other relatives working in cities, in mines, or on commercial farms. In rural communal areas, women have little access to waged labor; they make a living through subsistence farming, market gardening, selling beer and cooked food, hawking handicrafts, and individual or group-based income-generating projects such as sewing school uniforms, manufacturing ovens, and building toilets. During the hungry season, before the next harvest or during a drought or flood, the ruling party distributes bags of maize meal for food and seed corn for the next season. Even when the supplies come from donor countries to fight famine, they are typically delivered by government trucks. This may not buy loyalty, but few are willing to bite the hand that feeds them. The old saying about African peasants is true of Zimbabwe: they tell the opposition party, "I will vote for you, when you are in power." Joost Fontein suggests that in Zimbabwean politics there is a blurring of "spontaneity and enforcement" that encompasses people's awareness of the state's display of arbitrary force and their own aspiration for "good governance and a functioning state" (2009). I like this way of thinking about women and the vote because it moves the discourse away from the distribution of goods, recognizes the terror that visits the powerless, and addresses why some people try to find legitimacy in the state's actions. In Zimbabwe, democracy is an aspiration, but multiparty politics there leads to such disruption and conflict that many people prefer not to vote (Chikwanha, Sithole, and

Bratton 2004). And those who wish to vote are often thwarted by long lines, interference, and violence.

Within this context of political upheaval and economic decline, AWZ had funds to advocate for the "Engendered National Budget," called "the Gender Budget," as a part of a southern African regional effort to get women involved in good governance. When AWZ held its Gender Budget workshop in 2001, I found myself chairing the session. How could this be? I had sworn off public appearances on behalf of the group, after the editorial on me and the constant low-level aspersion of "Western influence." In 1984 I had represented the pro side in a debate that AWZ had organized and been interviewed on radio and for magazines, and I had written an article for AWZ for a news magazine. Most of the time, being a public face of AWZ had not bothered me much. I knew that I was working for and with Zimbabwean women, but a white American friend withdrew from the group right away—too many white women for her—she questioned the authenticity of the group. And a black American friend had qualms after a few weeks—she felt like an outsider, especially when she went into the townships and faced women who were afraid to talk to her without a party member present. I felt that I had learned something from the women's movement in the United States, something about consensus decision-making and about coalition building, which I felt could serve AWZ. That was 1984, but this was 2000, when the authenticity and legitimacy of the group was not in question. Its director was a black Zimbabwean as were all its officers, staff, and members.

In the year 2000, I was not at the head of the table to speak on the "Gender Budget." In fact, most of the meeting was conducted in rapid-fire chiShona and siNdebele, which I could not follow. I was there to represent the outside world, to indicate that what women say here has meaning and merit on a broader scale. So I agreed to chair the session, to make introductory remarks, and to thank the participants in discussions that I could not understand. Translators mostly translated from chiShona to siNdebele and vice versa. From my seat of honor, I gained a sense of the power of the women's voices. None who spoke was hesitant; the words flowed, and the women stood strong.

About 140 women from forty-eight of the fifty-two districts of Zimbabwe, including all major urban areas, participated at the workshop. It also drew from other NGOs—Women and AIDS Support Network, Zimbabwe Women Lawyers Association, and Zimrights (a human rights NGO). Members of parliament were invited through their party whips, but none from ZANU (PF) or the MDC attended. The Gender Budget workshop included a presentation on the national budget process by a UZ economics professor (presented mostly in English) as well as breakout groups on the following topics: benefits of gender analysis of the budget, areas of concern in the budget, and difficulties and challenges of lobbying for a gender-sensitive budget. No matter what its assigned topic, each group reported back pretty much the same thing: women were not valued or consulted as "stakeholders"; women are major consumers of services whose allocations are decreasing—health, education, gender and youth development—and government priorities do not match women's. These comments were written up in an internal document summarizing the workshop. Six of the fourteen recommendations coming out of the workshop had to do with improving health care and disbursement of the AIDS Levy; five concerned good governance, decentralization, transparency, accountability, and anticorruption; two argued for greater allocation to education in general and for adult education in particular; and one presented the need to increase participation of civic organizations in a bottom-up budget process. When I thanked the participants at the end, I said that the workshop was only the beginning of the process and that participants should be geared to take the process further.

Impressed by what I saw of the participant's strength and articulateness, I suggested to the AWZ leadership that we follow up the Gender Budget workshop with one-on-one visits of constituents to their MPs. This suggestion was unequivocally rejected at a meeting of the board of trustees with the director. Why was it a bad idea to bring a woman from the rural areas to the capital to talk with her MP? Two reasons: first, the MPs would not like it; and second, the women who are not chosen would not like it. On the first point, my colleagues explained to me that the woman might suffer reprisals. MPs would be hostile toward AWZ's interference, enabling women to bring grievances that could embarrass them. Second, we should not risk rekindling old hostilities in the rural areas by singling out a woman here or there to go to the capital to meet with her MP, which could lead to witchcraft accusations, jealousy, and animosity. I gave up.

AWZ did follow up on the Gender Budget workshop through a breakfast meeting with three female MPs, one MDC member, and two ZANU (PF) members. The modest breakfast took place in a meeting room in one of the international hotels. The MPs said that they agreed with much that had come out of the workshop but gave little advice about how we might proceed. The strongest bit of advice was to go where the decisions are made and the budget set, talk to the junior civil servants. We were told to expand our concerns beyond social welfare issues to include land, a central issue for the government since the constitutional referendum and the beginning of the farm invasions. And we were told that we had to get men into our groups; women and gender-specific issues are trivialized by MPs. This session was quite cordial, but it was as though we were strategizing with colleagues about how to be effective, not influencing political officeholders. We made no petitions and they made no promises.

The breakfast meeting of NGOs and parliamentarians in the Gender Budget campaign is an example of the interrelationship of civil society and government in its classic sense. Rosemary Coombes, in an overview of civil society in postcolonial settings, states, "In the Western history of civil society, self-governing voluntary associations are privileged as the institutions most likely to foster civil society, continually forging new interests and new identities" (1997, 6). These voluntary associations are thought to forge a space between government and society in which civil society can influence the actions of government. Of course, this is not a one-way street: the state also contributes to the production of the subjectivities and modes of being that constitute civil society. What does this breakfast meeting reveal about the interrelationship of civil society and government in Zimbabwe? In one sense, it shows the imbrications of government and civil society as women with multiple ties assume the binary of government and public. One of the MPs had been active at the university and in civil society in dealing with women's issues, another was like our director in being married to a government minister, and the third had built her reputation through community organizing and activism.

AWZ's unwillingness to push an agenda and its desire to maintain cordial relations allowed the director to fall into a comfortable conversation about the problems of women in society, especially of women like the MPs themselves—the parliamentarians were also fighting a male establishment. The director had argued that sitting at the table with the government opens up the possibilities for influencing its decisions; this did not seem to be the case with a breakfast meeting with women MPs who seemed either ineffectual or unwilling to risk political capital for women's issues. At this breakfast, the government was represented not by faceless functionaries, or by reams of paper, or spools of red tape, but by women whose good opinion the director valued. They were chewing over a common problem, not meeting as petitioner to government. I don't want to make too much of this encounter between AWZ and the women parliamentarians; they were not in control of the budget. I hold it up as an example of the normalization of relations between AWZ and the state and a flattening of distinctions between the two.

These relations between AWZ and the parliamentarians are a far cry from the state's blatant attempt to control civil society about five years prior, in 1995, through the Private Voluntary Organizations Act. This act is a legacy of the colonial period. In 1967, under the unilateral declaration of independence

(UDI), the Smith regime instituted the Welfare Organizations Act, to oversee the actions of organizations supporting the "terrorists" (freedom fighters) and their families during the liberation war. In 1995, the Zimbabwean government, under Robert Mugabe, amended and renamed the act the Private Voluntary Organizations Act (PVO). (I digress to point out that, of course, this was not the first time that the apparatus of the colonialists had been used against the people in a newly independent country: the dreaded police tanks that rumble through streets of postapartheid South Africa and the Law and Order Maintenance Act, which prevented freedom of assembly and speech under UDI in Rhodesia both served similar purposes in black-majority ruled countries.) The amended PVO Act gave the Department of Public Service, Labour and Social Welfare the power to suspend any or all members of executive committees of NGOs in the country and to appoint trustees to run the organizations (see Dorman 2003). I learned about this attack on NGOs in a letter from a founder and board of trustees member, while she was awaiting a supreme court decision on the constitutionality of the PVO Act. She explained that the director of the Associated Women's Club (discussed briefly in chapter 1), one of the oldest civic organizations for African women in the country, had been removed from her office; in her place the government had installed the organization's former director, a ZANU (PF) stalwart who had been dismissed from that very post for fiscal mismanagement.

Under the regime of PVO, AWZ was anxious: could it protect its mission, resources, and reputation? The Zimbabwe Supreme Court ruled in favor of the AWC on the grounds that the provisions of PVO did not allow for due process in the removal of directors (Dorman 2001, 179–82). That this one instrument was not successful in bringing civic organizations under the control of the state does mean that others will not be tried (see Dorman 2001). The regime's monopoly on broadcast media and its antagonism toward independent print media limits the scope of civil society. Yet the state and NGOs dance together. In some instances, the dance moves as smoothly as a waltz, but in others it resembles a square dance where the caller has gotten drunk on his own power to make dancers do his bidding.

The Remains of Socialism—Retrenchment Procedures

After Mugabe lost the constitutional referendum in 2000, after people loyal to him began occupying white-owned farms, and after the violence leading up to the parliamentary elections, foreign donors started withdrawing support from many local NGOs. At that time, AWZ found itself without enough money to run its offices. The Dutch, the Norwegians, and the Danish had pulled out; the Swedish were threatening to do so. The organization was suffering and so, it seems, was the staff: at this time of high inflation and low buying power, they asked for raises, even though their salaries were higher than many at other NGOs (as noted in an external study of the group), and other organizations were already talking of retrenchment. We weren't the only ones hit hard by the political and economic fallout of Mugabe-endorsed farm invasions. Our group had only one funded project to complete, after which we might have to scale down services or staff, sell off capital, or close our doors forever. In the previous section, I dealt with the political stress that the group felt; now I turn to the financial stress and how the NGO managed to survive in a period of economic freefall.

The AWZ offices were never what you could call "abuzz." During my time with the organization we had few visitors, though a stream of volunteers from U.S. universities came through yearly, and a fair number of researchers, interested in civil society, gender equity, and women's health, found the house in suburban Harare. At the main entrance, a receptionist greeted visitors. (She was sick; two of her children had died, "failure to thrive," it was called. Most people believed her to be HIV+. The director had begun to consider requiring a medical exam before hiring new staff. The board asked what the director would do if she were to learn that a job candidate was seropositive; would she refuse to hire the candidate? In response, the director raised the question of the cost of health care and retraining for staff but dropped the issue in the face of the board's insistence that there be no discrimination against seropositive candidates.) To one side of the receptionist was the library and archives room with its comfy, brightly upholstered chairs and functional office furniture. Doors leading to the Health and Legal Education coordinators' offices faced a hallway beyond the receptionist. The Legal Education coordinator reported that about sixty women per quarter came by the office with questions, and more than double that number called or wrote with queries about inheritance, marriage, remittances, property ownership, court cases, and other legal matters. At the rear of the house, through a separate entrance, the editors of the magazine worked. Their offices had the busyness of a publisher, checking on facts, searching out advertisers, and meeting deadlines. By comparison, back through the main entrance, down the hallway to the left of the receptionist, the director's office was calm and peaceful. Only the financial assistant, whose workspace was just outside her office, could be easily seen by the director.

It was the year 2000, and the group was in trouble. Donors were pulling their money out of the country. Without fail, the director and staff did all they could to please the donors. AWZ operationalized its mission statement in projects, usually workshops. "To promote, advocate, and defend women's economic rights" led to "The Engendered National Budget" workshop. "To develop and implement programs that address HIV/AIDS" generated projects on sexually transmitted diseases, AIDS education, and home-based care. The ideas for such projects originated with the staff, but they were developed in consultation with the funding agencies. Funding agencies from different nations were constrained by their own countries' notions of appropriate development assistance. As plans for the projects were laid out, staff members had to be cognizant of the donor countries' guidelines as well as the needs of Zimbabwean women that the projects were designed to help. Staff meetings, quarterly reports, and director's reports were all geared toward the funded projects. Each project was evaluated: What are the overall goals? What activities are involved? What objectives met, how assessed? Each budget was broken down into administrative and project costs. But donor agencies, besides being wary of Zimbabwean government policies, were also reluctant to fund overhead and administration. The group owned houses, vehicles, and office equipment; it had monthly bills for utilities, telephones, and other services. There were twenty people on the permanent staff: the projects could not get done without staff. Pay for staff and overhead had to come from somewhere. Everyone was scrambling to get more money. Everything in the country cost more—the rising cost of food was indexed in the paper through the rising cost of a shopping cart of food items, but most people talked about the rapid increase in the cost of tomatoes, a staple in Zimbabwean relishes.

The inflation rate had climbed so high that the trustees were having a hard time keeping up with yearly cost-of-living increases: last year's increase was 8 percent; this year's topped 25 percent. All the staff members who could were taking extra jobs as consultants while collecting their full salary at AWZ. The board of trustees tried to set up a policy restricting the number of hours to be spent on consultancies, establishing the organization as a whole as the consultant with a small percentage of the salary going to the lead person. In budget negotiations, staff members asked for increases in salary and in housing and transportation allowances. The board of trustees countered with a request for a retrenchment plan from the staff, suggesting that, in the meantime, they use their leave days in an effort to scale back retrenchment costs. (I learned from one of the MPs at the breakfast meeting in the follow-up to AWZ's Gender Budget workshop that AWZ was not alone in struggling to find enough money to lay off workers: some government offices could not afford the payouts to lay off employees.)

Inflation had eaten up AWZ's income and savings, but why were there so few new external donors? Most of the new project funding coming into the country seemed to be for HIV/AIDS prevention and care and for democratization.

For decades, Mugabe had buried his head in the sand regarding the AIDS epidemic. Now, when the epidemic had spread to all parts of the country and all segments of society, his health care system was bankrupt—nurses and doctors were scarce; few drugs and supplies were available in the hospitals; patients' families were responsible for bed linens and sanitation; and bodies were piling up in the morgues. The central government had levied a tax on all incomes to improve the situation, but the "AIDS Levy" was as unpopular as the "Development Levy," which yielded no discernible results. Few people believed that they would reap any benefit from the levy. Based on their experience of other taxes, many believed this one-time tax would go to the "haves" rather than the "have-nots": it would not be used to relieve suffering or to help caregivers. In this environment, international aid organizations and foreign national donors contributing through NGOs stepped in to fund HIV/AIDS prevention education, to work with people living with AIDS, to provide for AIDS orphans, to train family caregivers, and to supply hospice services.

Two sources of funding were readily available for Zimbabwe from foreign donors around the time of the constitutional referendum: funding HIV/AIDS education, prevention, and treatment and for democratization, especially to encourage a vote of no confidence in the Mugabe regime. When AWZ tried to jump on the democratization bandwagon before the referendum on the constitution, I visited a United States aid office to see if it would support our legal literacy program, an education program to apprise women of their civil rights. I was told that the agency would pay for the cost of a flyer urging a "no" vote on the draft constitution to go out in the next issue of our magazine. Joining others in the Women's Coalition, we were participating in the campaign to get women to vote "wisely" (rather than encourage them to vote against the referendum); the group declined the offer of support from the Americans.

The government-supported farm invasions, attacks on the independent press, intimidation and assaults on the urban population, and harassment and torture of MDC members curbed the spread of the party into the countryside and forced some agencies to be more circumspect in how they funded democratization projects—but that did not kill the fervor for change.

Donor agencies were not only uneasy about the political situation in Zimbabwe; they were also not sure of AWZ's effectiveness. Some were reluctant to fund administrative salaries, and others lacked confidence in the group's financial accountability. After an investigation by a major donor, the group had to go through a financial audit to satisfy external donors. The audit revealed no malfeasance but some sloppiness in bookkeeping. Auditors recommended hiring a supervisor for the financial assistant and separating the organization's executive and financial functions. AWZ vowed to comply, though hiring in the face of budget cuts was a long shot. With its clean bill of health, the group prepared to approach the Swedish International Development Cooperation Agency (SIDA), a longtime donor that had not renewed funds for the upcoming year.

I joined a delegation from the board of trustees to make a presentation to SIDA. The SIDA offices were downtown in a row of modern, clean, low-rise office buildings. We were taken into a glass-walled room with a long conference table, where we defended the proposal we had submitted for the next budget cycle. SIDA was adamant about what it would and would not fund: no salaries or operating expenses for the Harare office, but offices and telephones for provincial fieldworkers. AWZ argued against offices for fieldworkers, who were in all but one of the country's provinces. Typically, they work from home, except when they rent spaces for workshops and "awareness" meetings, which promote AWZ membership and addressed local concerns. SIDA was concerned about the lack of privacy for visitors at home offices and about the distances that some women would have to travel to get to a fieldworker's home. The SIDA proposal seemed reasonable; it advocated professionalization through a dedicated, centrally located office, preferably near a bus depot. But as those of us in AWZ knew, conditions in Zimbabwe were far from ideal for what SIDA was proposing. Both war veterans and the ruling party were on a rampage throughout the country, retaliating for the ruling party's defeat in the constitutional referendum by beating blacks, ousting whites from their farms, and occupying the farms. Aided by the military and the police, the veterans were harassing and torturing citizens in urban townships and rural administrative centers for supporting the opposition party. Over and over again, resources were commandeered for the ruling party. We thought that having a lone woman in an office would make available more resources to the ruling party—telephones, office equipment, the office itself. Regardless of these concerns, however, the office, accessibility, and privacy fit with a Swedish model of community development, and SIDA would not budge. We compromised and agreed to a trial of their plan in two or three districts.

With no money coming from the Americans (who seemed only to want to support the opposition party's efforts at democratization) and little from the Swedes (who wanted their version of the little community), we were unable to augment our dwindling operating budget. We had to lay off workers. The formal firing and retrenchment procedures for Zimbabwe are the last vestiges of the once and future socialist paradise, which guaranteed workers employment and a fair hearing. We did not fire any employees while I served on the board of trustees; I learned about that procedure later from one of the secretaries in my study of women office workers in the capital city. When she was fired, a workers' council was convened to listen to her side of the story and to her boss's side. According to her, the workers' council heard the boss's side first and knew what they had to do: it was a done deal; the deck was stacked against her.

At one point, Zimbabwe's procedures to dismiss or "retrench" even a single worker required government authorization, making the job-security regulations in that country "among the most onerous prescribed anywhere" (Fallon and Lucas 1993, 242). The Labour Act, which regulates dismissal and retrenchment, was amended in 1992, 2003, and 2005, each time making it easier for employers to sever ties with employees. When AWZ sought to reduce expenditures and reorganize in order to keep going with reduced function, I went to the Ministry of Labour and Social Welfare for a crash course on retrenchment. The board of trustees was required to present its plan to a workers' council—in this case, the assembled staff in the central office—and we had to come up with measures to avoid retrenchment. In the end, retrenchment seemed the only option. Now began the negotiations. Severance pay, relocation allowances, and other benefits, including cash in lieu of leave, were among the items that must be included in our retrenchment package, but there was no law on how to calculate these allotments. The monthly pay to employees included salary, transport allowance, meal allowance, housing allowance, and clothing allowance. The director got a car instead of a transport allowance, and the fieldworkers, who typically work from home, did not get a transport or meal allowance. All the group's employees received paid vacation and sick leave. The retrenchment packages for the seven laid-off staff members in the central office included three times their monthly salaries, cash in lieu of leave at the rate of one's day pay per day of accumulated leave at the time of the layoff, plus the number of years worked times twenty thousand dollars as severance pay (about four hundred U.S. dollars at the official exchange rate in 2000). Computers were given to some staff members, and the director was allowed to take one of the vehicles. The total retrenchment bill was close to 1.7 million Zimbabwe dollars; the yearly cost for keeping those staff members would have been around a half million Zimbabwe dollars.[9]

AWZ survived the cuts. The director took a retrenchment package, and the assistant director left for a position in another country. The very capable and personable health coordinator took over as director and has since served admirably in that capacity for several years.

The Personal and the Political

AWZ had an informational booth at the 1999 Zimbabwe International Book Fair, as did Gays and Lesbians of Zimbabwe (GALZ), even after Mugabe's infamous denunciation of homosexuals in 1995.[10] I had been in the country only a couple of months at the time of the fair and happily chatted with the representatives at both booths. I was surprised to see that a man was AWZ's sole representative. When I asked him if he were a member of the group, he replied, totally straight-faced, "I work for AWZ." That told me how much the group had changed in sixteen years. It hadn't been a volunteer organization for years; it employed men, and, I was soon to learn, a man sat on the board of trustees. At the book fair, not wanting to seem presumptuous or to appear a relic of a disowned past, I hesitantly explained that I had once been active in the group. He did not seem at all curious about this but pleasantly answered my questions and invited me to stop by the group's offices, which, incidentally, were within walking distance from my university flat.

I didn't go by the offices until after I had met with a friend who was a founder and member of the board of trustees. I had something to give to her. After all these years, I had brought videotape of the first AWZ workshop, a copy for her and one for the AWZ archives. As we looked at the tape, my friend brought me up to date on some of the participants. Several of the white founders had left the country for Australia, South Africa, or other African countries; two black Zimbabweans had returned after years abroad; others were still working in Zimbabwe; three had died, one from cancer and two others under dreadful circumstances in Harare. The two were the factory workers who had been instrumental in producing the play that was the centerpiece of the first workshop back in 1984. One was Dorothy Gona, who was last seen when she went to the bank to draw out money on a Monday at lunchtime. Though her body was never found, the police, her family, and friends presumed that she had been abducted and killed, not because of her activism, but because of the relative wealth the association provided. The other, Sheila Chikoore, was killed by her husband, who used her membership in AWZ as part of his justification. Three of the original members were now on the board of trustees. I was pleasantly surprised to learn that my friend and others thought that my major contribution to the group had been the introduction of consensus decision-making, which they still tried to follow—while most U.S. groups in which I participated had long given up on reaching consensus. An invitation was extended to me to join the board of trustees as an honorary member. I thought I had best introduce myself to the director before I said yes.

I met the director in her office and presented her with a copy of the videotape. In talking to her, I felt awkward: I didn't know this person or this new organization. Yet working with the group had been the high point of my career as a feminist activist. I had done nothing to compare to it at home, though I am

Figure 9. Dorothy Gona, labor and women's rights activist, Harare, 1985. Photo by Birgitta Lagerstrom.

proud of my work in addressing sexual harassment on my campus and in the University of California system as a whole. What did the director and I have in common? She knew the history that included my experience with the group, but I didn't know hers. She must have sensed my hesitation, because she started to tell me the story of her development of feminist consciousness. Her story was not about the state or laws or protests, but involved her sexual history. I've taught courses on sexuality for years, but when I noticed where she was going, I tried to stop her, for fear of discomfiting her or me. She said, "I tell my story"—she was not at all uneasy. Then she talked openly about sex and about claiming a right to sexual pleasure. The story that she told showed her understanding that the political does not stop at the front door or the bedroom door. It was a perfect example of feminist body politics: "The personal is the political"—a slogan from second-wave feminism in the West that captured the sense that contests for equal rights in the home and within sexual relationships were crucial to the struggle for equal rights in the public domain.

My own reaction to this encounter puzzled me then, as it still does now. When the director began her story, I suddenly remembered my students and colleagues reporting their experiences talking with girls in relief centers in other parts of Africa who had been raped and abused. Some of the girls were so practiced at telling their stories that visitors were a little taken aback. The girls seemed to withdraw into themselves and produce a horror story, complete with appropriate emotion. When the story ended, their demeanor and tone of voice quickly reverted to normal. Something like this happened with the director; it was a theater of authenticity. She did not give space for me to reciprocate; this was not a moment of mutuality. Berlant refers to moments when such stories are shared as "the strange sociability of contemporary trauma talk" (2011, 128). But something else was going on here. As I reflect on this now, I see the director accomplishing two goals in telling her story: she showed me that her feminism was cosmopolitan, and she drew me in as an intimate, making it possible to call on me later as a confidante and ally. Perhaps that strange conversation explains the moment that I started with in this chapter, the then director seeking me out in a crowd and embracing me as one of her supporters. Her understanding of power, agency, and politics was deep, and her ability to maneuver in the office, in local politics, and in international forums was astute. She went on to head other NGOs.

Cosmopolitan Feminism in Zimbabwe: Dangarembga's Fiction and the Director's Politics

The director's embedding her story in feminist body politics recalls what I see as a particular cosmopolitan feminism in Dangarembga's novel *Nervous Conditions* and her play, *She No Longer Weeps*. Dangarembga leads the reader to believe that feminist consciousness can be developed indigenously by interrogation of gender inequality in the division of labor, in access to education, in distribution of marital wealth and power, in the exercise of familial authority, and in the achievement of individual integrity. In the novel, a young woman who acknowledges that her problems are based in gender inequality must find strength and courage within herself to confront and overcome sexism. On the whole, women in the Sigauke family, around whom the novel is centered, combat sexism by speaking out. Speaking one's mind becomes an act of resistance in itself.

For Dangarembga, feminism stands for voice, personal integrity, assertion of self, socially productive uses of the erotic, and recognition of the value of women's productive and reproductive labor. Whether such feminist ideas and methods could have developed in remote areas of Zimbabwe without exogenous contribution, as the novel implies, is open to debate. In the novel, a bildungsroman, we see an indigenous development of feminism as the country cousin, Tambu, discovers sexism through her own experiences and as witness to those of her female relatives, especially her outspoken cousin Nyasha.

But Dangarembga's novel and play, her statements in interviews (Dangarembga 1991), and her own activities in the 1980s suggest that she has a literary feminist genealogy rather than independent invention. She has mentioned

Germaine Greer (Whyte 1989, 12) and Alice Walker and Mariama Bâ (Veit-Wild 1989, 106) as signal influences in her feminism. "The western white feminism does not meet my experiences at a certain point, the issues of me as a black woman. The black American female writers touch more of me than the white ones," Dangarembga said when directly questioned about her legacy of women writers (Veit-Wild 1989, 106). Among the black American feminist writers, one very important name goes unmentioned in Dangarembga's genealogy: Audre Lorde, the black poet, mother, lesbian, feminist, warrior, and activist whose writings helped shape black feminism in the late 1970s and 1980s.[11] Yet Lorde's brand of feminism, with its emphasis on speaking up, its caution against using the master's tools—for *Nervous Conditions* read "education"—for liberation of the oppressed, and its celebration of sensuality and eroticism, is present in both the novel and the play.

I want to denaturalize and historicize the feminist practices of "speaking up," "questioning authority," and "expressing yourself," all variations on popular women's liberation strategies in the 1980s. These strategies assume an individual who through consciousness-raising—or "conscientizing," a term I heard often in Zimbabwe in the 1980s—comes to understand the roots of her oppression and develops the courage to fight for herself. Contrast this to other African strategies women use to resist authority: "sitting on a man" (staging a sit-in), gossiping, running away, withdrawing from domestic duties, covert manipulation and recalcitrance, invoking the spirit of female ancestors, and using civil law against customary practices (all covered in Hodgson and McCurdy 2001). Not all these options were available to the characters of the novel and the play. And some of them, such as women's covert (as opposed to open and confrontational) actions were especially defamed in popular feminism in the 1980s. "Sitting on a man," occupying his homestead and thereby requiring his provision of food and hospitality, refers to historical cases in West Africa, but similar calls to arms for women have been noted in other parts of Africa (Van Allen 1976). A sit-in requires that women work in concert in support of an injured colleague, and *in Nervous Conditions* the Sigauke family is purposefully secluded. In a 1994 interview, Dangarembga explained: "This family is very isolated, and the reason why I chose such an isolated family is that it pushes all the conflicts I am talking about to an extreme situation which I could build on" (Petersen 1994, 347).

In the novel, though the female characters learn from one another, each woman is expected to act in accord with her own sense of integrity, to honor her own beliefs and conscience, and to speak up, if not for her own ends, then because her sense of self demands it. I suggest that this representation of feminist consciousness in *Nervous Conditions* could be seen as a paean to Audre Lorde, who in her essay "The Transformation of Silence into Language and Action" famously says, "Your silence will not protect you" (1984, 41). In *Nervous Conditions*, women and girls fail to contain themselves; they speak out. But speaking out in and of itself is not a surefire solution to the problem of sexism. Lorde never suggested that it was, but rather her work encourages using language to define oneself and to recognize the power within. Dangarembga does not parrot this slogan but examines and interrogates it. Speaking out does not automatically bring victory, as is made apparent through the nervous conditions of two female characters: Tambu's disassociative state and Nyasha's anorexia-bulimia. With these conditions, Dangarembga probes the limits of Lorde's dictum. Dangarembga's use of Lorde reveals both the liabilities of speaking up as well as its power. Silence will not protect you, but speaking, in and of itself, does not redress gender inequality. Yet despite persistent obstacles, Dangarembga's protagonists work with personal integrity toward "the transformation of silence into language and action."

Lorde also exhorts women to celebrate feelings and eroticism: "We tend to think of the erotic as an easy, tantalizing sexual arousal. I speak of the erotic as the deepest life force, a force which moves us toward living in a fundamental way" (Tate 1983, 99). The erotic as a wellspring of power that can fuel social change is represented in *Nervous Conditions* in the desire for bodily pleasure, sensuality of dance movements, and celebration of sexual appetite. But it is in explicit statements in *She No Longer Weeps*, which was written before the novel, that Dangarembga claims the erotic as a life force. The following passage from the play, in which Martha (the unwed pregnant daughter of a church minister) addresses her mother, is a clear example of the powers of the erotic: "I don't want to feel ashamed of myself because my mind is free—it's the celebration rather than marriage that becomes the important thing. I like to feel my life in every cell of my body—pleasure and pain, pleasure and pain, pleasure and pain.... I like to shudder with pleasure, and sob with desire" (1987, 31; ellipses added). In the quoted passage, Dangarembga correlates a free mind with erotic pleasure, but the reader must infer causality or directionality. Martha in *She No Longer Weeps* and Nyasha in *Nervous Conditions* both show desire for bodily pleasure, but the ontogeny of this desire is not developed in either work. The desire is strong and seemingly socially productive, given its associations with the other progressive causes each young woman embraces. Their feminism extols women as outspoken, proactive, and lusty.

While *She No Longer Weeps* begins with a feminist protagonist, feminism develops anew in the lives of the protagonists in *Nervous Conditions*. Though the convention-shattering opening line of *Nervous Conditions*—"I was not sorry when my brother died"—represents a stand against traditions of male preference, of female solicitude, and of family loyalty, the work of the novel is to show how a female-centered consciousness developed. In contrast, early on in the play *She No Longer Weeps*, Martha's stakes in feminism are clear, and her explicit goals are quite congruent with those that I am using Audre Lorde to represent. Dangarembga's protagonist wants to capture the power of the erotic for the new Zimbabwe; she wants to make the personal political; she wants women to have control over their own bodies, their labor, and their children; and she wants women to define themselves outside their relations to men.

Dangarembga's optimism did not seem to last long. Just four years after independence and during the time when she wrote the play, Dangarembga appeared to be already disillusioned with postcolonial sexual politics. In an essay titled "Seizing Power," Dangarembga and coauthor Juliet Baah parodied how socialist rhetoric and capitalist accumulation played out in the postcolonial intimate relationships: "For example, since socialization of the means of production is a basic aim of scientific socialism, socialist men in the transitional stages, who still regard women as mean-objects, will happily subscribe to the notion of socialization of women—joyfully and lustily throwing to the capitalist any shreds of decency and self-discipline they might have had in this respect. So we see a married man, enjoying an evening out with his 'sugar mummy,' who claims that this is an aspect of traditional socialism that was stifled by the present capitalist system" (Dangarembga and Baah 1984, 23). She uses the language of socialism and the figure of a radical feminist to satirize postcolonial society, but she also takes swipes at the terms themselves.

While the novel *Nervous Conditions* holds out some hope that by choosing self over security women may act to loosen the bounds of patriarchy, the play's climactic onstage castration both destroys and reaffirms male power: the husband is castrated, but the father is asked to call the police. The ending of the play could be read as triumphant, bringing to mind a Greek tragedy: Clytemnestra in Aeschylus's *Agamemnon*, thrusting her knife three times into her husband's body to avenge the sacrifice of their daughter. After this Clytemnestra faces the ultimate authority, the people (Hamilton [1937] 1965, 226). But I see the climax of *She No Longer Weeps* as Dangarembga's recognition of another kind of trap for women—one that she also explored in *Nervous Conditions*: Nyasha cries, "I'm not a good girl. I won't be trapped"; refusing to be trapped in the racist and sexist conventions of colonialism, she would rather be damned as the kind of girl who grows into a loose woman (1988, 201). Martha, on the other hand, tries to rejoice in being a "bad girl" and feels herself trapped in an emotional double bind: if she steels herself to go against society, she will become cold, no longer able to weep, but if she remains compliant and vulnerable, she will lose her integrity and a sense of her own power.

In the play *She No Longer Weeps*, Dangarembga portrays a woman taking charge of her own life and acting on her feminist values. Martha's feminist principles are tested in the new Zimbabwe, but the ordeals she must survive are based on family psychodynamics as well as the sociopolitical exigencies of postcolonial life. Women who embraced the status of legal adults, granted at the end of the colonial era, found it tough going in postcolonial Zimbabwe.[12] Their place at the table was set with conventional morality, judicial inaction, and deceptive progressive discourses. The Zimbabwean government too had a lot on its plate: dissidents in the southwest, a black middle class that wanted the perks of the ousted white rulers, and a powerful belligerent neighbor to the south—apartheid South Africa, intent on destabilizing the newly independent country. In this atmosphere, Dangarembga spoke up for women's liberation, but she also recognized that gender inequality and sexism were served up with large helpings of oppression from other social domains.

The director of AWZ was fully involved in a postcolonial Zimbabwe grown more callous and vengeful, and she tried to navigate between the contradictory demands of charity and self-promotion, body politics and realpolitik, and social networks and distant reference groups. She captained a group that had started as a multiracial feminist activist organization outraged over the treatment of women in Zimbabwe's capital city. It became a Zimbabwean membership organization with considerable international recognition; it presented workshops to address local issues, and it sought funds for projects from donor countries with their own agendas. Directors of such an organization must have their feet in two camps: they must sagely employ the rhetoric and principles of Western feminists and donors, and they must adroitly weave their way through national politics, networking with the power elite while attending to the needs and desires of local women. There are many ways to make mistakes in this situation: one could too fully adopt the outsider's perspective; one could throw oneself wholeheartedly into national contests over power and status; one could determinedly meet the project goals of donors and slight the needs of local women; or one could put the needs of local women above all else and lose the ability to keep the organization going. The group did not avoid all these pitfalls, but it has adapted and survived for more than thirty years and may yet go through further transformations.

Feminism in the Muddle

In the midst of turmoil, conventions offer comforts. This is the sense that W. H. Auden conveyed in his poem "September 1, 1939": All the conventions conspire /

To make this fort assume / The furniture of home; / Lest we should see where we are, / Lost in a haunted wood, / Children afraid of the night / Who have never been happy or good" (1979, 87). Concluding this discussion of one feminist and one feminist organization in turbulent times, I address the pull of conventionality in the AWZ director's conduct and, by implication, in the lives of other change agents who have been co-opted or have run out of steam. "One of optimism's ordinary pleasures is to induce conventionality, that place where appetites find a shape in the predictable comforts of the good-life genres that a person or a world has seen fit to formulate," Berlant asserts as she argues about the power of attachments as a force that moves one out of oneself (2011, 2). In Berlant's usage, attachment is a feeling state: an individual feels attached to desired things, people, or ideas. The irony in her conceptualization is that people are attached to what they don't have: it is the motivation for, the movement in the direction of an idea, thing, or person that identifies an attachment. Conventionality seldom looms large as an attachment—typically people do not move toward convention, but rather they rest in convention, stay in convention—it is what they take for granted.

But when the rug is pulled out from under one, as in periods of economic uncertainty and political unrest, convention beckons as a place of solace. In the director's case, the pleasure of conventionality is represented by her friendship with the women parliamentarians, by her desire for local prestige and power as a member of the Harare City Commission, and by her refusal to take a stand against government violence. Conventionality confers happiness in her marriage to a government minister, companionship with like-minded individuals, and refuge from political discord.

Berlant's work is about why and how people stay attached to good-life fantasies; here I am asking how succumbing to the allure of an attainable, conventional good life diverts attention away from a distant one.[13] The promise of feminism could lead a person to work tirelessly for a good life on a distant horizon, or it could inadvertently illuminate a closer object that seems more realizable—the lifestyles of friends and neighbors, the good life as opposed to the good fight. Women are not induced to settle for the conventional; they almost trip over it when their eyes are on distant prizes. The conventional is all around them; the conventional is ordinary. Berlant refers to a sense of resignation but not defeat among those who "ride the wave of the system of attachments that they are used to" (2011, 28). The promise of feminism does not block the view of the good-life genres of one's own society (whether they are attainable or not); rather we have to be induced to keep trying to realize the sought-after promise in spite of the familiar enticements of social life around us. Women's groups are important because they provide the pleasures of camaraderie and the satisfaction of small victories as alternatives to the conventional good life—but the process of living every day while trying to realize a promised goal can be disorienting and numbing. One response to the "depression, dissociation, pragmatism, [and] cynicism" that can follow ambitious optimism is to reward oneself along the way, but the danger is that the reward supplants the original goal.[14] Just ask the CEOs on Wall Street who in fulfilling their fiduciary responsibilities to stakeholders reward themselves mightily. One version of the good life in a kleptocracy, as Zimbabwe had become by the end of the twentieth century, involves employing political connections, business relations, and friends and family to attain material rewards and social standing. These are the conventions of the director's local reference group.

How does feminism figure into this muddle of competing loyalties and desires and failing economy and political instability? The director identifies as a feminist. We can see her feminism in her achievement of agency in the fulfillment of her sexual desires, in her management of an organization devoted to the empowerment of women, and in her cooperation with other women's organizations to change the constitution of the country for the benefit of women. She might best be characterized as a conservative feminist working with government institutions to slowly change the status of women. Her embrace of the conventional does not obviate her belief in the moral equality of men and women or that sexism hurts women—but it does keep the realization of feminism's promise to transform society through gender equity at a distant horizon.

CHAPTER 4

Mercy, Mercy, Mercy

Middle-Class Working Wives and Mothers in Harare

> "This business of womanhood is a heavy burden," she said. "How could it not be? Aren't we the ones who bear children? ... When there are sacrifices to be made, you are the one who has to make them. And these things are not easy; you have to start learning them early, from a very early age. The earlier the better so that it is easy later on."
>
> Tsitsi Dangarembga, *Nervous Conditions*

Mercy is the last of the four types of women I present in this book. Grouped under the sign of Mercy—a translation of the chiShona name Nyasha, the most popular contemporary female name in Zimbabwe—are working wives and mothers who represent the ideal qualities many parents hope to cultivate in a daughter: compassion, modesty, and obedience (Hungwe 2006). That these women earned wages in the year 2000 indicates how fortunate they were: Zimbabwe's unemployment rate was around 50 percent in 2000, and only about 44 percent of the labor force was female at that time.[1] Based on the millennium study I described in chapter 2, the working wives and mothers in this category generally occupy the middle of the middle class: they work as secretaries and personal assistants in industry and government offices; they own stoves, refrigerators, and CD players; most travel by bus or commuter omnibus.

I interviewed twenty women in this category in 2000–2001. From the registration list of the Fourth Annual National Secretaries Convention (2000), I randomly chose twenty-four names of women to interview, about one-tenth of the number registered.[2] Women who turned up in the sample were between 25 and 37 years old—with 29.9 as the mean and 29 as the mode and median.

Primarily they were married with children, having gotten married just before or just after they began their secretarial training; most had been working for about nine years. Most lived and worked in Harare—the registration list contained few cities outside the capital.[3] The sample was predominantly from the Shona ethnic group. Of the others, two women had Ndebele heritage; one was Malawian/Zambian; one was mixed race (called "coloured" in Zimbabwe), and one had an Asian surname (I was unable to reach her). With a few other women unreachable—changed jobs, not known, wrong number—I had lunch with the remaining twenty secretaries from the list and asked them questions from a sheet I shared with them. Our conversations were in English as were the sessions of the convention. The interview questions covered family, work histories, current duties, presentation of self, romantic relations at work and home, sexual harassment, and how HIV/AIDS affected their lives. This small sample may not be representative of all black middle-class women in Zimbabwe, but the secretaries I interviewed reveal variations on themes central to middle-class Zimbabwean women as represented in history by Michael West (2002) and in the last decade by Rekopantswe Mate (2002). Having a random sample expanded the usual ethnographic gaze beyond the informants that an anthropologist would get to know during fieldwork. I interviewed women whom I would not otherwise have come across and women who were not in friendship networks with one another.

The National Secretaries Convention and the Secretaries Summer School, where I met again with some of the secretaries I had interviewed earlier, are training and professionalization meetings. Guest speakers from Zimbabwe and South Africa gave talks on a range of topics, such as the appropriate procedure for laying off and firing workers in Zimbabwe and how to get ahead at work through skills and confidence. As I discuss later, I was a speaker at one of the conventions and at a summer school program. I can't be sure how the attendees at the convention were chosen by their various employers, but I believe that some firms used the convention as a perk for their employees and that others rotated which employee would come each year. From my visits to their workplaces, it was clear to me that not all the secretaries in one firm would attend in any given year.

The numbers of black women in the clerical and secretarial field increased significantly around 1975, when many whites began leaving the breakaway colony of Rhodesia as independence increasingly seemed thinkable.[4] Before that time, white women and black men had dominated the profession. Histories of women in clerical and secretarial positions in the United States and Britain suggest that women were originally seen as incapable of the concentration, discipline, and commitment necessary for the smooth running of an office (Fine 1990, 55). But once women entered the field (the invention of the typewriter drove this change), clerical and secretarial jobs were reconfigured as women's jobs by increasing rationalization, routinization, and mechanization of the jobs of stenographers and typists and by creating clearly separate career tracks for male and female clerks and bookkeepers (Fine 1990, 100). Before women entered secretarial and clerical positions in the mid-nineteenth century in Britain and the United States, male workers "had access to general knowledge of the working of the firm and were given a certain degree of autonomy and independence in carrying out their tasks" (Fine 1990, 7n17). Creating a separate track for women as stenographers, typists, receptionists, and secretaries limited their knowledge of the working of the firm and set their highest rank below that of men who could rise to middle management. This strategy made clerical and secretarial jobs dead-end jobs for women.

Because secretarial work combines some of the general expectations of women—especially that they be caring and self-effacing—I was interested in seeing to what extent women saw a blending of their domestic and professional duties. On the whole, I found that this was not the case for women: what they found most significant about work was that it was not home. Women, but not necessarily the men they worked for, had very different expectations about managing social relations at home and at work. They came to work with an expectation of gender equity, while at home they valued gender difference.

Figure 10. A secretary interviewed at lunch, Harare, 2001. Photo by author.

Women who work in the offices of downtown Harare and its industrial environs flood the streets at lunchtime and at the quitting hour—dressed in their companies' uniforms or in sensible shoes and polyester skirted suits with contrasting blouses, their hair flowing or tightly braided, either way with hair of black, brown, and blonde hair extensions. Most of them are married and head home at the end of the day via public transportation or private cars. At the turn of the twenty-first century, these women—like the feminist activists, the female war veterans, and the would-be models and beauty queens—had reason to hope. But they paint their vision on a smaller canvas than some of their female contemporaries. They want equal access to resources and upward mobility at work, and at home they seek shared responsibility for family well-being. Most are Christians, and that attachment limits their choices of dress, company, and leisure activities. Christianity presents itself to them not as new or modern but as proper and traditional. What is new to them is the prospect of gender equity in the office and the idea of partnership in decision making with their husbands, of joint responsibility and mutual pleasure. Few of these women call themselves feminists. They don't even tend to utter the phrase "I'm not a feminist, but . . ."—which in other places and times often precedes stirring feminist statements, such as the ones these Zimbabwean urbanites make about sexual harassment or being stuck in dead-end jobs.

They see the problems that women as a group tend to share both at home and at work and are willing, individually or in church groups, to make some changes in the direction of women's empowerment. Yet they are caught between self and security, as Dangarembga puts it. They seek home as a sanctuary even though it may be the scene of physical and emotional abuse and their greatest source of exposure to HIV/AIDS. With divorce infrequent, they are secure in their positions in their husbands' families, yet they want to shift some of their resources to supporting their own relatives and perhaps themselves. They are faithful spouses and would like to say the same about their husbands.

This chapter ranges over several topics that I asked about in interviews: advantages and disadvantages of being a woman, work ethic, sex in the workplace, marriage and fidelity, and togetherness and shared responsibility in marriage, deriving from my interest in how women entered a new field of endeavor and constructed new identities as secretaries, as well as whether they perceived continuity between their domestic roles and their workaday world. I was wrong about the continuity between domesticity and work, but the interviews and participant observation pointed to tensions over women's control of their sexuality and led me to probe Dangarembga's novels and those of the late Yvonne Vera, another noted black female Zimbabwean novelist, for resonances with the ideas and practices of sexual freedom and containment this research presented. Finally, I turn to Berlant, who suggests that making the present bearable is also a version of cruel optimism (2011). What ties all this together is my interest in understanding what role femininity plays in women's lives—or, to put it in the language that I have been using throughout this book: how the aspiration for a better life that is evident in women going to work affects their sense of themselves as workers, mothers, and wives. In Berlant's terms I want to understand what makes life bearable, how women think and feel about things that matter to them. I categorize five sources of women's power to shape their identities and the nature of their involvement with other people, ideas, and things. These sources of power are also attachments that I understand as motivational feeling states with which women orient their lives toward relationships that they expect to have satisfying outcomes. Attachments have different etiologies, coming from women's activities, feelings, and knowledges. From the interview data, I abstracted five attachments: moral superiority, maternal responsibility, Christian conduct, ethnic circumscription, and workforce professionalism. In the sections that follow, I describe how these attachments play out in women's lives, but at the outset, I want to note, because it might not be clear in my attempts to define general patterns, that individuals vary and social systems contain contradictions. Despite the human predilection for habit, we all improvise and some of us change. Zimbabwean women's sense of their femininity develops from their ideas about what it means to be a woman interacting with the hard facts of life and the matrix of changing expectations resulting from local and global influences, including, but not limited to, a declining economy that pushed women into waged labor, romantic ideals of companionship in marriage, and the AIDS epidemic that tested wifely obedience.

Sentimental Attachments: Family, Religion, and Ethnicity

According to Lauren Berlant, whose notion of "cruel optimism" provoked my examination of the promises of feminism, attachment is "an absorptive investment in something other than one's self" (2011). Attachments are necessarily optimistic since they move "you out of yourself and into the world in order to bring closer the satisfying something that you cannot generate on your own but sense in the wake of a person, a way of life, an object, concept, or scene" (2011, 2). I think of attachments as feeling states that signal relationships to other people, ideas, and ways of being. For instance, in what I discuss here, urban middle-class women are attached to Christianity in that their Christian belief announces who they are, how they stand in relation to the moral universe, and what they want or desire in their everyday lives. I see Christianity as a positive and intense attachment. On the other hand, women's attachment to their work world or to themselves as workers, though positive, is on the whole weaker, and their attachment to their ethnic heritage is much more varied: several spoke of their ethnic heritage, but some deemed it positive and others thought of it as negative, something they must overcome in their achievement of the good life.

In looking at the attachments that define the working women I studied in Zimbabwe, I found four recurrent themes that underpin their sense of themselves in the world and indicate how their engagements with the world shape their identities. These are the moral superiority of women, the responsibility of mothers, the guidance provided by religion, and the value of ethnicity as good rather than binding or something to be overcome. I argue that women are attached to these ideas, images, or positions in varying ways and that those attachments help define who they are or how they want to be seen by others. A pattern emerged in my research that revealed the women's deep attachment to a perception of themselves as gendered, rather than simply as generic persons. Although the specter of the loose woman haunts them, most generally they think of women as good, always doing the right thing. A few note the existence of stereotypes of women as unintelligent or useless, but women tend not to be defensive or weighed down by this negativity. Mothers are revered for their hard work and sense of responsibility in taking care of families.

My research suggests that women engage the world through their assumptions about female moral superiority and the value of religion and motherhood, and that they hold on tight to them in their presentation of the self. These are attachments that are positive and strong. Women's attachment to ethnicity is a different matter. More generally, the women I spoke with referred to ethnicity in terms of "our culture," "our Shona tradition," or "on our side [Ndebele]." In research on women and contraceptives in colonial Zimbabwe, Amy Kaler found that ethnic culture and tradition were powerful forces "dictating norms of conduct and belief and providing explanations for behavior and events" (2003, 11). Urban women in my study seldom mentioned their ethnicity as shaping who they are, and when they did, it was equally invoked as a positive and a negative force. Ethnicity is an attachment—it is one of the ways that women engage the world—but it lacks the power that it once had. In some ways, religion now trumps ethnicity. This works in two ways: religion may supplant ethnicity, as in the colonial vilification of traditional practices and beliefs, or it may incorporate ethnicity, as in African Apostolic churches that integrate traditional practices and beliefs.

Women can derive power from their attachments to the world. Of course, attachments have the power of defining the person, at least in part, but their symbolic and social capital may also give women leverage in interactions with others, especially with family members. In this section, I discuss women's sense of themselves in the world and their attachments to the world, and I explore the feminine modes of power that derive from these attachments.

"Women are good; men are bad" is a heteronormative sentimental bargain struck by husbands and wives that allows men to behave badly and women to feel superior to them. This bargain permits men greater freedom, while women are ceded the moral high ground, from which they make themselves feel better, criticize men, and forgive them. Moral superiority is one source of women's conventional power. Even if this power fails to curb husbands' excesses, it binds sons to their beleaguered mothers and across the generations establishes a basis for guilt and compunction in husbands. I could see the dynamics of these feelings at work in a group of young men, fifteen to nineteen years old, that I interviewed. These young men mentioned different ways of proving one's manhood: fistfights, dominance over other men, sexual intercourse with a girlfriend, and taking on men's responsibilities. While at home, brothers are expected to look after and protect their sisters, and as adults, they have to make sure that their mothers are housed and fed. These young men were critical of the behavior they see in their fathers' generation. One summarized the situation in many marriages when he said: "The mother will be doing everything at home, yet the father will be drinking." Another felt it was not fair to wives for men to spend their wages at bars: "The girl friend gets chicken, but the wife gets *sadza* and *kapenta* [staple stiff cornmeal porridge and dried sardines]." Coining a phrase, one of the city high school students spoke of "social workers," men who go out with many women. "In the streets, the social workers are infected by AIDS and when they go home they expect their wives not to ask them to use a condom and this is very unfair." The oldest man in this group of interviewees, nineteen years old and a devout Christian, agreed that some men abuse their power as head of the household. But he argued passionately that a man who loves his wife would treat her with respect, not squander money, or commit adultery. Would these young men succumb to the pervasive narrative of bad men and good women? I contended in an argument with a Zimbabwean friend that they are brave, new men with feminist promise, but she countered that they would become just like their fathers. If she is right, then they will carry with them a residue of compassionate feelings for their mothers' situations that will yield their wives a degree of power and complacency even as husbands enjoy and feel the sting of patriarchal privilege. Having developed empathy for their mothers in regard to their father's misconduct, they will know how their bad behavior hurts their wives.

"Moral superiority" is an attachment to the world, a way of making sense of the options presented to women, and it forms the core of the identity that many women value. Women I interviewed characterized women as conscious, sensitive, and responsible in caring for their families, in contrast to men's weakness, irresponsibility, and self-indulgence—especially as shown in their male drunkenness, infidelity, and negligence. They identified women's distinguishing qualities as strength, endurance, and responsibility: strength expressed as ingenuity, practical knowledge, and resilience; endurance as patience and stamina in facing hardships; and responsibility as consciousness of, sensitivity to, and willingness to act to meet the needs of others. Invoking the most common example of men behaving badly, Barbara, an executive secretary at a bank, said, "I think women live better than men. Women can take up difficult situations and men cannot. Women can really stand up and look after a family; unlike men. . . . Women are more responsible. Do you know that men can go drinking when there is nothing at home? But a woman will never do that." Of course, there are women drunks in Zimbabwe, and women who abandon their families, but those women fall under another widespread narrative or discourse, that of the loose woman, which I will examine later in this chapter. Both the evil of the loose woman and the morality of the good wife are undergirded by Christianity. Barbara, who painted the picture of the hardworking wife and the derelict husband, was just a bit more extreme than most in saying, "I think we are most favored by God. . . . Because when Jesus died, two women were the first to see that Jesus had arisen."

I never heard women in Zimbabwe put down their gender in the offhand way that I do sometimes in the United States, such as, "Isn't that just like a woman," in reference to a mistake of misjudgment a woman made, or "Well, I'm a woman," in excusing a failing or an indulgence. This is not to say that women had only positive things to say about being a woman—a couple thought that women were petty, and another said that women could not be trusted as friends. But mostly they were not reactive or defensive about what it means to be a woman and seldom invoked negative stereotypes. Nonetheless, two women did make universalizing statements about female subordination—"society in general just looks down on women," and "they [men] tend to say that our minds are not bright." After those statements, each speaker went on to talk about the problems women have getting ahead in the business world. One told a story about a bus accident to indicate what women can do and how little men think that they can: When the bus broke down, men expected women to be "useless," but women "did everything," while the men went off to look for help. When the men returned and found the repairs done, they apologized to the women. Even if some women recognized a universalizing discourse of women's inferiority, most women had a way of separating their sense of themselves from these broader social notions of women's inferiority. They were neither positively nor negatively attached to them.

Motherhood and mothering evoked the most emotional portrayal of women, but even this was underpinned by a mother's chief characteristics of being responsible, caring, and strong. Praising mothers who stayed in their marriages and kept their families together, one interviewee put it this way: "Women are strong. We work hard for our families." The women whom they admired were their mothers, especially the single mothers—two credited their divorced mothers, because of the strength and independence they showed in getting divorced and their success at home and at work. One woman said of her mother, "She is a very hardworking woman. I admire everything she is. I always wish I could be like her, even the way she brought us up. She's a hard worker; she's a fighter. She divorced my father when I was only two years old." This veneration of motherhood is the foundation of Women of Zimbabwe Arise (WOZA), one of the activist groups discussed in chapter 2 and is prevalent in feminism in other parts of Africa.

The sentimental attachment to mothering and motherhood shared by working women in Harare is not out of step with that of other African feminists. Anthropologist Filomina Steady (2006), who studies feminism and women's collective action across the continent, points to motherhood as an arena of empowerment based on the social category of mother where women's power is derived not from their affiliation with men but from their own economic roles and contributions to the development of their society. Molara Ogundipe-Leslie (1994), in her overview of African feminism, presents a similar focus on motherhood, but she found that motherhood as biological reproduction had primacy for African feminists. She criticized those who believed that if you are not married, do not have children, you are not human. Yet she gave credence to a holistic approach to African feminism that held that women's biological roles should be distinctly valued because women as mothers contribute to the production and reproduction of their society and to the economic fulfillment and independence of women (210–25). Within the Zimbabwean context of increasing uncertainty about the future, children offer moments of emotional satisfaction that can inspire efforts to work toward a better life. African women's famed resilience comes from this ability to see a brighter future through the gloom of the present. Only a couple of women voiced criticism of the responsible-mother ideal. Both were married women who loved and sacrificed for their children. One felt that she was a failure, especially when compared to her single mother, who was a successful businesswoman and a loving mother, and the other said that she found it a burden to have responsibility for the family. Her expression of this latter sentiment suggests that more women feel the same way but are not willing to admit that they are turning an obligation into a virtue. The venerated mother is an image and a discourse that contribute to the power or symbolic capital that women can wield in social relations. The honor and prestige of motherhood accord women respect in many quarters, including in relation to husbands.

Of course, one's sentimental attachment to motherhood has particular cultural content, but few alluded to that specificity when speaking of mothering. Zimbabwe is not unlike other African countries where "subordinate and domesticated women have . . . come to symbolize African culture" (Berger 1988, 31). This was obvious in a playful interview that I conducted with the husband and wife who were the gardener and a housekeeper in the university flats where I lived. I asked them whether they preferred living in the rural areas or the city. The wife answered first, saying that she preferred the city, but her husband interrupted her before she could list her reasons. Criticizing his wife and defending his culture, he said, "In our culture, she is supposed to say the rural areas." Rural women tend the home and fields for husbands working far away in mines and factories, and they keep culture alive through their attention to the elderly and participation in ceremonies to honor the ancestors. Only a couple of women in my study had come from what Rudo Gaidzanwa called SRB (severe rural background—sons and daughters of poor rural farmers), though many came from provincial towns: life in a farming family was not their own or their mother's experience (2001). They were also not inclined to hold tight to ethnic identity.

Typically absent from the women's statements about who they are was mention of ethnicity. No one specifically identified herself as Shona or Ndebele: only two people explicitly explained their orientation or behavior in terms of "African culture" and "our culture," and another explicitly distanced herself and her family's practices from "our culture." One woman assessed "Shona" women's church organizations positively, and another, trying to address how men and women are different, blamed men's "cultural background" or home training for their shortcomings. Failure to learn the lessons about how to be a good woman was one of the accusations hurled at "loose women," girlfriends, and mistresses of married men. Proper ethnic upbringing should teach women to control their appetites and to contain themselves. Clearly the concept of culture and the distinctiveness and boundedness of African culture was a part of some women's repertoire, but culture and ethnicity contributed just one thread into a weave in which Christianity is dominant.

Two women highlighted their attachment to Christianity in telling me about problems at work. The first was Clarissa, an ambitious young woman who believes she was victimized because she was a Christian working for a Jehovah's

Witness. (I don't know how widespread in Zimbabwe is the belief that Jehovah's Witnesses are not Christian, but it was firmly held by this interviewee.) She stated: "The people there, most of the staff members are Jehovah's Witnesses. I'm a Christian myself. You know what it's like. It's like tribalism. You get some organizations that tend to lean towards something. . . . It actually affects staff members. I hadn't realized that my predecessors [in the same position at the firm] had gone through the same kind of treatment that I went through." Clarissa was quite agitated when she talked about this, and I could get very little of the particulars of her "treatment" there. Besides a bad working relationship with a woman boss and hints from a Christian friend to be more accepting of Jehovah's Witnesses, what they held against her, according to Clarissa's own report, was that she did not respond to emails from her boss regarding Jehovah's Witnesses; she had "Christian" emails on her computer, and she had lunchtime fellowship meetings with a "Christian" staffer. Clarissa fought for her position when she was being forced to resign but ultimately lost her case. As she saw it, she was forced out because she was a Christian. At the time of the interview, she was working for a Christian NGO.

The second woman who spoke of her religion in connection with her employment was Lillian, a thirty-three-year-old Apostolic Christian (a combination of Shona and Christian beliefs and rituals) who attends weekly church services and meetings of a women's group at church. Her Christian belief seemed to be a sword for fighting disease and affliction and a shield against the ravages of modern life. She joined the church when her second child was very sick—his cure was "a miracle." When she refused her previous boss's sexual advances, "He had to look for someone else. I said to myself thanks to God for our religion." About deciding what to wear to work, "Now, I'm guided by Christian life. We don't have to put on those minis [mini-skirts]. I have to wear something decent."

No woman interviewed mentioned that she did not regularly attend church, and only one explicitly said that she had turned against the church—she was angry at the hypocrisy of her stepfather, an officer in her church who had not supported her after her mother's death.

In sum, moral superiority, maternal responsibility, and Christian conduct were overriding concerns of the black middle-class women whom I studied, but that does not mean that all these women abided by the highest of their own precepts. Sometimes they only resorted to these attachments to find comfort in moment of crisis, and a few women found all three too confining. For most, these ideas and the behavior they prompted gave women some leverage in their relations with others and helped them make meaning of the lives that they lived.

Women in the Office

In this section, I address women as workers: they spend six to eight hours a day at work, and while none directly implicated herself as an alienated worker, only a handful identified their work or their desire to work as an intense and positive attachment. Women do not have the same sentimental attachment to their identities as workers as they have to the identity of moral woman, responsible mother, good Christian, or ethnic-group representative. One woman, who probably spoke for many, said, "Most of the time we just think that coming to work is because... you need the money" (Zifikile, a twenty-eight-year-old who works as a secretary for a manufacturing firm and is married with two children). For others, being a worker is a more significant component of their identity: "You come to work. You lead your own life. It is important to be a working woman rather than staying at home and being a housewife" (Agnes, a twenty-five-year-old secretary to a general manager, with one child and another on the way). Felicity, at thirty-seven the oldest of the secretaries that I interviewed, said, "I feel proud about being a secretary because I am just as good as a manager. In fact, I call myself a manager also. I manage the office. Like at the moment, my boss is new in the organization. I've worked with him for only three months, and we've not had any problems in our office. No breakdown, no nothing. We are just continuing as usual. I know most of the things that men do. I am experienced with the job. I've been doing it for the past four years so there is nothing really new. We just continue as if nothing changed. So I am proud of that." In response to my questions, most interviewees immediately said that being a secretary was no small thing to them. Then a few hesitated, adding that they did not want to be just a secretary; they wanted to move into administration or management. They had a sense of accomplishment—and they also saw the limitations of the positions that they occupied.

Finding a job is increasingly hard in Zimbabwe; keeping it has its own challenges, including tedium and sexual harassment, and moving on presents inevitable uncertainties. Several of the women whom I interviewed said that they were referred by an employment agency, usually for their first job. By the time of their third or fourth job, a few had inside tips and connections. One secretary explained that some employment agencies have associations with particular secretarial colleges. Another noted that employment agencies were popular; she further qualified her point, stating, "But I think the trend has changed. It is now who you know, who can organize a job for you." Two contrasting cases from very different people illustrate how women handle getting, keeping, and moving on in employment. Chiedza, a divorced mother who lived in the city center, came from a well-to-do family in a provincial town. She was one of three hundred applicants for her present position and had worked there for nine years as personal assistant to the director of an NGO that promotes staff development. At the time of the interview, Chiedza was preparing to take an exam to become a chartered secretary and had enrolled in a correspondence course to complete an MBA. Her situation differed considerably from that of Clarissa, who wanted greater experience in the business, greater exposure to the workings of the business, and greater scope for engagement of business issues, and could never find satisfaction.

Clarissa, married with two sons, was a member of what some Zimbabweans disparage as "the nose brigade," because of their British or American accents. She quoted a colleague's description of her: "She comes from a private school. You can tell from her accent. Everything about her is from a private school." Clarissa's first job came as a result of her college "attachment" (internship), and after being at the company a short time, she was chosen to be personal secretary to a divisional director. With this experience, she tested the market to see what else she could find, using her college's employment agencies and answering ads in the newspaper. She took a position in the financial industry as senior management secretary to the chief of internal audit. There she met her husband. With the "policy silent" on married couples working in the same division, they both stayed there. But after three years she and her husband did not want to stay at the same firm, so she sent her CV to other companies. "Secretaries normally find it easier to move around than men. The market, I think, now is really, really tight. It is difficult for anybody, a lot of people, no matter how educated you are," she said by way of explaining why she moved and not her husband.

Her third job was as a marketing secretary with a manufacturing firm. This was her second time working for a white man: "They lay their cards on the table. They tell you that you are going to be earning $20,000. You don't have to nag him tomorrow and say look you promised me an increment, you know, that kind of thing. I never had a problem with him." In this job, Clarissa gained "exposure" to the workings of the company and took on the role of the internal sales representative. Working against the dead-endedness of the secretarial position, she concluded, "Sometimes it is not about the money. Sometimes what you want is exposure. The one thing that I noticed within the profession is that a lot of people don't seem to be willing [to work harder and to take chances]. Secretaries might have a problem in wanting to learn more about the organization, but the bosses also have a problem. They don't allow you to go beyond your typing."

After three years at that job, she felt she needed more of a challenge and joined a tourist company, to which she was referred by a friend—but she still had to pass a clerical test and take minutes at a meeting as a part of the interview process. There she felt victimized as a Christian, as I discussed earlier. When pressured to resign, she refused and demanded a disciplinary hearing before a workers' council according to Zimbabwean fair-labor practices. The council ruled against her: she had an "attitude problem" was what she got from the hearing. She found new employment, but it was not clear that she would find the challenging and rewarding work she seeks.

Besides complaints about the lack of opportunities for promotion in secretarial work, women also identified gender inequality as a problem at work. Though "gender equality" and "gender sensitization" were major campaign platforms during the liberation struggle and afterward in numerous NGOs that target women's social problems, the term "gender" seldom appears in the record of my interviews with high-ranking secretaries. Without using the term, Felicity, the office manager whom I discussed earlier, clearly identified discrimination according to gender. She believed that men and women have equal capacity, but they are not equally compensated: "Sometimes people look down upon you like what I noticed at our workplace. There is a certain grade that is entitled to have company cars. So if a female employee is promoted to that grade, they would give a car allowance but not a company car. I don't know why. I have noticed, but I have never asked why." Two other women, Chiedza and Barbara, do use the term "gender." Chiedza, the divorced mother (who was not looking to get married again), described the problem women encounter in the workplace: "The main problem is gender inequality, because you will find traditional people just assume that women are not capable of [inaudible] or of becoming leaders. You really have to prove yourself wherever you go. In fact, you have to work twice as hard as your male counterparts. I think that's a problem." Barbara, who believed women are favored by God, addressed general stereotypes of women as unintelligent and in relation to gender inequity at work: "Women are even more focused although they tend to say our minds are not that bright." The major problem that women face, she said, is that "they are looked down upon even in workplaces. We do not have a director that is a woman. That is a gender issue. It is a problem." The woman she admired most was a senior manager: "She is good. She's strict, but she knows her work. She is very intelligent. I wouldn't mind being like her. She is the only case."

In the office, this discourse of difference is joined with a discourse of gender equity that is absent in the home. The language of gender equity and gender inequality comes from the liberation struggle, the government press's feature stories on successful women in business and politics, and the large number of NGOs that have identified women as a special category regarding human rights, land, law, and health, among others (see the introduction to this volume). By the turn of the twenty-first century, NGOs had stopped using terms such as "gender discrimination," the term in the United Nations' Convention on the Elimination of Discrimination against Women (CEDAW, 1979); they had started using "gender sensitization" to refer to efforts to bring women's issues into political discussions, and "capacity building" to highlight what is needed in order to bolster the presence of women in decision-making processes. Their use of the term "gender" and Felicity's analysis according to gender, without naming it, reflect both the reach of the promise of feminism and its lack of punch. That is, while one of the goals of feminism—to identify and fight discrimination against women—lurked in the secretaries' discourse, they as individuals, and certainly as the groups gathered for the convention, had little ability to effect changes in the institutions in which they worked.

Gender discrimination was just one of the problems that women encountered at work. While most said that they worked for the money, some wanted greater recognition for their skills and effectiveness, and others strove to break out of dead-end jobs. Those who wanted more than the routinization of the secretarial world also exhibited greater intensity and more positive attachment to their work identities, yet only one in this group was able to break the glass ceiling on women's promotion in business.

Sex at Work

Working away from home, but especially in an office, with a male boss imperils women's reputation as good and respected women. Women working as secretaries pose a particular paradox in Zimbabwean society. They appear to be free women, or "loose" in Zimbabwean English parlance: that is, they are in the public sphere without a male guardian and outside the company of female relatives, they interact with non-kin men, and they even take orders from them. Many are attractive and pay attention to their appearance (see my discussion of beauty in chapter 2). In their freedom, in their associations, and in their appearance, these women seem to share attributes of the prostitute. The women that I studied were aware of these possible references, and they were critical of secretaries who use sexuality to curry favor or for job advancement. Most of the secretaries in my sample were married women who were anxious to be respectable in suspect circumstances. Generally, they felt that since men cannot control their sexual urges, it is the duty of women to avoid tempting them. These secretaries had business-only attitudes and used their Christian beliefs and practices to protect them from men's advances in the office. They dressed conservatively; they had Christian desktop decorations; they went to Christian fellowship meetings at lunch; and they shared inspirational Christian email messages. This could be seen as an update of the respectability campaigns that women embraced when they first started living in the city (see chapter 1). But this is not about domesticity: the upshot of this respectability campaign, so to speak, is that in the office women hold on to a sense of themselves as better than men, responsible and strong in opposition to men's weakness and self-indulgence.

I became interested in sexual harassment when I learned how pervasive it was from a factory worker active in AWZ in 1983. As she put it, when you try to get onto the work site to apply for work, the guard at the gate asks for sex. The intake officer asks for sex to forward your application. Once hired, you have to have sex with the foreman to keep your job. In 1984, I wrote an article on sexual harassment for a popular Zimbabwean magazine. In 2000, I presented a workshop to the National Secretaries Convention and to the Secretaries' Summer School on sexual harassment.

Though about half the women I interviewed had suffered some form of sexual harassment, they did not conceive of it as an aspect of gender inequality or gender discrimination. As I reflect back on it, I think that they saw sexual advances from bosses and coworkers as the price they paid for freedom or an occupational hazard. In Zimbabwe there is has no law against sexual harassment, but cases can be taken under the unfair labor practices provision of the Labour Relations Act. Some women have won such cases against employers; one was a case of "indecent assault" that was taken to a criminal court. But in another much-publicized case, when a woman claimed that her boss propositioned her, she was fired, and she got no relief in the courts. In my presentations on sexual harassment at the secretaries' convention and summer school, I used the definition of sexual harassment that was suggested by the Women's Advisory Council of Zimbabwe: Sexual harassment is any repeated and unwanted verbal, physical, or gestural sexual advance, sexually explicit derogatory statements, or sexually discriminative remarks made by someone in the workplace that are offensive to the worker involved, that cause the worker to feel threatened, humiliated, patronized, or harassed, and that interfere with the worker's job performance, undermine job security, or create a threatening or intimidating work environment.

To deal with sexual harassment at work, I encouraged women to speak up and to actively try to end unwanted attention. They should tell someone about it when it happens and should keep a diary of incidents that could be used to support their accusation. In addition to using Zimbabwe's Labour Relations Act, women seeking redress for injury they have suffered from sexual harassment could appeal to the company code of conduct and/or union contract. They could also bring their case before a worker's council, the government ombudsman, and criminal or civil court. During discussions at the public meetings and in private interviews, several secretaries thanked me for putting a name to what they had experienced.

A 1997 study conducted in Harare estimated that one in three working women was sexually harassed.[5] The study surveyed women from ages seventeen to sixty-one in a wide range of employment including managers, secretaries, factory workers, general hands, and maids. The women who were most vulnerable, most likely to be sexually harassed were divorced, widowed, or separated; temporary or seasonal workers; new to the job; and with less education, Form 2 or below. The most common perpetrator of sexual harassment was the supervisor, in 54 percent of the cases, and coworkers in others. Over half the women who had been sexually harassed said that they never reported it.

In what follows I present three cases that show a range of women's responses to sexual innuendos and sexual propositions by their supervisors at work. As Zifikile, in the first case, came to see that she had experienced sexual harassment, she then recognized it as rife. Instead of needing laws and policies to mitigate harassment of women in the workplace, she believed that it could be handled by women displaying the right attitude. Margaret, a well-spoken young woman from a middle-class background, suffered demotion because of her refusal of a sexual proposition. In the last case, Beatrice, the menaced secretary, had the tools at hand to seek recourse for the psychological trauma she suffered at the hands of a predatory boss.

ZIFIKILE: STAYING CLEAR OF SEXUAL HARASSMENT IN A CHARGED ENVIRONMENT

Her first name, "Zifikile," suggests that she had Ndebele heritage; this ethnic group comprises about 15 percent of the Zimbabwean population, compared to the Shona's 83 percent (whites, Asians, and mixed-raced people make up the remaining 2 percent). She was a twenty-eight-year-old woman, had been working for six years, was married with two daughters, ages four and one. Many women pointed to men in general as irresponsible, but she more openly complained that her husband drank beer whenever he got money; she was left alone with the children on Friday nights and Saturdays, and on Sundays, "Maybe he stays at home. On Sunday, he's now tired, sleeping the whole day."

Until she heard me speak at the National Secretaries Convention, she was unsure of what sexual harassment entailed: "Like you were saying the other time, we only learn some of the things that they are sexual harassment. People just come and pass on comments. I think it is very common there [at her workplace]." She was aware of a coworker who was given a final warning because she did not submit to sexual advances: if she made the smallest mistake in her work, she could be fired. But on the whole, Zifikile felt that "you have to tell them straight so that they understand that you are not interested in that kind of [talk]." Sexual innuendoes and unwanted sexual attention were rife in her government utility firm: "Not serious ones but just small ones like someone just coming in and saying a comment or something: 'Wow, you are coming so big.' [She did not elaborate on the sexual reference in this comment.] Those sorts of comments. So many of them." She tried not to respond, to brush them off, and then to talk straight. This, she said, worked.

MARGARET: WALK AWAY FROM THE JOB

Margaret, a proudly betrothed woman, who at twenty-six was one of the youngest women whom I interviewed, was still living at home in a rural suburb with her parents, both schoolteachers. She had been in the workforce for about seven years. Margaret was very talkative. Prompted by the memory of my presentation at the convention, she immediately began to tell me about how she had been sexually harassed at work. She worked for a private firm as personal assistant to the CEO. When she turned down his proposition, she was demoted: "I was actually PA [personal assistant] to the chief executive. And what he did, I was demoted to a junior office to say she can't do anything; she's clumsy and things like that. So I then said to myself, I can prove myself. I will do better things. So I left that job." Margaret felt that she had no other recourse: "I left the job. . . . Remember in Zimbabwe; we really didn't have a strong body that would represent your case. And I wasn't prepared to go through that channel. And, you know, it was just something. And I was too young then. I was still trying to gain myself and groom myself. And, you know, it wasn't right and it wasn't a good environment for me. So I said I just have to cope." Because many people in the company were related by kinship, Margaret felt that she had no one who would listen to her complaint.

BEATRICE: USING THE COMPANY'S CODE OF CONDUCT

Beatrice, a charming, soft-spoken woman, was twenty-nine years old, married, with two children. A member of Zimbabwe's small coloured community, estimated to be about eighty thousand people in 2000, she had grown up in various coloured neighborhoods and lived in Arcadia, one of the oldest of the community's suburbs. She worked as secretary to the director of marketing in a manufacturing firm.

Beatrice had had little problem with sexual harassment until after I spoke at the convention. What happened after she heard my talk did not involve her interpreting past behavior as sexual harassment, as was the case with Zifikile; rather her first instance of sexual harassment occurred just days after she heard my talk. While she was on a business trip, a man from upper management propositioned her at dinner and called her on the phone in her hotel room. When she put him off, he came to her door and demanded to be let in. Beatrice was terrified; she spent the night in the bathroom and never opened the door until morning. She called me as a friend, seeking advice. Fortunately, she was a good student; she had already consulted her multinational company's code of conduct and found rules against sexual harassment. She pursued the case and reached a reasonable settlement, the terms of which she could not disclose.

All the secretaries whom I interviewed had heard my presentation at the National Secretaries' Convention. That presentation had not directly addressed sexual harassment but rather had suggested ways of organizing one's thoughts to make an oral statement. To kick off my presentation, I had asked two of the convention's organizers to participate in a skit that involved sexual harassment, after which I asked the audience to make notes about the important issues to be covered and to make oral presentations in small groups. I circulated among the groups and gave feedback on their speaking style, use of eye contact, and pauses. I purposely included sexual harassment as a topic because I wanted to understand to what extent unwanted sexual attention was a part of women's work life. In the concluding large-group discussion, women turned away from sexual harassment and to other women's use of sexuality to get ahead in the office. Other women's dress and conduct were topics easily discussed in public; only in private did women bring up their own experiences of sexual harassment.

I have included a subsection on women who use sex at work because this behavior raised the ire of many women I encountered—from neighbors, each of whom told me privately that the other cheated on her husband and used sex to get ahead at work, to women on the staff of a medical school, who complained that other women were using sex to get promoted. I believe that instrumental sex in the workplace outraged their sense of women as better than men, threatened the moral superiority that they used to make men repentant, and encouraged a use of the power of sexuality, which is not equally available to all women.

ON USING SEX TO GET AHEAD

According to the 1997 National Training and Research Center report mentioned earlier, at least a third of women in Zimbabwe suffered unwanted sexual attention at work, but, it seems to me, more women seemed to think that others got ahead by using sex. It was the most heated topic in workshops and talks that I did on the subject of sexuality or sexual harassment. In 1984, as a Fulbright

Fellow at the University of Zimbabwe, I gave a talk to the medical school about the social construction of human sexuality. During the course of the talk, when the topic of sexual harassment came up, women angrily complained that other women used sexuality to get ahead, and while men, not at all defensively, said they did not offer quid quo pro (job benefits in exchange for sex), they gladly had sex with women but did not offer raises or promotions in return. Twice in 2000, during my presentation at the Fourth Annual National Secretaries Convention and at the summer school conducted by the same agency, women fumed about other women who dressed in skimpy clothes and threw themselves at men in the office. Among the women I interviewed, only one did not condemn those who had sex with male coworkers, bosses, or married men. Veronica, a beautiful single woman who lived alone and was in a five-year relationship with her boyfriend, volunteered that some of her friends liked sexual advances in the workplace—it's a "challenge," she said, and "makes you feel very attractive."

Grace Mutandwa, a columnist for a Zimbabwean weekly newspaper who interviewed secretaries at the same convention from which my sample was drawn, elicited a response that could be categorized as a complaint of sexual harassment: "Well, one girl frankly told me that if you want to keep your job and be assured of hefty salary hikes, then 'you gotta put out.'"[6] But Mutandwa did not see it that way. Perhaps in keeping with the trope of the loose woman, the writer described the two women she interviewed as "shamelessly vulgar," adding no value to the organizations they worked for. Mutandwa is not alone in reviling women who appear to use sex to get ahead—it was what I heard in every discussion on sex in the workplace in 1984 and in 1999–2001.

Imagine my surprise when I encountered a public gathering of women who thought otherwise. In a workshop on cosmetics, a session at the Third Annual National Secretaries Convention, which I attended the year before my interviews began, women cheered when the leader hinted broadly that perfume is one way to seduce the boss. Some howled with delight when she suggested that a nice afternoon pick-me-up could be an arm massage given by the boss. Women office workers I interviewed a year later did not agree. They thought of their work strategies, not in terms of sexuality, but rather in terms of their skills and knowledge; they saw themselves as competent managers who were adept in handling business and personnel issues. Many were highly placed assistants who felt their work to be vital to their companies. These secretaries did not see sex as a part of the work contract, yet they were basically from a similar pool to those at the beauty workshop. Honoring my interview data, I could extrapolate from the numbers and suggest that 10 percent of women working as secretaries might relish office romances, given that two of twenty had had an office romance. Of course, it could be that those women who chose to attend the beauty and makeup session were a skewed sample, which is more likely than that my random sample was skewed. Most evident in my sample was a high level of professionalism among the secretaries. It could be that more single women attended the earlier convention and that bosses awarded this benefit in exchange for sex, but none of the interviews a year later point to that conclusion.

I belabor this point about sex as a part of the work contract because the major study of women office workers in a central African city, Ilsa Schuster's groundbreaking *New Women of Lusaka* (1979), concluded that women office workers traded sex for perks. There are few studies of women office workers in Africa and even fewer of women working at the top of the secretarial ladder. Schuster argues that Zambian women office workers saw the exchange of sexual favors for occupational advantages and gifts as expected, commonplace, and often desirable. Women office workers in Lusaka profited from this exchange until they married and were left at home, finding love and emotional involvement in their children, while their husbands dated younger women. I must acknowledge that the majority of working women whom I interviewed were already married, in contrast to the situation in Zambia a generation before. Zimbabwe's historically high level of literacy for men and women, its generous maternity-leave policy, and the declining economy, as well as changing tastes and desires fueled the two-income family. The unmarried women whom I interviewed included a woman engaged to be married, a divorced woman, and a sexually active single woman with a boyfriend. Unlike the Zambian case, of the married women I interviewed, only one had met her husband at work. None of them explicitly condoned sex with bosses or coworkers. How do I explain women's professionalism and the lack of their instrumental use of sexuality in Zimbabwean workplaces?

I hold that women's disapproval of sexual license in Harare was influenced by highly effective domesticity campaigns dating back to the late 1940s and by even earlier women's township-based religious and social clubs and associations, which set a high standard of respectability for married women.[7] In teaching African women domestic skills, Homecraft clubs (discussed in chapter 1) had emphasized monogamy as a sign of progress for women.[8] While I argue against critics of the Homecraft movement who suggest that the clubs withdrew women from the public domain, I agree with these critics that Homecraft bolstered monogamy, the home, and the nuclear family. The same set of values were in play in the church clubs, where marriage accorded women membership but bad behavior—not keeping a clean house, drinking or selling beer, and certainly adultery—was reason for expulsion. In urban areas, respectable women were expected to avoid association with the prostitute and the beer seller. Married women formed clubs that helped assimilate newcomers into city life, taught domestic skills, and gave women a voice with city government. The ideology of domesticity was not confined to the private domain, but Homecraft and other clubs, in bringing women together in new associations, had schooled them in interacting across social barriers. The clubs also gave them a social platform for their voices as women and introduced them to systematization of everyday knowledge. Combined with Zimbabwe's emphasis on education and upward mobility, the ideology of domesticity fashioned the strain of professionalism that I found among working wives and mothers.

Women outside the middle of the middle class might be less reluctant to employ instrumental sex and might also, at a later time, wrap themselves in the cloak of respectability. Mary Adams, writing about sexuality as play for teen-aged girls in an economically distressed peri-urban area outside Harare, concluded that girls who go to town to help their families by selling—usually vegetables and cooked foods for their mothers—also engage in prostitution (2009). But that sexual work is seen as play, and many of the reputable women of the community have such experiences in their backgrounds. My participant observations in groups at the university, at the secretaries' convention, and in conversation with neighbors suggest that a counter-hegemonic discourse valuing instrumental sex coexists with that of women as morally superior. Luise White's (1990) work on prostitution in colonial Kenya as well as Mary Adams's in present-day Harare suggest that some women engage in prostitution to meet the expectation that they be caring daughters: they bring funds into the family not by going on the marriage market—bringing wealth into the family by way of the gifts of a groom to his bride's family—but by directly converting their sexuality into money through prostitution.

Home as Workplace

The women I studied were attached to a view of themselves as responsible mothers and respectful wives. At work, they were also capable and efficient employees who cautiously hoped for gender equity, while fending off unwanted sexual attention. At home, where women were the employers, there were noteworthy reversals of their concerns about gender equality and about sexuality. No longer did they speak of gender equity. The discourses of gender difference rather than gender equity came to the surface: women must be strong and responsible to take care of the family, while men, who provided housing and material comforts, were indulged and pampered. Some women said that their husbands pitched in with cooking, gardening, and taking the children to school, but none said that she had expected it or explicitly asked that husbands undertake these tasks. Women did not complain about husbands' not doing chores around the house or not doing a fair share of child care. What they complained about was men's drinking, staying out late, and unfaithfulness. This too was part of how men differ from women.

My interviewees hired maids or house girls to help with the housework, child care, and cooking—and then as employers, women worried that their husbands would be sexually attracted to the maids. A secretary's workday typically begins at eight o'clock in the morning and ends around four or five o'clock in the afternoon. Most secretaries' double day was alleviated by their hiring domestic workers.[9] All the women I interviewed, except for a single woman living alone in a rural suburb, had full-time help to clean the house, wash the clothes, look after the children, and prepare the meals. The secretaries most often shared cooking, cleaning their bedrooms, and washing; they especially washed their own clothes and their husbands' underwear.[10]

Women liked to cook for their husbands: "the way to a man's heart is through his stomach" resounds here. One or two women indicated that their husbands might complain if they did not cook dinner at least some of the time. Working women were cautioned by their mothers, but mostly aunts and grandmothers, to make sure that they cooked their husbands' meals and not to let the maid do all the cooking. If they were lax here, maids could usurp their positions.

Several women adamantly wanted to keep the maid out of the bedroom. Though Zifikile, a twenty-eight-year-old secretary, married with two children, let her maid wash her husband's underwear, she did not allow her to clean the marital bedroom. Felicity, the office manager, washed her husband's underwear and also did not let the maid clean her bedroom: "I don't like the maid to [clean my bedroom]. I feel it is private property. She just does for the children. And for my bedroom, dressing room, and bathroom, I do it on my own. Sometimes I do it at night; if I come back from work and prepare my clothes then I go and clean my bathroom, bedroom, dressing room, and everything. So she doesn't do anything." Besides concern with intimacy, keeping the maid out of the bedroom also is an indication of the distrust of maids as thieves. This distrust is as much about wealth differences between maids and their employers as it is about domestic workers having sticky fingers. Though working women don't feel guilty about hiring domestic help, the differences in their lifestyles make the employers concerned about what will go missing. To thwart the tendency for things to walk away from the household, many women try to hire relatives, over whom they hope to have greater leverage.

One woman complained that her husband criticized her as "not a good woman" because she was sloppy in her personal habits and clumsy in cleaning the house (she had been brought up with maids who did the housework), but no one told me that husbands would complain if wives did not wash their underwear. Washing the husband's underwear was something that wives did on their own initiative, but with great social pressure from other women. There are many overlapping reasons for the value placed on this one object and this one action. It is a mark of intimacy that women struggle to maintain in a home turned into a workplace. On the one hand, the husband's underwear may stand for his genitals: washing the underwear echoes an older custom of washing the husband's genitals after sexual intercourse. But on the other, washing his underwear may stand for more general submission to the husband: Gaidzanwa's research on men and women at the University of Zimbabwe shows that male students ask female students to wash their clothes as a sign of women's docility and commitment (2001, 125). Women let the maid wash their husbands' underwear only at their own risk.

Zifikile, who protects herself from sexual harassment at work by straight talk, took the risk; she defiantly did not wash her husband's underwear. As the subject of working women's household tasks came up in the interview, she told me: "Yes, [the maid does wash my husband's clothes]. But I hear so many

Figure 11. Maids at the back of the university flats, Harare, 1984. Photo by author.

people [exclaim], 'She washes your husband's clothes.' They say, 'Hah! Why are you letting her do that?' I don't think there is a problem with that except if she is not cleaning them well."

In sum, tension between the wife and the maid structure interactions in some households. The secretaries' anxieties about themselves as good women came to the fore around the issues of the duties and responsibilities of the maid. Caring for the house, washing her husband's clothes, and cooking his food are tasks central to women's desire to be good wives. When I asked women why they washed clothes themselves instead of assigning the task to the maid, most answered that they wanted to have it done right, so the clothes would look like new, or to keep clothes fresh. They wanted to show that they were as good as the maid at doing housework, they wanted to set the standard, and they wanted to be seen as good housekeepers. Even with the additional tasks that working wives and mothers undertook, having a maid definitely gave them more free time. It allowed them time to enjoy their husbands and family in leisure activities, but it also threatened the intimacy of their marriage.

The Working Wife and Mother: A New Style of Marriage

Marriage as an institution both intimate and social is an excellent place to study the changing ideas that women have about how the roles they play vary as political and economic systems change around and through them. In this section, I show some of the new expectations that women bring to marriage. Most still have bridewealth (money and gifts given to the bride's family by the groom's) paid for them, but they incorporate that tradition within modern practices that give prominence to the nuclear family over the lineage or clans and that value shared responsibility of husband and wife over the husband as head of the household. Neolocal residence, shared household responsibilities, and joint family activities connote an ideal of family togetherness that young women tried to establish in their marriages. In sociological parlance, these were companionate marriages based on monogamy, fidelity, and the importance of emotional ties between husband and wife above all other relationships. Husband and wife are companions, friends whose relationship is founded on romance, love, and sex (see Cherlin 2009, 68; Hirsch and Wardlow 2006). Such marriages contrast with patriarchal husband-headed models in which husbands do not approach wives as equal partners; they also are at odds with the idea of marriage as the joining of two families. *Parade* magazine's millennium supplement, "Portraits of the People of Zimbabwe," notes that a little over 50 percent of people in the middle-class categories believe that men should be bosses at home and are the head of households. Varying data are reported in each profile. This statement about the highest group (group 7) is curious: "Fewer think that men should have the final say (62%)."[11] This leads me to conclude that while men generally may not be thought of as the boss, they are the final arbiters of decisions in the family.

Companionate marriages are not new to Zimbabwe, but they are also not widespread or universally valued. The introduction of companionate marriages can probably be traced to the missionaries during the Rhodesian colonial period and to the women's clubs in and outside the churches. Opposed to polygamy and bridewealth (*roora* [chiShona] and *lobola* [siNdebele]), women's clubs promoted what Sita Ranchod-Nilson (1992) calls the "incorporated wife," and Teresa Barnes (1999) identifies as the "respectable," "well-known," and "proper" housewife.[12] In clubs, women learned cooking, housecleaning, child care, hygiene—all intended to create a proper home for the upwardly mobile male head of household. In chapter 1, I argued that these clubs also gave participants a chance to associate with women beyond their kin groups and new possibilities for agency (see also Shaw 2008). These clubs and other social forces shaped the pattern of marriage that contemporary working women struggle to maintain; they are part of the history of the construction of companionate marriages in Zimbabwe.

When the ideal of companionate marriages spreads to new territories, those who adopt the practice view this pattern of marital relations as modern, as opposed to marriages that are arranged, negotiated through bridewealth or dowry, or based on sex segregation, or extended family residence (Hirsch and Wardlow 2006). Moreover, in situations where companionate marriage represents change from an older form, it is associated with increasing individualism, commodified social relations (as in the purchase of love tokens or in furnishing a nuclear family home), and a narrative of progress in gender relations. When a woman marries in customary marriage in Zimbabwe, a man "buys her womb," a Zimbabwean director of an international education program told a group of American students in 2000. Representing the two major ethnic groups in Zimbabwe, she was an Ndebele married to a Shona; she was referring to the practice of a man giving bridewealth to a woman's family as a part of traditional marriage negotiations. These goods—in the past, cattle and other movable property, once widely distributed among men and women in the bride's family—now come in the form of money, houses, cars, appliances, and furnishings and are mostly kept by the bride's parents. While many women interested in achieving progress in gender relations decry bridewealth as buying women, some women save money with their fiancés to be able to give bridewealth to the woman's parents, and others want at least a token of bridewealth to be given to their parents in recognition of the parents' contribution to their daughter's upbringing. Bridewealth marks the transfer of power over the woman from her father to her husband. It also is a means of legitimating her children, who will belong to her husband's lineage. The Zimbabwean director of the overseas program expressed a widespread sentiment in connecting bridewealth to the womb: a woman was expected to give birth as many times as she could. She was also expected to work for the clan and to inherit no property at the death of her husband.

Though the 1982 Legal Age of Majority Act made women legal adults at age eighteen, women of all ages still seek their parents' permission to marry, and marriage is still typically negotiated by an exchange of money or other property between men. At a constitutional seminar on "Gender and Customary Law" in 1999, this view of customary marriage was not so much disputed as it was updated and broadened by two of the leading feminist scholars in Zimbabwe, sociologist Rudo Gaidzanwa and law professor Amy Tsanga, who described what they called "the new patriarchy." They noted a crisis in patriarchy as customary norms change under capitalism. Bridewealth has been changed to the benefit of the bride's parents, not the extended family or the bride's brothers. Families still give and accept bridewealth, but without the expectation that it entails residing at the husband's father's home or patriarchal authority. Among the changes presented for discussion was the assertion that custom has eroded among the poor but is kept afloat by the rich. Businessmen and small-scale commercial farmers more often practice polygamy (for instance, the rate of

Figure 12. Rural entrepreneur, owner of a cotton farm and resort hotel, and his two wives, managers of farm workers and finances. Photo by author.

polygamy in town is 3–4 percent, but the rate in developed resettlement areas and small scale commercial farms is 15 percent): well-off men "marry labor." Because men are better placed to profit from the market economy, many women see that their best choice may be traditional marriage; people say they like customs because the market system is failing them, Gaidzanwa concluded.

The women I interviewed in 2000 were among the segment of the population for whom the market system was working. They and most of their husbands were gainfully employed. Most of them lived in a nuclear family, in a single-family household. This differs from the pattern for many Zimbabwean women in the colonial and postcolonial eras. As a settler colony, Zimbabwe had many white-owned large-scale commercial farms. Whole villages were incorporated into these schemes, and relatives from afar sometimes joined others in laboring in this feudal system. In manufacturing, industry, and mining, male migrant labor was central to the economy for much of the colonial period. This is much the same as in other African countries where men went to mines, factories, and farms, while women stayed in the rural areas rearing children, protecting patrimony, and taking on much of men's domestic labor. Husbands' visits home were often timed to the harvest: they would oversee any sale of surplus crops and take charge of the proceeds. In the first decades of the twentieth century, when the cycle of agricultural labor permitted, wives went into urban areas to stay in townships with their husbands. This practice was then against the law, and the fight to stay in the city as proper wives was one of the first protests taken up by urban women (Barnes 1992, 1995, 1999).

During a post–World War II boom in the urban population, Africans organized for "marital rights for township men and for township residence rights for women" (Barnes 1999, 134). Teresa Barnes (1999) and Terri Barnes and Everjoyce Win (1992) show that, when established in urban areas, black women formed self-help groups and joined men in unions and political organizations. Early in the 1950s, township women were introduced to Homecraft clubs, which had social goals (see chapter 1), to improve health care and sanitation, as well as individual goals for the woman and her home, to establish a proper Christian home (especially monogamous marriage), and to enhance her hygiene, appearance, and confidence.[13] Black women joined the groups to improve their standard of living and to enrich their lives. These clubs not only helped women to improve their abilities but also allowed them to "display ever more finely honed domestic skills" (Barnes 1999, 161). Women interviewed here belong to the generations who are the daughters and granddaughters of those whose Christian values and desire "to live a better life" urged them to be homemakers in nuclear families.

Faced with the changes in postcolonial Zimbabwe, the generation of women studied here lives with the paradox of liberation rhetoric and reactionary policies, with the corrosive effects of economic decline, and with the seeming permanence of the AIDS pandemic. The liberation armies achieved some of their successes in the rural areas by making alliances with women rather than men, and women joined the armed forces as active combatants during the 1970s, though many female combatants had limited opportunities for training and advancement. In spite of the rhetoric, the values most commonly acted on for women combatants as well as for women not engaged in the struggle emphasized women's responsibility for pleasing men, providing food, and taking care of the home and children.[14] Women in this generation are surrounded by competing narratives on differences between men and women, on women's "empowerment" and "capacity-building," as well as romantic tropes in which a woman must find herself and the love of her life.

At close to thirty years of age, the average office worker I interviewed was born during the liberation struggle and educated in the first decade of the Zimbabwean nation. The lives and aspirations of these women were shaped by the desire for companionate marriage, relative economic prosperity, and Zimbabwe's inclusive educational policy.[15] Later in Zimbabwe's dire economic circumstances—they were less dire but definitely challenging when I began this study—most women wanted to engage in some form of income-generating activity that would take care of living expenses, in particular to provide money for school fees for children. Only a lucky few had wage labor or held salaried positions in the public or private sectors.

I concluded that their goal was companionate marriage from what they did not say as much as what they did say. In the 1980s, urban women complained first about the demands of their husbands' mothers and sisters, about the deference these relatives demanded and their imperious rule over the women's marriages. For instance, in 1983, in a spirit-possession ceremony undertaken to resolve problems in an extended family where daughters were at about the same level of education and employment as secretaries, the spirit of the deceased grandmother (speaking through a sister) pointed to the young wife of a brother as having too much pride and too little generosity. Those complaints thirty years ago might also be evidence that some women were trying to establish a new kind of marital partnership but clearly with limited effect. What did secretaries complain about twenty years later?—money and husbands' absences. In my interviewees' complaints about the irresponsibility of men, I heard them saying that they depended on their husbands for emotional and financial support. None echoed Maiguru from Tsitsi Dangarembga's novel *Nervous Conditions* in her grumbling that her money props up his family while she has no say in the matter. However, several did say that relatives—his and hers—expected too much of them (housing job seekers, paying school fees for brothers and nephews, provisioning rural relatives) since both husband and wife were employed. Women's emphasis on the nuclear family decenters what Dangarembga calls "the patriarchy," the authority of the husband's male and female relatives, who have a claim on all the resources of their kin.

Household bills were divided between husband and wife and paid individually—seldom did husband and wife pool their money in joint accounts. Barbara, a thirty-four-year-old with two children, explained to me that while the bills are paid separately, women have to be patient and negotiate to be able to get the things needed in the home: "It's only women who make a home. For people to call a place a home it is because there's a woman. Yes, we have difficulties. You don't talk to him when he is in a bad mood because . . . men don't want to buy furniture. All they want is [to] give me the money. So we sit down and talk and say, yes, this is my salary and that is his salary. These are our bills. What extra do we have? . . . You really need to sit down and talk. That is how a home is supposed to be handled because if you go your own way and he does his own [shakes her head]."

Women feel responsibility for their families and are increasingly willing to negotiate with men to find ways to both share their sense of responsibility and gain control of more resources for their families.

Togetherness, Infidelity, and AIDS

I have argued here that togetherness—shared responsibilities of husband and wife and joint familial activities—are part of a new style of marriage that many, but not all, women value. In this section, I pit togetherness against infidelity, especially husbands' unfaithfulness, and suggest that they both factor in companionate marriage. Husbands and wives are doing more together, but wives still have little confidence that their husbands will be faithful to them. In the time of AIDS, this is more than depressing; it is downright dangerous.

Togetherness—a term popularized, if not coined, by *McCall's*, an American women's magazine in the 1950s (Miller 1995)—is probably the most public change brought about by the development of companionate marriage in Zimbabwe. Companionate marriage, in Zimbabwe, is marked by husbands and wives sharing leisure activities as well as the budget and household chores. In addition to travel to the husbands' natal home, family outings included local excursions to parks and lakes as well as national tourism. Families also prayed together at churches, and in one instance, husband and wife attended a couples' club at their church. Several women said that they participated in athletic activities with their husbands—jogging, tennis, and golf—though one said that she just watched golf, and another intimated that her husband had to drag her out to jog. Contrary to much literature on married life in Africa, a handful of women mentioned that their husbands take them out to dinner, to movies, to visit friends, and dancing. In a deliciously humorous treatment of the economic collapse of Zimbabwe, a white Zimbabwean relates how his parents saved their property by turning it into a bar and motel that was used for trysts with girlfriends and mistresses (called "little houses") on weekdays, and on weekends some of the same men would bring their wives for drinks and dancing (Rogers 2009).

Although women in this study reported a greater degree of togetherness than the ethnographic record typically shows for the region, on the whole, they also intimated that their husbands were unfaithful to them. Togetherness did not go hand in hand with fidelity. Only one woman said that she had no doubt that her husband was faithful to her. "I am a very faithful wife. I wish my husband to be the same," as another interviewee put it, is a more representative statement. Women are not happy about their husbands having sex with other women, but they do expect it. In contrast to a recent *New York Times Magazine* article that suggests that the goal of a stable marriage might be met by openly telling one's spouse about the desire to have one's sexual needs met outside the conjugal bed and setting the guidelines for doing so (Oppenheimer 2011), my guess is that Zimbabwean sexual mores more resemble those of Mexicans for whom "silence is golden" or "don't ask, don't tell" is the policy (Carrillo 2002). This pretense of ignorance endangers the lives of women in the AIDS pandemic. Noting the high rates of HIV/AIDS in the heterosexual population, AIDS researchers have concluded that Africans are no more promiscuous than other populations, but for many reasons, including men having more than one wife and brothers inheriting their deceased brothers' wives, men are more likely to be in coterminous multiple relationships.[16] Their data suggest that women as well as men may be in such relationships; my data, with the exception of the one case that I discuss later, includes no women who have sex with multiple partners (see Hunter 2005).

Women in the recent nationwide study in Zimbabwe report "being married to be the biggest HIV/AIDS risk factor in their lives" (Chiroro, Mashu, and Muhwava 2002, 1). My interviewee Barbara, the thirty-four-year-old mother of two, a Methodist who went to lunchtime prayer meetings twice a week, believed that God can prevent a woman from getting AIDS: God protects the righteous. The following is a snippet of my interview with her:

> CAROLYN: One of my friends went to a gospel concert... last year. I think there was a gospel singer named Rebecca?
> BARBARA: Malope.
> C: She said if you believe in God, you are protected from AIDS.
> B: Yes.
> C: Do you really believe that? Really?
> B: You know all we need to do is to ask God. Your husband goes out there. All you need is to pray to say, "God, I need your protection." So anyway, God somehow makes them not get infected. But I've heard the preacher preach [that also].

Barbara's take on AIDS was not unique. Rather it engaged the positive pole of a common discourse on AIDS: God protects the righteous and punishes the sinner. This view of the pandemic coexisted with a discourse of "innocent victims," AIDS orphans and children afflicted with AIDS-related conditions. Some interviewees looked on the AIDS pandemic as a sign of the moral crisis of the country, while others concentrated on personal and familial health concerns, getting tested for the virus, taking care of needy family members, and attending funerals.

I asked questions of all the interviewees about the number of intimate partners they had at the same time; only one admitted to having more than one at a time. Most addressed the question head-on, and a few said that having more than one boyfriend at a time would cause problems. Lillian, a thirty-three-year-old married woman with children aged twelve, six, and three, told me that she had had an extramarital affair, with an ex-boyfriend, shortly after she was married. What she didn't tell me was that she was HIV+ and showing signs of AIDS, and that her second child was also HIV+, though I have no doubt that this is true—her child seemed to fall into the "failure to thrive" category of children born HIV+. In keeping with what I learned from other women, I believe she mentioned her boyfriend because she understood AIDS as God's retribution for her loose morals. Lillian dealt with AIDS by joining an apostolic church, where the women's organization at the church taught her how to be a good wife, and the pastor's healing hands brought about a "miracle cure" for her child when he was gravely ill. At the interview, Lillian looked good, with a trim body in loose-fitting clothes and a head full of synthetic hair. Her husband warned her against wearing her natural hair short with the words, "All the people will see how you are suffering." Thinning hair is one of the signs of AIDS that Zimbabweans most take note of.

In many ways, AIDS was invisible in the cities of Zimbabwe. The disease, which at its worst lowered the life expectancy for women to thirty four years, affected an estimated one in three people in Zimbabwe in the prime of their lives.[17] AIDS was overwhelmingly present in the overburdened hospitals and cemeteries. But even though the disease was devastating the country, the streets of the capital city of Harare were filled with prosperous-looking young men and women. The city's look of health resulted from people who were too sick to work leaving the city for the rural areas. Their vacated jobs were readily taken up by the vast number of well-trained and educated people seeking employment. Since the Zimbabwean president Robert Mugabe bulldozed the homes of urban dwellers in slums and middle-class neighborhoods alike because the cities were the hotbed of the opposition, many healthy urbanites also retreated to rural areas. Remittances from the millions of emigrants who left the country added a glint of prosperity to a country in economic meltdown and ravaged by despotic rule.[18] Most women in the city wore wigs and had synthetic hair extensions braided onto their hair, not just because of AIDS, but because it was stylish. However, as the economy declined, fewer women were able to afford these hairstyles. It was not until a student from the United States, not yet in Zimbabwe two weeks, was diagnosed with AIDS that I began to think about the connection between AIDS and hair extensions. The student, a member of an overseas study program that I was associated with in Zimbabwe, was among the first to arrive from the States. She was thin and trim, accustomed to running four miles a day and boxing at the gym, with long blonde hair, held in place by a wide headband. She was the picture of health, except for a nasty cut on her lip, which she attributed to a fall while rollerblading. When she suddenly became ill, the doctor we took her to listed the symptoms that made him say, without a blood test, that she had AIDS: a particular form of pneumonia, swollen lymph glands, fever, diarrhea, gastrointestinal pain, oral yeast infection, weight loss, and thinning hair. "I see seventy cases like this every day," he told the director of the overseas program, adding: "She has a strong immune system. A Zimbabwean would be dead before this stage."

My student did not accept the diagnosis—she had an explanation for each ailment and resisted seeing the pattern. She almost had me convinced until I went to her dorm room to remove her belongings, since we were sending her home. In her closet and suitcases were three wigs, including the flowing hair that she had sported at the airport. She had an explanation for her thinning hair, too: anemia.

Thinning hair is the quintessential sign of AIDS in Zimbabwe. It is mentioned in songs, in everyday speech, and in newspaper articles. Where thinning hair is a sign of illness, long, lustrous hair is a sign of health. Carter Wilson, author of *Hidden in the Blood* (1995), about an AIDS clinic in Mexico City, once told me that fat men had a certain cachet in the gay community during the height of the U.S. AIDS epidemic because if thin meant disease, then fat meant health. When I see African women with full heads of hair (even if not their own), I wonder if something similar is not at work here. Hair is cheaper to buy than a membership in a fitness center, and it takes a lot less time to get a new hairdo than a massive body. Thick, full, flowing hair, in the midst of the AIDS epidemic, is "the picture of health."

Death from AIDS is seldom mentioned in the media. There are no obituary pages as such in the *Herald*, Harare's major newspaper (and the government paper), with a circulation of 550,000 at the turn of the century. The first page of the classified section contains death notices, birth notices, birthday greetings, condolences, and commemorations. Most of the photos on these pages are of young people; only every now and then does a grandmother or a grandfather's picture appear. While friends and relatives use these pages to send messages of condolence to bereaved families, many of the messages are addressed to the deceased. Family members remember the anniversary of the death of their loved ones—one, two, even ten years after the event. Often addressing the deceased in the second person, their messages tell the deceased of their love and their sense of loss. Children despair that their fathers never got to see their accomplishments, and widows ask their deceased husbands to guide and protect the family. AIDS is never mentioned on these pages where relatives lament that they still do not understand why their loved one was taken away from them. Even in the rare obituaries of musicians, journalists, and leading citizens, the cause of death is typically not mentioned. People thirty years old die after "a long illness" or "a short illness," and sometimes of tuberculosis.

HIV/AIDS, glossed in Zimbabwean English as "the virus," was talked about during the time of this research, 1999–2001, but some in Zimbabwe as in the United States doubted that it was sexually transmitted or that it was a single disease. Besides being whispered about at funerals, AIDS appears in popular music and in health articles in newspapers and magazines, and is talked about on talk-radio programs. During the peak of the pandemic, a news magazine and a women's magazine ran stories that engaged the debate on the causes of AIDS and the mechanism of its spread. Criticism of AIDS research and the AIDS establishment, which has been growing among young people in the United States, is also present in Zimbabwe. Just before I went to Zimbabwe in 1999, outside the office of the Names Project in San Francisco, the organization responsible for the AIDS memorial quilt, I saw a sidewalk stencil that posed the question: "Do you still believe in the AIDS myth?" Similar sentiments abound in Zimbabwe: citing Peter Duesberg, John Lauristen, and Zimbabwean medical director, Richard Ngwenya, among other international and local authorities, the Zimbabwean women's magazine *Mahogany* has referred to "so-called AIDS" and headlined topics such as "AIDS is not an infectious disease" and "There is no such thing as AIDS." This magazine and others have also catered to a different view, carried ads for AIDS testing, and in the past run thoughtful articles about the extent of the AIDS epidemic in Zimbabwe.

Popular music took up the issue of AIDS. Musicians sang about the scourge taking over the country, about increased rape and sexual abuse of young girls (whose purity either removed the risk of contracting the disease or was believed to wipe away the disease), and about the depletion of energy and resources from AIDS. The answers they and many others suggest are a return to cultural values and a new fundamentalism that promotes female virginity and control of youth and women.

After more than a decade of the government's denying that AIDS existed in Zimbabwe, the ABC ("Abstinence, Be Faithful, Condom Use") education and prevention program is widely used by NGOs, which, even before the collapse of the Zimbabwean economy, were the leaders in AIDS education and prevention in the country. The campaign is up against stiff competition from local and global beliefs and practices. For men, being able to have more than one partner, proving masculinity by producing many offspring, and brooking no opposition to their decisions are valued and sought-after goals (Chiroro, Mashu, and Muhwava 2002). Condoms, in a belief similar to that of some black Americans, are seen as a plot to lower the black birthrate, and some Zimbabwean men believe that condoms distributed in the country are impregnated with the AIDS virus. Patrick Chiroro and his colleagues' study found that "over 90% of men and male youths believe that condoms are infected with sexually transmitted diseases, including the HIV virus. This was thought to be particularly the case with condoms that are supplied through hospitals and clinic and by peer educators" (2002, 23). According to this study, men believe that if they have sex with the same partners (not with only one partner but with the same set of partners), they do not need to use condoms, and that any woman who asks them to use a condom is promiscuous. In focus groups men reported that refusal to have sex is the number one reason for beating their wives and girlfriends, and that they would not tell their wives if they were HIV positive.

The emphasis of marital togetherness combined with husbands' infidelity marked a style of marriage that maintained privileges from the past while latching on to practices and ideas of companionate marriage. To some extent, companionate marriage in Zimbabwe was consciously placed within a narrative of progress in gender equality, but women called on it and a variety of other discourses to form their ideas about life and to live their lives. Experiences at work brought to the fore the question of gender equality within the hierarchy of the office and the possibility of upward mobility outside the feminized secretarial ladder. In light of the power imbalance between their husbands/fiancés and themselves, women often claimed a moral high ground in relation to men: women were responsible, putting the family before their own pleasures, while men were irresponsible. Married women had unprotected sex with their husbands whom they believed to be unfaithful, not only because they wanted to show loyalty and obedience or because they might be beaten and reviled if they did not, but also because of their own ideas about what it means to be a good wife. As they weighed gendered demands (such as never declining to have sex with their husbands), they were forced to consider the consequences of exhibiting the qualities that had conventionally ensured social security and symbolic capital—the qualities of a good wife, especially endurance. They weighed the value of being a good wife under circumstances in which being a good wife might jeopardize their ability to be caring and responsible mother to their children. They weighed the value of being a good wife under circumstances in which becoming a mother, one of the central tenets of womanhood for many in Zimbabwe, is itself fraught with danger. Many women prayed for themselves and their husbands, but they could not face the issue of using condoms without themselves being labeled loose women.

The Loose Woman Speaks

The loose woman—also referred to as common, whore, prostitute, mistress, or girlfriend—is the nemesis of the respected, responsible married woman: poor, migrant husbands spend money on these women instead of sending funds to their wives in the rural areas, and rich, salaried men keep women in flats and private homes, using funds that could be put to other uses at home. At work, women complain about loose women getting ahead through sex, while their virtuous hardworking colleagues are overlooked. These vilified women seldom speak out in public to explain or justify their conduct. But a very public defense of the loose woman did appear in the newspapers late in 1999 in the form of a series of letters responding to a news story about a wife and her friends assaulting her husband's mistress. A similar incident had occurred at the UZ flats where I lived. A wife and her husband's girlfriend had gotten into a yelling match that escalated into a physical fight. I had missed the incident, but everyone I knew in the complex told me about it. The mistress of one of the UZ lecturers came to see him: he was the husband of Chipo, whom I wrote about in the introduction to this book; they had three daughters, and he was dying of AIDS with a particularly virulent strain of tuberculosis. Chipo met her husband's girlfriend in the courtyard, and a screaming match ensued. The girlfriend was sick, her body wasted with AIDS, but she put up a good fight, declaring that her child was the lecturer's only son and should inherit from him. Chipo had been in and out of the hospital with various ailments (the topic of much gossip in the complex), but she was plump and healthy looking. The two women came to blows before neighbors separated them, and the girlfriend went home without seeing her dying lover. I heard this story secondhand, as I did another story about a girlfriend of another UZ lecturer asserting her rights to be with her dying lover. In the latter case, after staying with him in hospice care, she relinquished his body to his wife and family and did not attend the funeral.

Given the open secrecy of men's extramarital affairs, it is surprising that few wives are ever knowingly in the company of their husband's girlfriends, and although a wife sometimes knows the identity of her husband's mistresses, most never confront them. Girlfriends accompany men to night clubs and on business trips, and they entertain their lovers' male friends and the girlfriends of those men. Girlfriends and wives lead separate, if similar, existences. One of my unmarried acquaintances in Harare, who had a teen-aged son with her married lover, lived in a well-appointed suburban home, as essentially a second wife. She wrangled with him for luxuries and complained to me that the money kept her in the relationship, much like a privileged professional woman in the United States, who, in conversation with me, referred to herself as in golden handcuffs—tied to her way of life because of the goods and privileges that it bought.

A series of letters to the editor in the *Herald*, the government-funded daily newspaper, brought the wives and girlfriends together.[19] On the newspaper's editorial pages, over a three-week period, married women and girlfriends of married men developed the metaphor of men as dogs, each group making special claims to the affection and loyalty of married men. In what follows, I have distilled the letters into a conversation between a loyal wife and an understanding girlfriend. An amused man, a righteous man, a bitter wife, and a happy ex-wife are sideline kibitzers. All the statements contained in this conversation were taken verbatim from the *Herald* editorial pages in November 1999.

> **UNDERSTANDING GIRLFRIEND:** It is so sad that you so-called married women claim that your husbands are snatched away from you by girlfriends. . . . Didn't your aunts advise you that keeping quiet is the best solution? . . . Have you

ever asked yourself why [your husband has a girlfriend]? If you do not feed dogs, they will definitely go and look for food somewhere else.

LOYAL WIFE: What amazing pets dogs are! They are loyal, obedient, loving, responsible and to some extent, submissive and ravenous. But no matter how well you feed dogs they will still go and scrounge in the rubbish bins. It's in their nature.

UNDERSTANDING GIRLFRIEND: A dog is a dog no matter the breed or pedigree and it is a proven fact that these apparently loyal dogs have been known to breed with all sorts that tickle their fancy.

RIGHTEOUS MAN: Girlfriends, forget about sex life, become nuns and leave married women to enjoy their married life. I advise all women to lobby the Constitutional Commission to have prostitution legalized with formal brothels established. This may help stop you from grabbing other women's husbands. Who your customers will be, I do not know.

LOYAL WIFE: Our husbands pass you by like service stations. You are not there to stay.... The reason they go to girlfriends is maybe to run away from solving problems at home. But they come back anyway.... They keep you in the dark corners where you belong (as pretty as you are) while he takes me to meet important members of his family to which he does not take you.... Where is Monica today? Hillary and Bill Clinton are still together happy ever after.

AMUSED MAN: I wish that our new constitution could allow us to marry our loving and caring girlfriends.

LOYAL WIFE: To be proud to be a mistress shows that you were not brought up properly by your parents. They have the same loose morals as you.... Our aunts are enlightened. They are aware of the dangers of promiscuity. Your aunt has a great deal to do.... It is people like you spreading AIDS and breaking up families.

UNDERSTANDING GIRLFRIEND: Unlike dogs, men get fed up and will divorce the "holier than thou art" wives and marry the girlfriends you despise so much. ... We are not prostitutes but women like the rest of you but unfortunately you think you are all better than the rest for the simple reason that you are married.

BITTER WIFE: You should fix your husband by going after his money or his pride. Spend his money so that he has nothing left to spend on girlfriends or give him a taste of his own medicine and see how he enjoys having a competitor. Do not be soft on these men.

HAPPY EX-WIFE: I am glad that married women publicly admitted that they stayed with dogs, their husbands. That is why I never want to own one again after having tried every trick for 15 years. Most women stay in those bitter marriages for the letters MRS and the fear of society. . . . Leave him and get on with your life if he is not worth it. Using protection and feeding just one stray dog in a while is no big deal. Left the dog to protect myself.

Girlfriends are women without moral superiority, which undermines their claims to womanhood, making them abject. They try to make up for their lack of moral high ground by being responsible mothers and compassionate partners. Sustaining relationships that come close to the ideal of companionate marriage, girlfriends offer solace and sexual excitement to their married lovers and seek for themselves a feeling of being cherished and taken care of. The girlfriends discussed here are not town wives (sometimes called *mapoto*, woman of the pots and pans), who are temporary partners taken by men working away from home in factories and mines. The institution of the town wife is a form of prostitution wherein a woman may live with a man for weeks or years, continuously or seasonally, providing domestic services—cooking, laundry, and cleaning—as well as sex. When a town wife's relationship ends, she seeks out another or may go into other forms of prostitution. Mary Adams's (2009) study of women in the peri-urban community of Epworth, just outside Harare, suggests that young women who go to the city as petty traders may serve as prostitutes or town wives but later marry and settle in their natal community without ignominy. Girlfriends, of the type writing in the newspaper, do not tend to move on to other relationships, which is one of the reasons they may appear more mercenary than wives. They have staked their survival on a relationship with no familial or community support in which they have little recourse if the man decides to leave.

The colloquial terms men use to objectify the girlfriend–married lover relationship in Nigeria—girlfriends are "handbags" (attractive accessories) and "razor blades" (bleeding a man of money and sexuality)—capture much of the Zimbabwean phenomenon (D. Smith 2006). Men show their economic prowess by having attractive girlfriends; the women, because they have little familial and social support, try to get as many things and as much money as they can. One of the young men whom I interviewed, the oldest and most Christian, thought that this mercenary orientation could be generalized to all girls. When I asked him what he thought women want, he replied: "Girls mostly, they are like prostitutes, most of them like money, especially those who are in the rural areas." None of the other young men shared such a negative view of young women, but all of them said that girls wanted boys to spend money on them. The youngest asserted, "They will be looking for money and for you to take them to Nando's [fast-food restaurant] or movies. And when your money is finished, they will leave you and go for someone else." The subtext of their statements is that they, as high school students and the newly unemployed, cannot compete with the employed and wealthy—that women will not choose to be with a man who cannot offer reliable support. Also underlying understanding of courtship and sexual relations that the boys pointed to is a phenomenon that one of the secretaries described to me. Lillian avowed that she was "guided by Christian life" in deciding what to wear and with whom to sleep; she coyly saw women's advantage in the sexual power they have over men: "A woman can do whatever you want to with a man. Sometimes they go out of their way to please [women]."

Some women see their sexuality as power, but men may use it to have power over women, as illustrated in two studies of masculinity and femininity at a college and a university in Zimbabwe. Rob Pattman (2001) studied a teachers' college in the southeastern province of Masvingo. There male students divided themselves into two groups: beer drinkers and churchgoers. Both groups had the same opinion of the women on their campus who spoke up in class, were independent minded, went to night clubs, or wore trousers and miniskirts. They were called prostitutes and Western; they were said to have abandoned their culture. The churchgoers avoided this type of woman, but the beer drinkers delighted in dancing, drinking, and having sex with such women. The gendered cultural imaginary of both groups included an assertive masculinity in which men are free and active subjects and women are objects of desire, threatening coevals, or malleable potential mates. Pattman concludes that masculinity in the college cohort is predicated on dominating women and women's bodies.

Among students at the leading university in Zimbabwe, UZ, similar standards hold. Gaidzanwa's (2001) five-year study identified different patterns of masculinity based on socioeconomic class, home area, age, commitment to religious fundamentalism, and political activism. Hegemonic masculinity, represented by men born in townships (high-density urban areas) and in rural areas (severe rural background, sons of poor farmers), is politically militant, violent, and aggressive. Fundamentalist Christian masculinity, another pattern of masculinity found at the university, opposes any pedagogy that questions the rightness of male dominance. A gentlemanly masculinity, a third pattern, appears regardless of age, class, religion, or ethnicity, expressed by men who volunteer to perform errands and guarantee safe passage to women. Among this third group is a smaller segment identified by class, from elite boys' schools, who "exhibit pronounced verbal politeness" (117). In contrast to the rigid divisions among men, Gaidzanwa's research finds femininities to be fluid. Women students from severe rural backgrounds and women from high-density urban areas all aspire to the material well-being and consumption patterns of middle-class women of "the nose brigade," so called because of their control of the English language and their British intonation pattern. Gaidzanwa concludes that "a common feature among these femininities is that they focus on earning the admiration of men on and off campus," though male students are often overlooked in favor of wealthy businessmen and government employees. Women want to earn good degrees, get highly paid jobs, and attain status, "but many student women are also expected to prove themselves on the marriage market" (121).

Both men and women students use sex as a means to a committed relationship. In addition to hand washing a boyfriend's clothes and having sex at his will, some women will engage in unprotected sex to prove their commitment to a man and will "fall pregnant for" a man before he graduates in order to push him toward marriage. From the man's point of view, pregnancy "accomplishes the triple goals of curtailing her desirability and mobility on the sexual marriage markets, testing her docility and submission to the man's wishes and demonstrating her ability to bear children" (Gaidzanwa 2001, 125). The pattern for women identified at the university—in a committed relationship by her last year or showing her commitment by "falling pregnant"—is borne out by my research with women office workers. Typically their final credential was the high school O-level, and many were pregnant in their last year of high school, married shortly after leaving school, and then chose to get secretarial training. Gaidzanwa and her graduate students at the University of Zimbabwe seem to contend that no matter what their other accomplishments, the pressure is on women in Zimbabwe to prove their femininity through marriage and reproductive fertility.

Premarital sex does not in itself deny a woman access to moral superiority, but if her sexuality and fertility are not claimed by a husband, she can fall into the category of loose woman. Women who openly control their own sexuality and do not marry are most likely candidates for opprobrium. Casting her net wider than the university and college students mentioned earlier, Kaler (2003) found that young women in Zimbabwe are increasingly opting to have children as single mothers and to slacken their ties to their natal families by marrying without parental permission and bridewealth. In doing this, women jeopardize their power and authority within what Dangarembga calls "the patriarchy," the senior members in an extended family in which women and men engage in decision making and women oversee their nieces' moral education.[20] While some anthropologists note that women as sisters are relatively more powerful than women as wives, the Shona in Zimbabwe present an interesting intermediate position: women do have authority as sisters, but their influence is weighed against their conduct as wives—their being dutiful wives enhances their voice in decisions involving their brothers and their brothers' children (Shaw 2007). By this logic, divorced women and unmarried mothers have little say in their natal families' decisions: because they control their own sexuality, they are morally suspect.

Novels written by Zimbabwean women provide another way of studying the feminine moral ground and its prospects of change. To most women, "loose woman" is an abhorrent identity, not one with a strong or positive attachment. Tsitsi Dangarembga in *Nervous Conditions* shows how broad the category "loose woman" is, potentially embracing a surprising range of qualities: educated, streetwalker, elite, beautiful. Zimbabwean novelist Yvonne Vera portrays some of these qualities in her novel *Butterfly Burning*, in which the protagonist is a child of prostitutes (birth mother and nurturer) and is named for one of the distinguishing characteristics of the loose woman, Phephelaphi: one who does not settle; one who flits about. Using works by both novelists, I consider the interior lives of loose women. Both novelists depict ambitious and sensual women and assess the trope of the responsibility that so defines the Zimbabwean wife and mother. Dangarembga's and Vera's works point to the pleasures and dangers of sexuality and pull the reader in close to the power of the erotic in shaping women's quest for the good life.

In *Nervous Conditions*, Dangarembga presents stories of women who seek intellectual rather than physical fulfillment, of ambivalence toward the body and sexuality, and of distrust of maternity under patriarchy. All her major characters fail to contain themselves as they try to restrain honest emotions, reproachful words, individual conscience, fleshy body parts, sensuous movement, and sexual desire. Tambu, the country cousin, finds beauty in the hills and sensuality in the river once she leaves the confines of her parents' home, more a workplace than a place of rest. Swimming is one of the few activities in which she allows herself to feel bodily pleasure. Lucia, the protagonist's maternal aunt, is not ashamed of her appetite for sex, but the willful daughter of the headmaster, Nyasha, the city cousin, is defeated by her budding sexuality. Despite the fact that the play came before the novel, Martha, the protagonist in Dangarembga's little-known play, *She No Longer Weeps*, is so much like Nyasha in *Nervous Conditions* that it is as though that character is given a second life. Martha is decidedly loose, enjoying sex, getting pregnant out of wedlock, defying her father, taking lovers, and finally castrating her child's father. The violent revenge at the end of the play does not leave its perpetrator satisfied; instead she is delivered, meek, into the hands of her father and the law. She had grown cold living on her own terms and become unhinged at the thought of losing her child because of her failure to contain her sexual desire. Another spectacular failure of containment comes in the opening lines of *The Book of Not*, the second in a proposed trilogy that started with *Nervous Conditions*: "Up, up, up, the leg spun. A piece of a person, up there in the sky" (Dangarembga 2006, 1). Tambu's younger sister, a combatant in the liberation struggle, had her leg severed when she stepped on a land mine as she moved toward her wayward lover, after the villagers noted the smug, satisfied look of the young woman he had chosen over her. Sex is dangerous: women who cannot control their bodies will suffer.

Yvonne Vera's five novels use women's bodies to portray Zimbabwean history from the colonial period through independence, chronicling the nineteenth-century uprising against colonialism as the efforts of a woman who does not accept her femininity (*Nehanda*, 1993), the inchoate violence of the liberation struggle through infanticide and child abandonment (*Without a Name*, [1992] 1994 and *Under the Tongue*, 1996), the rhythm of township life and the pressures of ambition and reproduction (*Butterfly Burning*, 1998), and the genocidal terror of rape and death after liberation (*Stone Virgins*, 2002). In her works, sexuality and reproduction are intertwined and antithetical: sex is not transcendent, home does not fulfill, and children do not redeem. City women who free their sexuality from domesticity and male dominance do so at the cost of their reputations, motherhood, and, sometimes, their lives. The love affair between an older sister, Thenjiwe, and her enthralled lover in *Stone Virgins* is probably Vera's most realized representation of woman as subject of her own desire. Thenjiwe is immediately attracted to the appealing stranger; with him, she has a "weightless courage to be loved" and "forgives the desire sparking in her own fine limbs" (29). Their lovemaking is intense and satisfying, but it does not take her out of herself or prevent her imagining a world beyond his reality. This sister is raped and beheaded by a solider driven mad by his participation in the massacres in the western region of Zimbabwe. Thenjiwe's young sister, who has suffered physical and psychological injuries during the attack, ends up in the nurturing care of the older sister's lover.

Both writers try to deflate the loose woman trope, but in some ways reinforce it: Nyasha, who as a teenager wants to explore sex, goes mad; Martha, who defies her father and lives independently, grows cold and violent; and Thenjiwe, who enjoyed the feeling between her thighs, literally loses her head. There are no easy answers here.

I cannot leave this discussion of the loose women in Zimbabwe without mentioning the most famous of all, the country's first lady, Grace Mugabe. What I recount here is what I heard recited in many circles in the capital city. It is a story of a woman's sexual license and her rehabilitation, and of her excesses in piling up goods and her desire for power. It starts when she was a married woman, working as a secretary (some say a typist) for President Mugabe when he was married to his first wife, Sally Hayfron Mugabe. Though Sally was much loved as a hero of the revolution, she was a Ghanaian and thought of as an outsider. Sally had one child with Mugabe, a son, who died in Ghana while Mugabe was imprisoned in Zimbabwe during the liberation war. Before Sally's death, the president displaced his secretary's husband. Of the children born to them, one was born while Sally was still alive and another within months of her death from kidney disease. Grace Mugabe and the president married four years after Sally died.

As first lady, Grace Mugabe is constantly in the news but, until recently, not publically engaged in politics. The media showed her in fabulous clothes and especially big, fancy hats; they reported on her interests in diamond mining, inspected the mansions she built, speculated on her properties overseas, and marveled at or rebuked her for her extravagant shopping sprees around the world. When scores of Zimbabwean elites were targeted in sanctions for human rights violations and election irregularities in the country, her name was at the top of the list of individuals whose assets overseas were frozen and who were prevented from visiting the United States and participating European Union countries. In 2014, Grace Mugabe entered presidential politics as the heir apparent to her husband. Very cannily, during his more than thirty years of rule, President Mugabe never explicitly named a successor, but he gave hints, and a roving spotlight landed on one and then another of his cabinet ministers. The first lady is not a cabinet minister, but she has been acting like a candidate for presidential office in attacking the person whom many had thought most likely to succeed Mugabe, Vice President Joice Mujuru, the female ex-combatant who has occupied several posts in the cabinet since independence.[21] In a battle that will probably tear the ruling party asunder, Grace Mugabe could become president of Zimbabwe.

Before the first couple married, women were contemptuous that Grace, a married woman, allowed herself to be drawn into a relationship with the president. But he was the president and all powerful; he could be forgiven. Few women see even a shred of sexual harassment in the case. For most, Grace could not be forgiven; she was shameless, greedy, and lacked charity. Some women held a different opinion: they saw her as clever, a woman who understands feminine power and used it to reach the highest realms in the nation. To the extent that her fertility was claimed through marriage to the president, Mrs. Mugabe is not very different from the university women studied by Gaidzanwa (2001) and her students or the petty traders whom Adams (2009) studied: all were sexually active, either in the interest of marriage or they were redeemed by marriage. Spronk's (2003) young middle-class women in Nairobi walk a similar line between valuing sexual pleasure and preserving their image as proper marriage prospects. There are differences in these stories of sexuality and rehabilitation, and the main one people remember is that Grace was married at the time that Mugabe chose her. She yielded to temptation: she was no better than a man.

Having It All?

In Western countries in the 1980s, many women wanted to have it all—to be powerful leaders in the boardroom, sexy wives in the bedroom, and caring mothers at home. Expressing much the same sentiment, a quotation from Nigerian feminist Amina Mama (2001) appears at the end of the 2011 report of the Zimbabwe Feminist Forum: "As a result of the accumulated experience generated by the democratic praxis of women's movements, feminist theory has developed a sophisticated understanding of power that can usefully be brought to bear on considerations of identity, an understanding that highlights the workings of power from the bedroom to the boardroom." The women discussed in this chapter want to have it all, too, but their "all" is different. They want to be respectable and competent workers, responsible mothers, and dutiful wives. Working women have to contend with the possibility that they will be seen as prostitutes because they leave home and go to work among strange men; they must cope with men's sexual advances, which often are tied to their viability in the workplace. Women's sense of moral superiority and their belief that men cannot control their urges allow some women to navigate this terrain without feeling personally affronted. Many wrap themselves in Christianity to settle any problems. Others take a more secular stance but remain on guard for any reproach to their dignity at work. Women are not lax in their surveillance and discipline of other women, through gossip and exclusion. Some denounce those who use sex to get ahead, in an attempt to control the behavior of others and to maintain a standard of appropriate feminine behavior. The freer women are to move about and associate with others, the more important it is to them to signal their status as "good women." This would explain why working women with household help persist in doing domestic tasks themselves. Washing husbands' clothes and cooking their dinners communicate wives' standing as good women.

The interviewees in this chapter do not identify as feminists, nor do they have their eyes on that distant prize. For most, their visions of the good life are closer, more conventional—respectability in society, reciprocity in marriage, upward mobility at work—but also not easily attainable. External forces affect the possibility of reaching their goals, which would require not only a political will but also major changes in the expectations of men and women, as well as in the political economy that profits from the social and economic inequality of men and women. Moreover, women's attachments to their own moral superiority and to themselves as distinctly responsible might have to change. Ogundipe-Leslie, whose social-transformation approach to African feminism emphasizes cultural change and interdependence of women and men, takes women to task for not giving up some of their privileges and strongly held beliefs (1994, 210–26). According to her, women must educate themselves about the rights and responsibilities of being independent in a liberal democracy, and women must stop exploiting men financially or burdening men while talking about equality.

Ogundipe-Leslie is especially hard on married women with children, whom she calls "Married Women, Inc." for their unbending rules of exclusion against single and childless women. The issues she addresses, which speak more directly to West African social and cultural understandings, might not all be relevant to the working wives and mothers whom I got to know in Zimbabwe, but the feelings and orientation of women in the suffrage movement of the First Wave of feminism in the West come closer. Historian Paula Baker (1984) argues that British suffragists and antisuffragists all agreed that women belonged in the home, where they could exercise moral influence and ensure national virtue and social order. As women struggled to gain the vote at the turn of the twentieth century, many feared "women's loss of position as society's moral arbiter and enforcer," and some female antisuffragists forecast social disorder and political disaster with the loss of women's moral superiority (Baker 1984, 620). In the Zimbabwe case, if women give up their feelings of moral superiority, they fear the breakup of their marriages and the loss of fathers' interest in their children. Women may want greater reciprocity in marriage, but they have to weigh the cost of acting as though women are morally equivalent to men.

These changes are not easy to make, because they threaten women's sense of themselves as women, based on ideals to which they have become attached. Berlant (2011) argues that we can become so committed to our attachments that we are reluctant to change even when those attachments prevent our attaining satisfaction. Sometimes problematic attachments are what give us the will to live on; this she calls cruel optimism. In such cases, "the very vitalizing or animating potency of an object/scene of desire contributes to the attrition of the very thriving that is supposed to be made possible in the work of attachment in the first place" (25). Women's attachment to their own moral superiority unconsciously detracts from their achievement of reciprocity in marriage, while keeping them in marriages that do not satisfy them.

CHAPTER 5

Reflections

Promises of Freedom and Feminism

> Quietly, unobtrusively and extremely fitfully, something in my mind began to assert itself, to question things and refuse to be brainwashed, bringing me to this time when I can set down this story.
>
> Tsitsi Dangarembga, *Nervous Conditions*

Quiet, unobtrusive, and fitful is how Tsitsi Dangarembga describes the burgeoning of feminist consciousness in Tambu, the narrator and country cousin, in *Nervous Conditions*. Fitful—disturbed, restless, and irregular—might best sum up feminism in Zimbabwe: disturbed by their place in society, women, restless for a better life, seek change, which comes irregularly, and when it does come, the change can be discomfiting. There is no single path to feminism; the roads can be rough, and the goals varied. In this work, I have tried to show that feminism, the development of consciousness of sexism and the willingness to join with others to end discrimination against women, is not always quiet. Sometimes it blares as in the liberation war or in street protests. At other times it is unobtrusive, as in women's inklings that something is wrong at work, without having the words to name that something. Feminism stirs the promise of a better life, but the economy, politics, and society often do not conjoin to realize that promise.

Lauren Berlant's "cruel optimism" engages the dark side of good-life promises: the bad that can happen as we strive for a better, more satisfying something. While I have spent most of this book ruminating about cruel optimism as a promise of a future good life that is thwarted by the political economy, state spectacles of violence, and conventional attachments, Berlant is decidedly not future oriented. As she puts it, "Cruel Optimism gives a name to a personal and collective kind of relation and sets its elaboration in a historical moment that is as transnational as the circulation of capital, state liberalism, and the heterofamilial, upwardly mobile good-life fantasy have become" (2011, 11). She contends that the forces or situations that make optimism turn cruel also make life unbearable. The fact that most people live the unbearable is a testament to their optimism and to the power of certain kinds of conventional attachments. Reflecting on the varied worlds of women in Zimbabwe, I found that for some feminism is a mishmash of contradictions in the historical moment, and for others, it exists as a gravitational pull toward a shiny object in the firmament. In my work on the lives of working wives and mothers, I found glimmers of the promise of a feminist future, but those bright points were at times overshadowed by the attractions of more-conventional feminine powers. I tried to show in the discussion of the director of the feminist NGO AWZ that the conventional has its own delights—contentment, fellowship, prestige—but the conventional was not so satisfying among the married women office workers, who strive to be strong, responsible, and superior even as their husbands and the state fail them. In Zimbabwe, the slashing of government spending on social services has affected women's everyday lives, but, more importantly, economic collapse, increasing authoritarianism, and state-sponsored violence have removed some of the comforts of the conventional. Still optimism does not die.

Zimbabwe is paradoxical, as are many developing countries, with massive poverty at the bottom and fantastic wealth at the top. I write this in 2014 in the United States, where disparity between rich and poor is at its greatest. But Zimbabwe's middle class, which I have chronicled here, is far smaller, less established, and more vulnerable than its counterpart in the United States. There the middle class is seriously dwarfed by people outside the cities who live as subsistence farmers—without electricity or water on tap and dependent on remittances from distant family members. High-ranking officials and businesspeople who are loyal to the regime have plenty. Others, including most civil servants, feel lucky to have jobs even though their earnings, when they get them, are meager. Much will change in the country when President Mugabe leaves office or dies, but the histories of other African countries point to some continuing problems: a bifurcate legal system that leaves control of many laws, especially those affecting marriage, in the hands of customary courts, and other laws, especially those governing crimes and contracts, under the gavel of civil officials; an economic system based on export from agrarian and extractive industries that limit wide-scale participation; and an educated population with little chance of getting good jobs. These are the conditions that women in

Zimbabwe will continue to face as some try to make the best of what is, while others strive for a better future.

Zimbabwe, a country that came into being at the height of the second wave of the women's movement, was already influenced by worldwide feminism. With the promise of greater freedom to come under Marxist rule, women went to war as combatants in liberation armies, and those at home saw the gerontocratic patriarchy turned topsy-turvy as women's skills and resources gave them an edge with hungry and underfunded armies. "Freedom," "emancipation," and "liberation" were the terms used to raise the consciousness of the masses about the potential fruits of the anticolonial struggle for urban workers, rural peasants, and women. News of women's participation in the liberation struggle that reached the outside world carried images of women at the battlefront and stories of equality among female and male combatants. Though the reality was quite different, many women who were engaged in fighting colonial oppression did catch a glimpse of a better future. Under these conditions, feminism had a premature birth in Zimbabwe—but the political will, economic restructuring, and social consciousness that it needed to flourish were missing or in limited supply.

Perhaps it is best to speak of Zimbabwe feminisms in the plural, nourished from different sources, with varying goals. The activists in WOZA share a focus on women as mothers with women's movements in other African countries. They have taken to the streets to march for peace and recognition of their rights as citizens, calling on women as mothers to pressure the government to create an environment without state violence and with provisions of food, shelter, and education that would allow women to effectively care for their families. WOZA's source of power emanates from the moral authority of the mother to shame the men running the country. Another source, colonial clubs that taught women homemaking skills, surprisingly laid a foundation for the development of a kind of feminism in Zimbabwe. Homecraft clubs left a legacy of action for African women who broke with traditional dispositions; they became accustomed to and began increasingly to desire contact with other women, the support of non-kin, and the enjoyment of new skills and products. Building on their new associations in townships, churches, schools, and clubs, women created organizations of and for women. In later years, a Marxist stance on the emancipation of women shaped the conduct of the liberation struggle and influenced the formation of the Women's League, though its organization, leadership, and programs did not reflect egalitarian or socialist principles. After independence, the Women's League of the ruling party largely controlled women's public voice, but as NGOs began to form, some stood in opposition to the government and unabashedly addressed "unsafe issues" such as rape, abortion, and prostitution as well as human rights and the call for good governance. Intellectuals joined the battle. Novelist Tsitsi Dangarembga, employing feminist ideas centered on women finding their voices and exercising agency, explored the psychological, the sensual, and the political in women's search for freedom. Novelist Yvonne Vera's brand of feminism made her leery of sexuality and reproduction as marks of womanhood; at every turn she reminds the reader of the cultural politics of violence and oppression. At universities and in journals, professors and lecturers developed theoretical approaches to feminism and worked with NGOs to advocate for women's rights. NGOs today address a broad range of feminist issues, from agricultural practices to widow inheritance.

In my writing about feminism's contribution to women's power and about conventional feminine powers in Zimbabwe, it has been hard for me to avoid generalizations—especially when using ideal types to represent the variety of women. Here I want to make clear that I understand that diversity exists even within women's prime attachments. The conventional, for example, includes improvisation: manipulating, stretching, or contracting the rules and understandings in accord with the moment. An example of this is the variety of types of Kitchen Teas, a kind of event that draws from Shona habits of informal, non-perduring groupings of people for particular purposes. The Kitchen Tea itself is a modern convention, which usually reinforces women's containment of themselves, with its towel-wrapped gifts, each a reminder that women kneel before men. But the event can be stretched to promote women's standing up to their husbands, and the dancing at these parties lets loose women's sensuality, another aspect of women that convention decrees should be contained in public.

There are moments in this book when I point to divergence from women's core set of attachments—intense and positive attachment to their own moral superiority, maternal responsibility, and Christian conduct. For instance, Lillian, who had more than one lover at the same time, did not think of herself as morally superior, but she did repent of her sins in a church that required good Christian conduct from her. Another woman told me that she found it a burden to be responsible for the family, turning her back on one of women's main attachments and sources of power. Another woman foreswore the church and Christian belief, but she, like many others, felt that women were morally superior to men. Most women did not mention ethnicity in discussing their conduct, but one invoked it three times during her interview. Few interviewees were highly attached to seeing themselves as workers, but one sought further education in order to have a more challenging career, and another left a dead-end job to find one that gave her greater exposure to the workings of a business. As I finish my reflections on what I learned about middle-class women in Zimbabwe, I want to underscore what the examples above indicate: women come in more than four types; they contain contradictions; and they incorporate global issues while holding on to local ones.

Evidence from interviews, participant observation, social sciences, history, and fiction shows that feminism has seeped into every segment of society. It was not always front and center; sometimes it lurked in the background, and at other times it left traces in decisions that seemed to deny it. The director of the feminist NGO closely studied in this volume used feminist body politics in her story of the personal as political, capturing the sense of empowerment that comes when women exercise authority over their own bodies. Working wives and mothers wanted gender equality at work to gain more pay and greater chances for upward mobility. Without explicitly mentioning feminism, they noted that their ability to leave home and go to work is a positive change that allows them to live better lives. Those who worked in high government positions sometimes lost sight of the continuing battle for women's emancipation or found that following the rules of the game required them to downplay their concerns about women and gender. At home, for most women, differences from men—rather than moral equivalence between the genders—prevail. In fact, in the domestic domain, many women feel that they are morally superior to men, who are easily tempted and are irresponsible, in contrast to women's sense of responsibility to the family. While they desire a better life, some women do not see that their own attachment to moral superiority and responsibility might prevent their movement toward that goal. Girls and women who produce and participate in beauty and modeling contests want power; most recognize gender inequality and use either their beauty or their ability to inhabit a fantasy to assert their will in the world.

Movement is at the heart of the promise of feminism. Feminism is an idea that can motivate change, an opening to a view of a better, more satisfying life for many. The promise of feminism, as in the sense that something is going to happen or must happen, may be more pervasive than feminist accomplishments, and the promise can outlive particular organizations and movements. Getting to feminism is like climbing a mountain that you have seen from afar. It requires traversing familiar territory with new insights as well as exploring the not-yet-known. Past experience might recall unsteady footing, marshy meadows, rickety bridges, loose boulders, and thin air. Optimism about attaining the goal turns cruel when everything seems to conspire against your reaching the peak: the weather is wrong—too hot, too cold, rainy, snowy; you packed too much or too little. But you persist in doing just what you have always done, even though your joints are calling out for respite, and your shoulders ache from the tension you are carrying. Offering the comforts of the conventional good life, the warming hut, the shady grove of trees, or the rock by the creek tempts you to halt this weary slog. The peak seems to recede as you turn a corner or reach its base. This is the promise of feminism, a motivating force that pulls you toward a more satisfying life that is not under the control of any individual but can be reached by determination of individuals at the right time, in the right environment, none of which can ever be fully known.

Notes

Introduction

1. Dangarembga has mentioned Germaine Greer (Whyte 1989, 12), Alice Walker, and Mariama Bâ (Veit-Wild 1989, 106) as her feminist influences. Yet Audre Lorde's brand of feminism, with its emphasis on speaking up, its caution against using the master's tools for liberation of the oppressed, and its celebration of sensuality and eroticism, is present in traces in both her novels and the play examined here (1982 and 1984).

2. The "better life" quotation is taken from *To Live a Better Life*, the title of an oral history of women in Harare written by Teresa Barnes and Everjoyce Win (1992).

3. The 2009 film, produced by Laura Cohen and Joe Winston and directed by Joe Winston, is based on a book by Thomas Frank, *What's the Matter with Kansas?: How Conservatives Won the Heart of America* (New York: Henry Holt, 2005).

4. This quotation comes from the Bread and Roses Collective, *Women in Struggle* (London: Bread and Roses, 1978), 6–7. It is quoted in Seidman (1984).

Chapter 1. Sticks and Scones: The Homecraft Movement in Colonial Zimbabwe

1. The "Homecraft Movement" refers to secular women's organizations, which included Federation of Women's Institute's Homecraft Clubs and the Federation of African Women's Clubs, both run by white women. Hinfelaar (2001, 73–74) found a great deal of overlap in membership between the church-related and secular women's groups.

2. That Great Zimbabwe was built and occupied by one or more groups of the people now classified as Shona is debated, though its indigenous African origin is not. See

Beach (1998) and the following commentary in that issue of *Current Anthropology* for an excellent overview of debates on the who, what, and how of this fantastic ruin.

3. Ranger (1994, 293–95) reports that in eastern Zimbabwe centralized villages, bringing together several kin groups, broke up early in the colonial period. May (1983, 30–31) concludes that women gathered together in extradomestic, communal activities could have influenced men's actions through their gossip networks.

4. Ranchod-Nilsson (1992, 20) uses the term "incorporated wife" to refer to European women whose identities are largely based on their husbands' occupations and social standing. A similar notion was being taught to the wives of the emergent African middle class.

5. Much of my reporting on the activities and goals of the FWI comes from a study of its journals housed in the National Archives of Zimbabwe (NAZ) or at its headquarters in Harare. There are gaps in the NAZ's holdings of the journal, which changed its name from *Rhodesia Home and Country* to *Home and Country* between the 1940 volume and the 1951 volume. I was unable to ascertain if the journal was published in the missing years. At the NAZ, I consulted journals for the following years: 1936–40, 1951–53, 1957, 1960, 1962, 1966–69, 1974–79, 1981, 1987, 1991, and 1997. I found copies of the journals from 1998–2000 at the FWI Harare headquarters.

6. See Muchena (1980) 1984. In 2001, I interviewed Amy Tsanga, professor at the University of Zimbabwe's law school and head of a women and law NGO about this topic.

7. See Crehan's (2002, 131–37) discussion of Gramsci's notion of intellectual. See especially Gramsci (1971, 97). David Moore (1991) applies Gramscian perspectives in the study of the formation of the Zimbabwean ruling class.

8. Hinfelaar (2001, 50) lists eight rules for daily conduct, such as sweeping, cleaning, praying, not brewing or drinking beer, and eight rules for the conduct of meetings, including six-month trial membership, wearing uniforms, and removal for misconduct.

9. Barnes (1999) and Barnes and Win (1992) document black women's organizations during the colonial period. They show that when black women went into urban areas, they formed self-help groups and joined men in unions and political organizations. Hinfelaar (2001) chronicles the history of two women's church groups, one started in 1919, and Urban-Mead's 2004 PhD dissertation suggests that secular women's clubs in the late 1950s inspired women's church groups.

10. *To Live a Better Life* is the title of an oral history of women in Harare written by Teresa Barnes and Everjoyce Win (1992). In an article attributed to Mrs. Nhari, a complaint is lodged that women in the "highest category" are treated by Europeans the same those as in "the lowest" (*Home and Country* 9 [1962]: 1).

11. David Moore (1991, 479–84) uses letters to the editors of newspapers to support his conclusion that educated Africans saw themselves as superior to the uncultured masses. Also see Hancock (1984, 20) for a statement of middle-class exasperation at living "cheek by jowl with skoiaan queens and Africans straight from the bundu," expressed by Jasper Savanhu just before his election to the federation's parliament.

12. "Kitchen Parties Food for Local Women," *Herald*, Monday, May 11, 1992, 6.

13. See Bourdieu ([1980] 1990). When Shona women married, they typically left their natal homes and resided viri-patrilocally, with their husbands' kin. As the in-marrying "outsider," these women were likely to be accused of witchcraft or blamed as negligent when things went wrong.

14. Later the coming together of black and white female aristocrats was central in the promotion of women's groups in African townships. One township resident put it this way: "I think [the Women's Club movement] was inspired by the work of the then Governor in this country—Kennedy . . . Lady Kennedy, she was sort of a moving spirit and sort of paired with Mrs. Mangwende" (Barnes and Win 1992, 157–58). Helen Vira Mangwende, a teacher and wife of a chief, founded the Federated African Women's Clubs (now Association of Women's Clubs [AWC]) in 1953. After her untimely death in 1955, the administration of the organization was taken over by white women.

15. On duty to educate, see *Home and Country* 1 (1937): 2; and 1 (1939): 4; on adverse effects see 1 (1938): 3; and on Africans as a childlike race, see 1 (1940): 5.

16. Pape (1990) details charges brought against black men, showing that few cases came before the court and that the charges were broad, the evidence flimsy, and the punishment severe. He concludes that "black peril" scares solidified racial and class differences and helped construct a white and male supremacist social order.

17. Articles in the FWI journal support this position as does, Jock McCulloch (2000, 103–6), who concludes that the 1930s FWI resolutions were motivated by the members' concerns over white prostitutes, who in taking black customers were seen as degrading the prestige of all white women, and by the existence of mixed-race children of black mothers, who were evidence of the degeneration of the white race.

18. Pape (1990, 717–19) reports on two commissions to study the plausibility of recruiting women as domestic servants. One was the Standing Committee of the Federation of Women's Institutes of Southern Rhodesia, and the other was the government Departmental Committee on Native Female Domestic Labor.

19. See West (2002, 71) on the colonial policy of territorial segregation "aimed at thwarting the rise of an urban-based African middle class" and efforts before World War II to train those educated women who would be wives of the rural African elite.

20. Barnes (1992, 1995) covers the history of colonial attempts to contain African women in the rural areas and women's and men's efforts to be treated as resident families instead of visiting laborers in urban areas.

21. Hancock (1984, 16–17) covers the economic and political underpinnings of the Federation. Sylvester (1991, 36–45) examines the contradictory tendencies in settler politics and economics. Though the Federation formally recognized black trade unions, Raftopoulos (1997, 56) characterizes the Federation as "largely based on the self-interest of the colonial power and the settlers in the colony."

22. This interpretation follows Burchell, Gordon, and Miller 1991.

23. Ranger (1968, 237) writes, "In Zambia and Malawi the issue of Federation acted as a decisive stimulus to nationalist politics. . . . In Southern Rhodesia the coming of

Federation and its doctrine of 'partnership' in fact delayed the formation of the sort of united movement foreshadowed in 1948."

24. For a discussion of the changed gender relations brought about by the liberation forces, see Lan (1985).

25. Dangaremgba's 2006 novel starts with a scene in which a headmaster is beaten by members of the liberation army at the instigation of a jealous relative. Jacobs (1995, 255–57) elaborates on concatenations and contradictions in the liberation ideologies: liberation armies tried both to uphold African custom and to argue on behalf of wives against their husbands.

26. Staunton (1990). Two nationalist parties and their armies fought against the Rhodesian Forces, ZANU and ZANLA led by Robert Mugabe and ZAPU and ZIPRA led by Joshua Nkomo.

27. Nhongo-Simbanegavi (2000, 52–59) mentions that the ZANLA liberation army also wanted women recruits to learn Homecraft skills.

28. Though the AWC is a separate organization, founded by an African woman, in the 1950s and 1960s it was closely associated with the FWI and the Homecraft clubs. The AWC had a regular column in issues of *Homecraft*, the magazine for black women published by the FWI.

Chapter 2. Flame, Nyaradzo, and Pretty: Black Women and Girls in Harare with Reason to Hope

1. See Zimbabwe National Statistics Agency, 2010–11.

2. "Portrait of the People of Zimbabwe," *Parade*, Harare. My clippings of the magazine did not contain the date of publication; the editorial office in Harare does not have copies of the issue, nor does the National Archives of Zimbabwe. The present editor of the magazine concedes that December 1999 is a good approximate date.

3. After the first two years in high school, students take the General Certificate of Education (GCE), Ordinary (O) Level exam. If they do not score well on this exam, students who can afford it leave secondary school for teaching, nursing, technical, or business training. After two more years of secondary school, students take the GCE Advanced (A) Level. The Secretary of the Year for 2000 left her convent school with 11 O-level and her grades—eight As, two Bs, and one C—were published in newspaper articles about her.

4. Seidman reports, "Nearly three quarters of the women in the Mozambique camps were between fifteen and twenty-four years old in 1978, and another quarter were between twenty-five and twenty-nine" (1984, 426).

5. A number of important works have been written about female combatants in the Zimbabwe liberation struggle. Among the best are Lyons (2004), Nhongo-Simbanegavi (2000), and Zimbabwe Women's Writers (2000). I am interested in Bond-Stewart and Mudimu's 1985 booklet because it came out soon after the war; it was constructed by the female ex-combatants, and it is filled with their own reflections.

6. Staunton's *Mothers of the Revolution* (1990) details the stories of women caught up in the war in various ways and evaluates their participation in the war. Kriger's (1992) investigation of the village support system during the liberation struggle might have contributed to these participants sense of entitlement.

7. Casey Kelso, circa 1981. The text of this interview was given to me by Kelso, a journalism student at my university, who conducted the interview. It was undated, but I believe it came into my possession in 1982. Kelso and Metz (1984) published an interview with other female ex-combatants.

8. On Mujuru's fighting in Zimbabwe, see Lyons 2004, 112.

9. In 1988, the two major parties in Zimbabwe, ZANU and ZAPU, combined to form ZANU (Patriotic Front). Since that time ZANU (PF) has been the ruling party.

10. This information is available from the UZ website: http://uz.ac.zw/law/women/staff.html.

11. Olivia Muchena is an MP in the ZANU (PF) party. She has served as minister of science and technology development, minister of agriculture, and minister of state in the Office of the Vice President. In the MDC Party's court challenges to the 2000 parliamentary elections, Muchena was the highest-ranking parliamentarian to be found guilty of condoning election violence. In contravention of the law, she did not step down from her position, nor did she abstain from running for office in the next election (Solidarity Peace Trust 2005). She was minister of community development and women's affairs in the power-sharing government negotiated after the 2008 elections.

12. http://www.africanfeministforum.com/wp-content/uploads/2012/06/Feminists-ReBuilding-Zimbabwe-20114.pdf, accessed April 24, 2014.

13. Nafis Sadik, executive director of the United Nations Population Fund, speech at the United Nations Conference on Women in Beijing, China, in 1995.

14. *The Southern African Feminist Review* (*SAFERE*), sponsored by Southern Africa Political Economy Series (SAPES) Trust and its Gender Project and Southern African Research Institute Policy Studies (SARIPS), was produced in Zimbabwe and primarily edited by Patricia McFadden. The Zimbabwe-based journal included country profiles, interviews, poems, and articles by authors from South Africa, Namibia, Botswana, Zambia, Zimbabwe, Kenya, Cameroon, and the United States. Topics ranged from pan-African feminism to literature and from the arts to food security, elections, and constitutional reform in Zimbabwe. Editor McFadden explained that the policy was to present young feminists and at least one male writer in each issue and to openly address unsafe topics, including antiestablishment politics and sexuality.

15. In other cases, sex is said to cure the rapist as well as the victim of rape. Child rape increased because of the myth that sex with a virgin cures AIDS. Some traditional healers and evangelical prophets have been accused of engaging in coerced sexual relations with clients or members of the congregation who sought healing from them.

16. For a discussion of Mugabe's statement that gays are lower than pigs and dogs, see Aarmo 1999.

17. The name "Women's Coalition of Zimbabwe" is now being used by an organization with nine chapters in Zimbabwean provinces. This coalition focuses on advocacy, policy, and peace building and was active in the constitutional reform movement that ended with a new constitution in 2013. The board members of the Women's Coalition of Zimbabwe includes directors of organizations that deal with human rights, women and land, disabled women, and children. The successor organization to Homecraft clubs, JP/V, is among the organizations working with this coalition.

18. Williams's speech can be found on the WOZA Web site at http://wozazimbabwe.org/?p=486.

19. President's Obama's speech can be found on the WOZA Web site: http://wozazimbabwe.org/?p=549.

20. Magodnga Mahlangu's speech can be found at the WOZA Web site: http://wozazimbabwe.org/?p=482.

21. The disparity between judges and popular preferences has a history: a Miss Teen Queen Beauty contest in 1989 ended in an uproar as the majority of audiences protested that the contest was won by two young coloured women and one Indian (Matereke and Mapara 2009).

22. Zana'Kay (http://zanakay.wordpress.com/) writing on the Web site http://snowdroponline.com/the-new-miss-zimbabwe/.

23. Article in *Parade*, October 1999.

24. http://allafrica.com/stories/201207290338.html, accessed April 25, 2014.

25. http://www.mafaro.co.uk/2013/03/miss-zimbabwe-returns-from-shambles-of.html, accessed April 25, 2014.

26. Article carried in the *Daily News*, September 11, 1999.

27. From "A Mysterious Marriage," by Freedom Nyamubaya, in her book, *On the Road Again*, quoted in the report of the Zimbabwe Feminist Forum 2011, *Feminists (Re)Building Zimbabwe*. http://www.africanfeministforum.com/wp-content/uploads/2012/06/Feminists-ReBuilding-Zimbabwe-20114.pdf, accessed May 27, 2014.

28. *Feminists (Re)Building Zimbabwe*. http://www.africanfeministforum.com/wp-content/uploads/2012/06/Feminists-ReBuilding-Zimbabwe-20114.pdf, accessed May 27, 2014.

Chapter 3. Women against Government: An NGO under Stress

1. After crushing the opposition party, ZAPU, Mugabe announced that there was room for all under the ZANU-PF (Patriotic Front) umbrella. ZANU-PF and ZAPU signed a unity accord in 1987 that essentially absorbed ZAPU into the ruling party.

2. One handbook, developed for the Swedish International Development Cooperation Agency (SIDA) and used by women's groups in Zimbabwe, contains definitions of and tools for measuring empowerment through workshops (Oxaal with Baden 1997).

3. Two slogans were popular at the time: "Zimbabwe did not come for men alone," and "Independence is not only for one sex." The latter is the title of a volume on women

taking up the challenge to work for gender equality in the immediate aftermath of the liberation struggle (Bond-Stewart 1987).

4. The 1977 Termination of Pregnancy Act allows abortion only in cases when the mother's life is endangered, if the child may suffer permanent physical or mental defect, or if the fetus was conceived through rape or incest.

5. B. Raftopoulos, "Civil Society, Governance and Human Development in Zimbabwe" (unpublished MS, n.d.), quoted in Dorman 2003.

6. In 2005, the MDC split into two parties: MDC-T and MDC-N. Policy disputes within the parties, as well as charges of the use of violence and intimidation, have further divided the opposition parties.

7. Some issues, such as declaring Zimbabwe a Christian nation, which had many supporters in the country, were never put to the question.

8. Shereen Essof (2012, 101–8) reprints the Zimbabwe Women's Charter.

9. This was before the collapse of the Zimbabwe dollar, when the Zimbabwe dollar was trading on the official market at about Z$55 to US$1; on the parallel market, the Zimbabwe dollar could trade for two or three times that amount.

10. The book fair had gained international notoriety years before when Mugabe, seeing an exhibit for GALZ, had declaimed that homosexuality was "un-African" and that homosexuals were "lower than pigs and dogs." For a critical discussion of this, see Aarmo 1999.

11. In an interview Dangarembga lamented that in Zimbabwe Western feminists have a bad name: "People think about lesbianism, about breaking up families and . . . I actually don't understand it, quite frankly" (Petersen 1994, 347). Here I would like to note that while solidarity with other women is part of the process of breaking silence for Lorde, Dangarembga only minimally develops this through her juxtaposition of women in the novel.

12. The Legal Age of Majority Act (LAMA), which was passed shortly after Zimbabwe won independence, gave majority status to men and women at the age of eighteen, making it possible for women to vote, sign contracts, hold bank accounts, gain legal custody of their children, and arrange their own marriages. LAMA has always been controversial, and in the 1999 Zimbabwean constitutional reform exercise, repeal of the act was called for by men and women in the parental generation. Many feared loss of control over their daughter's sexuality and loss of bridewealth payments and seduction damages.

13. Berlant sees good-life genres—romantic love, upward mobility, political engagement—as increasingly unavailable in the contemporary United States. In contrast to the United States, the good life of upward mobility and political sway may be more attainable for some in Zimbabwe because of the power and wealth of an ever-growing technocratic and political class, from both government and private sectors.

14. The full quotation is as follows: "Fantasy is the means by which people hoard idealizing theories and tableaux about how they and the world 'add up to something.' What happens when those fantasies start to fray—depression, dissociation, pragmatism, cynicism, optimism, activism, or an incoherent mishmash?" (Berlant 2011, 2).

Chapter 4. Mercy, Mercy, Mercy: Middle-Class Working Wives and Mothers in Harare

1. http://www.issafrica.org/AF/profiles/zimbabwe/Economy.html, accessed June 21, 2014.

2. All the names used in this chapter are pseudonyms chosen to correspond to the women's use of ethnic or English names.

3. Industries that the women in this study worked for include telecommunications; banking, finance, and insurance; manufacturing of tobacco, beer, plastic, and electronics; and among the NGOs, protection and support for women survivors of domestic abuse and an evangelical consortium.

4. Most women in Zimbabwe are not engaged in paid employment; they are farmers or work in the informal sector. In 2007, most Zimbabweans, women and men, worked in the informal sector, if they worked at all: Zimbabwe's unemployment rate was estimated to be 80 percent. That was not the case in 1999–2001, when this research was conducted.

5. This unpublished study of sexual harassment in Harare was undertaken by Naira Khan for the Training and Research Support Center. I found the report at the Zimbabwe Women's Resource Center and Network in Harare.

6. Grace Mutandwa, *Financial Gazette* (Harare), April 27–May 3, 2000.

7. See Barnes 1999; Hinfelaar 2001; Ranger 1994.

8. See chapter 1, this volume, as well as Ranchod-Nilsson 1992 and West 2002.

9. It is very likely that maids also employ someone to look after their children or leave them in the care of relatives. Without having researched the topic, my best guess is that most women working as household helpers are literate but not educated beyond primary-school levels. Zimbabwe has a minimum wage for domestic workers, though few can demand it or get it in a tight labor market.

10. Washing machines are common only in the wealthiest households, well above the level of the secretaries. I think many women believe a person is better than a machine at getting clothes clean.

11. "Portrait of the People of Zimbabwe," *Parade*, Harare, Zimbabwe Publishing House. My clippings of the magazine do not contain the date of publication; the editorial office in Harare does not have copies of the issue, nor does the National Archives of Zimbabwe. The present editor of the magazine concedes that December 1999 is a good approximate date.

12. Ranchod-Nilsson (1992, 20) uses the term "incorporated wife" to refer to European women whose primary identity is largely based on their husbands occupations and social standing. A similar notion was being taught to the wives of the emergent African middle class.

13. *Home and Country* 1 (1952).

14. Nhongo-Simbanegavi (2000, 52–59) mentions that ZANLA wanted women recruits to learn domestic skills and participate in the Homecraft movement. The rhetoric of equality did not match the reality in division of labor or respect.

15. According to UNICEF statistics, Zimbabwe is one of the most literate countries in sub-Saharan Africa, with a literacy rate of 85 percent in the 1980s.

16. Gisselquist et al. (2003) argues that transmission through health care caused more AIDS cases in Africa than did heterosexual transmission.

17. *Independent*, March 17, 2007.

18. In 1999–2001, the HIV/AIDS infection rate in Zimbabwe was close to 30 percent of men and women between the ages of fifteen and forty-five. I had expected to see evidence of AIDS's destruction all around the capital city. The effect of AIDS was probably most evident in the number of street children, though I recalled seeing as many in Nairobi in the 1970s, but not in Harare in the 1980s.

19. I chronicled twenty-six letters from November 5 to November 19, 1999, when the editor called a stop to publishing any more.

20. There is no distinctive term for "the patriarchy," but a lecturer in African studies at UZ gave a Shona sentence that summarizes patriarchal practices as follows: Customs that give anyone perceived as being in one's father's or husband's line respect or higher status (Pedzisai Mashiri, personal communication). More generally, such a group might be called *Vana Vanyamunhu*, children of one man (see Mutswairo et al. 1996). In *Nervous Conditions*, this one man would be the narrator's grandfather, whom we know of only through the grandmother's stories.

21. See chapter 2 on Mujuru's service as a liberation war combatant. She is the minister of community development and women's affairs mentioned in chapter 3.

Works Cited

Aarmo, Margrete. 1999. "How Homosexuality Became 'Un-African': The Case of Zimbabwe." In *Female Desires: Same-Sex Relations and Transgender Practices across Cultures*, edited by Evelyn Blackwood and Saskia Wieringa, 255–80. New York: Columbia University Press.

Adams, Mary. 2009. "Playful Places, Serious Times: Young Women Migrants from a Peri-Urban Settlement, Zimbabwe." *Journal of the Royal Anthropological Institute* 15 (4): 797–814.

African Rights. 2000. *Zimbabwe: The 2000 Elections, Making and Breaking the Rules*, Discussion Paper No. 9. London: African Rights: Working for Justice.

Auden, W. H. 1979. *Selected Poems*. Selected and edited by Edward Mendelson. New York: Vintage Books.

Baker, Paula. 1984. "The Domestication of Politics: Women and American Political Society, 1780–1920." *American Historical Review* 89 (3): 620–47.

Barnes, Teresa. 1992. "The Fight to Control African Women's Mobility in Colonial Zimbabwe, 1900–39." *Signs* 17 (3): 586–608.

———. 1995. "So That a Labourer Could Live with His Family." *Journal of Southern African Studies* 21 (1): 95–113.

———. 1999. *"We Women Worked So Hard": Gender, Urbanization, and Social Reproduction in Colonial Harare, Zimbabwe, 1930–1956*. Portsmouth, NH: Heinemann.

Barnes, Terri, and Everjoyce Win. 1992. *To Live a Better Life: An Oral History of Women in the City of Harare, 1930–70*. Harare: Baobab Books.

Beach, David. 1998. "Cognitive Archaeology and Imaginative History at Great Zimbabwe." *Current Anthropology* 39 (1): 47–72.
Berger, Iris. 1988. "Women of Eastern and Southern Africa." In *Restoring Women to History*, edited by Elizabeth Fox-Genovese, Susan Mosher Stuard, with the assistance of Rufus Fears and Marc Mayer, 3–56. Bloomington, IN: Organization of American Historians.
Berlant, Lauren. 2011. *Cruel Optimism*. Durham, NC: Duke University Press.
Bond-Stewart, Kathy. 1987. *Independence Is Not for One Sex*. Harare: Zimbabwe Publishing House.
Bond-Stewart, Kathy, and Leocardia Chimbandi Mudimu. 1984. *Young Women in the Liberation Struggle: Stories and Poems from Zimbabwe*. Harare: Zimbabwe Publishing House.
Bourdieu, Pierre. (1980) 1990. *The Logic of Practice*. Translated by Richard Nice. Cambridge: Polity Press.
Boyce Davies, Carole, and Anne Adams Graves. 1986. *Ngambika: Studies of Women in African Literature*. Trenton, NJ: Africa World Press.
Burchell, Graham, Colin Gordon, and Peter Miller. 1991. *The Foucault Effect: Studies in Governmentality; with Two Lectures by and an Interview with Michel Foucault*. Chicago: University of Chicago Press.
Burke, Timothy. 1996. *Lifebuoy Men, Lux Women: Commodification, Consumption, and Cleanliness in Modern Zimbabwe*. Durham, NC: Duke University Press.
Carrillo, Hector. 2002. *The Night Is Young: Sexuality in Mexico in the Time of AIDS*. Chicago: University of Chicago Press.
Cawthorne, Maya. 1999. "The Third Chimurenga." In *Reflections on Gender Issues in Africa*, edited by Patricia McFadden, 55–83. Harare: SAPES Trust.
Chennells, Anthony. 1982. "Settler Myths and the Southern Rhodesian Novel." PhD diss., University of Zimbabwe.
Cherlin, Andrew J. 2009. *The Marriage-Go-Round: The State of Marriage and Family in America Today*. New York: Alfred A. Knopf.
Chikwanha, Annie, T. Sithole, and M. Bratton. 2004. *The Power of Propaganda: Public Opinion in Zimbabwe*. Afrobarometer Paper No. 42. Cape Town: Institute for Democracy in South Africa.
Chiroro, Patrick, A. Mashu, and W. Muhwava. 2002. *The Psyche of the Zimbabwean Male with Respect to Reproductive Health, HIV/AIDS, and Gender Issues*. Harare: University of Zimbabwe and United Nations Population Fund.
Coombes, Rosemary. 1997. "Identifying and Engendering the Forms of Emergent Civil Societies: New Directions in Political Anthropology." *Political and Legal Anthropology Review* 20 (1): 1–12.
Crehan, Kate. 2002. *Gramsci, Culture and Anthropology*. Berkeley: University of California Press.
Cvetkovich, Ann. 2012. *Depression: A Public Feeling*. Durham, NC: Duke University Press.
Dangarembga, Tsitsi. 1987. *She No Longer Weeps*. Harare: College Press.
———. 1988. *Nervous Conditions*. Harare: Zimbabwe Publishing House.

———. 1991. "This Year, Next Year..." *Women's Review of Books* 8 (10–11): 43–44.
———. 2006. *The Book of Not: A Sequel to* Nervous Conditions. Oxford: Ayebia Clarke.
Dangarembga, Tsitsi, and Juliet Baah. 1984. "Seizing Power." *Social Change and Development* 1 (9): 23.
Dorman, Sara Rich. 2001. *Inclusion and Exclusion: NGOs and Politics in Zimbabwe.* PhD diss., University of Oxford.
———. 2003. "NGOs and the Constitutional Debate in Zimbabwe: From Inclusion to Exclusion." *Journal of Southern African Studies* 29 (4): 845–63. http://www.jstor.org/stable/3557390.
Dowden, Richard. 2009. *Africa: Altered States, Ordinary Miracles.* New York: Public Affairs.
Essof, Shereen. 2001. "African Feminisms: Histories, Applications and Prospects. *Agenda* 50:124–27.
———. 2012. *Shemurenga: The Zimbabwe Women's Movement, 1995–2001.* Harare: Weaver Press.
Fallon, Peter, and Robert E. B. Lucas. 1993. "Job Security Regulations and the Dynamic Demand for Industrial Labor in India and Zimbabwe." *Journal of Development Economics* 40:241–75.
Fine, Lisa. 1990. *The Soul of the Skyscraper: Female Clerical Workers in Chicago, 1870–1930.* Philadelphia: Temple University Press.
Fontein, Joost. 2009. "Anticipating the *Tsunami*: Rumours, Planning and the Arbitrary State in Zimbabwe." *Africa* 179 (3): 369–98. Project Muse. doi: 10.3366/E0001972009000862.
Freire, Paulo. (1973) 2003. *Pedagogy of the Oppressed.* New York: Continuum.
Gaidzanwa, Rudo. 1985. *Images of Women in Zimbabwean Literature.* Harare: College Press.
———. 2001. "Masculinities and Femininities: An Introduction," In *Speaking for Ourselves: Masculinities and Femininities amongst Students at the University of Zimbabwe,* edited by R. Gaidzanwa, 1–9. Harare: University of Zimbabwe Affirmative Action Project, Gender Studies Association, and Ford Foundation.
Gelfand, Michael. 1979. *Growing Up in Shona Society.* Harare: Mambo Press.
Gisselquist, David, John J. Potter, Stuart Brody, and François Vachon. 2003. "Let It Be Sexual: How Health Care Transmission of AIDS in Africa Was Ignored." *International Journal of STD & AIDS* 14:148–61.
Gordon, Colin. 1991. "Governmental Rationality: An Introduction." In Burchell, Gordon, and Miller 1991, 1–52.
Gramsci, Antonio. 1971. *Selections from the Prison Notebooks.* Edited by Quinton Hoare and Geoffrey Nowell Smith. London: Lawrence and Wishart.
Guy-Sheftall, Beverly. 2003. "African Feminist Discourse: A Review Essay." *Agenda* 58:31–36. http://www.jstor.org/stable/4548092.
Hafkin, Nancy, and Edna Bay. 1976. *Women in Africa: Studies in Social and Economic Change.* Stanford, CA: Stanford University Press.
Hale, Sondra. 2001. "The State of the Women's Movement in Eritrea." *Northeast African Studies*, n.s., 8 (3): 155–77.

Hamilton, Edith, trans. (1937) 1965. *Agamemnon*, by Aeschylus. In *Three Greek Plays*, translated and edited by Edith Hamilton, 161–239. New York: W.W. Norton.

Hancock, Ian. 1984. *White Liberals, Moderates and Radicals in Rhodesia, 1953–1980*. New York: St. Martin's Press.

Hedru, D. 2003. "Eritrea: Transition to Dictatorship, 1991–2003. *Review of African Political Economy* 39 (97): 435–44.

Hinfelaar, Marja. 2001. *Respectable and Responsible Women: Methodist and Roman Catholic Women's Organizations in Harare, Zimbabwe (1919–1985)*. Zoetermeer, Netherlands: Uitgeverij Boekencentrum.

Hirsch, Jennifer S., and Holly Wardlow. 2006. "Introduction." In *Modern Loves: The Anthropology of Romantic Courtship and Companionate Marriage*, edited by Jennifer S. Hirsch and Holly Wardlow, 1–31. Ann Arbor: University of Michigan Press.

Hodgson, Dorothy L., and Sheryl A. McCurdy. 2001. *"Wicked" Women and the Reconfiguration of Gender in Africa*. Portsmouth, NH: Heinemann; Oxford: James Currey; Cape Town: David Phillips.

Holland, Heidi. 2008. *Dinner with Mugabe: The Untold Story of a Freedom Fighter Who Became a Tyrant*. Johannesburg: Penguin Books.

Hughes, Richard. 2003. *Capricorn: David Stirling's Second African Campaign*. London: Radcliffe Press.

Hungwe, Chipo. 2006. "Putting Them in Their Place: 'Respectable' and 'Unrespectable' Women in Zimbabwean Gender Struggles. *Feminist Africa* 6:33–47.

Hunter, Mark. 2005. "Cultural Politics and Masculinities: Multiple-Partners in Historical Perspective in KwaZulu-Natal." *Culture, Health & Sexuality* 7 (3): 209–23. http://www.jstor.org/stable/4005492.

Jacobs, Susie. 1995. "Gender Divisions and the Formation of Ethnicities in Zimbabwe." In *Unsettling Settler Societies: Articulations of Race, Ethnicity, and Class*, edited by Dairva Stasiulis and Nira Yuval-Davis, Sage Series on Race and Ethnic Relations 11, 241–62. London: Sage.

Kaler, Amy. 1997. "Maternal Identity and War in Mothers of the Revolution. *National Women's Studies Association Journal* 9:1–21.

———. 2003. *Running after Pills: Politics, Gender, and Contraception in Colonial Zimbabwe*. Portsmouth, NH: Heinemann.

Kelso, Casey, and Cara Lise Metz. 1984. "Too Liberated?" *Connexions: An International Women's Quarterly* 11:12–13.

Kennedy, Dane. 1987. *Islands of White: Settler Society and Culture in Kenya and Southern Rhodesia, 1890–1939*. Durham, NC: Duke University Press.

Kriger, Norma. 1992. *Zimbabwe's Guerilla War: Peasant Voices*. Cambridge: Cambridge University Press.

Lan, David. 1985. *Guns and Rain: Guerillas and Spirit Mediums in Zimbabwe*. London: James Currey; Berkeley: University of California Press.

Lorde, Audre. 1982. *Zami: A New Spelling of My Name*. Trumansburg, NY: Crossing Press.

———. 1984. *Sister Outsider: Essays and Speeches by Audre Lorde*. New York: Crossing Press.

Lyons, Tanya. 2004. *Guns and Guerilla Girls: Women in the Zimbabwean Liberation Struggle*. Trenton, NJ: Africa World Press.

Mama, Amina. 2001. "Challenging Subjects: Gender and Power in African Contexts." *African Sociological Review* 5 (2): 63–73.

Mano, W. 2004. "Renegotiating Tradition on Radio Zimbabwe." *Media, Culture, and Society* 26 (3): 315–36.

Mate, Rekopantswe. 2002. "Wombs as God's Laboratories: Pentecostal Discourse of Femininity in Zimbabwe." *Africa: Journal of the International African Institute* 72:549–68.

Matereke, Kudzai, and Jacob Mapara. 2009. "Shona Ethnoaesthetics: Beauty and the Shona Proverbs." *Journal of Pan-African Studies* 2 (9): 197–218.

Matshe, Thoko. 2001. "A Woman Leading." *Southern African Feminist Review* 4 (1): 61. Proquest.com.

May, Joan. 1983. *Zimbabwean Women in Customary and Colonial Law*. Harare: Mambo Press/Homes McDougall.

McCulloch, Jock. 2000. *Black Peril, White Virtue: Sexual Crime in Southern Rhodesia, 1902–1935*. Bloomington: University of Indiana Press.

McFadden, Patricia. 2000. "Interview: with Priscilla Misihairabwi." *Southern African Feminist Review* 4 (1): 47. Proquest.com.

Mikell, Gwendolyn, ed. 1997. *African Feminisms: The Politics of Survival in Sub-Saharan Africa*. Philadelphia: University of Pennsylvania Press.

Miller, Laura J. 1995. "Family Togetherness and the Suburban Ideal," *Sociological Forum* 10 (3): 393–418. http://www.jstor.org/stable/684782.

Mlambo, A. S. 2002. *White Immigration into Rhodesia: From Occupation to Federation*. Harare: University of Zimbabwe Press.

Moore, David. 1991. "The Ideological Formation of the Zimbabwean Ruling Class." *Journal of Southern African Studies* 17:472–95.

Muchena, Olivia. (1980) 1984. *Report on Women's Organizations in Zimbabwe: An Assessment of Their Needs, Achievement, and Potential*. Harare: Centre for Applied Social Science, University of Zimbabwe.

Musemwa, Muchaparara. 1995. "The Ambiguities of Democracy: The Demobilisation of the Zimbabwean Ex-combatants and the Ordeal of Rehabilitation, 1980–1995." In *Dismissed: Demobilization and Reintegration of Former Combatants in Africa*, edited by J. Cilliers, 44–57. South Africa: Halfway House, Institute for Defence Policy.

Mutswairo, Simon, E. Chiwome, N. E. Mberi, A. Masasire, and M. Furusa. 1996. *Introduction to Shona Culture*. Kadoma: Juta Zimbabwe.

Nhongo-Simbanegavi, Josephine. 2000. *For Better or Worse: Women and ZANLA in Zimbabwe's Liberations Struggle*. Harare: Weaver Press.

Ogundipe-Leslie, Molara. 1994. *Re-creating Ourselves: African Woman & Critical Transformations*. Trenton, NJ: Africa World Press.

Oppenheimer, Mark. 2011. "Married with Infidelities." *New York Times Magazine*, July 3.

Oxaal, Zoe, with Sally Baden. 1997. *Gender and Empowerment: Definitions, Approaches and Implications for Policy*. BRIDGE Report 40. Brighton: Institute of Development Studies.

Oyewumi, O. 1997. *The Invention of Women: Making an African Sense of Western Gender Discourses*. Minneapolis: University of Minnesota Press.

Page, Gertrude. 1907. *Love in the Wilderness: The Story of Another African Farm*. London: Hurst and Blackett.

Pape, John. 1990. "Black and White: The 'Perils of Sex' in Colonial Zimbabwe." *Journal of Southern African Studies* 16 (4): 699–720.

Pattman, Rob. 2001. "'The Beer Drinkers Say I Had a Nice Prostitute, but the Church Goers Talk about Things Spiritual': Learning to Be Men at a Teachers' College in Zimbabwe." In *Changing Men in Southern Africa*, edited by Robert Morrell, 225–38. Pietermaritzburg: University of Natal Press; London: Zed Books.

Petersen, Kirsten. 1994. "Between Gender, Race, and History: Kirsten Holst Petersen Interviews Tsitsi Dangarembga." *Kunapipi* 16 (1): 344–48.

Raftopoulos, Brian. 1997. "The Labour Movement in Zimbabwe: 1945–1965." In *Keep on Knocking: A History of the Labour Movement in Zimbabwe 1900–1997*, edited by Brian Raftopoulos and Ian Phimister, 55–90. Harare: Baobab Books.

Ranchod-Nilsson, Sita. 1992. "'Educating Eve': The Women's Club Movement and Political Consciousness among Rural African Women in Southern Rhodesia, 1950–1980." In *African Encounters with Domesticity*, edited by Karen Tranberg Hansen, 195–217. New Brunswick, NJ: Rutgers University Press.

Ranger, Terence. 1968. "African Politics in Twentieth-Century Southern Rhodesia." In *Aspects of Central African History*, edited by Terence Ranger, 210–44. Evanston, IL: Northwestern University Press.

———. 1994. "Protestant Missions in Africa: The Dialectic of Conversion in the American Methodist Episcopal Church in Eastern Zimbabwe, 1900–1950." In *Religion in Africa: Experience and Expression*, edited by Thomas D. Bakely, Walter E. A. van Beek, and Dennis L. Thomson, 275–312. London: James Currey; Portsmouth, NH: Heinemann.

———. 1995. *Are We Not Also Men? The Samkange Family & African Politics in Zimbabwe, 1920–64*. Harare: Baobab Press; Portsmouth, NH: Heinemann.

Rogers, Douglas. 2009. *The Last Resort: A Memoir of Zimbabwe*. New York: Harmony Books.

Rosenblatt, Tanya. 2008. "The Beauty Premium: Physical Attractiveness and Gender in Dictator Games." *Negotiation Journal* (October): 465–81.

Rutherford, Blair. 2004. "Desired Publics, Domestic Government, and Entangled Fears: On the Anthropology of Civil Society, Farm Workers, and White Farmers in Zimbabwe." *Cultural Anthropology* 19 (1): 122–53.

Saidi, William. 1988. *The Old Brick Lives*. Gweru, Zimbabwe: Mambo Press.

Schmidt, Elizabeth. 1992a. *Peasants, Traders, and Wives: Shona Women in the History of Zimbabwe, 1870–1939*. Portsmouth, NH Heinemann; Harare: Baobab; London: James Currey.

———. 1992b. "Race, Sex and Domestic Labor: The Question of African Female Servants in Southern Rhodesia, 1900–1939." In *African Encounters with Domesticity*, edited by Karen Tranberg Hansen, 221–41. New Brunswick, NJ: Rutgers University Press.

Schuster, Ilsa. 1979. *New Women of Lusaka*. Palo Alto, CA: Mayfield.
Schwarz, Bill. 2011. *The White Man's World*. Oxford: Oxford University Press.
Seidman, Gay W. 1984. "Women in Zimbabwe: Post-Independence Struggles." *Feminist Studies* 10 (3): 419–40. http://www.jstor.org/stable/3178033.
Shamuyarira, N. 1966. *Crisis in Rhodesia*. New York: Transatlantic Arts.
Shaw, Carolyn Martin. 2007. "'You Had a Daughter, but I Am Becoming a Woman': Sexuality, Feminism and Post-Coloniality in Tsitsi Dangarembga's *Nervous Conditions* and *She No Longer Weeps*." *Research in African Literatures* 38 (4): 7–27.
———. 2008. "Sticks and Scones: Black and White Women in the Homecraft Movement in Colonial Zimbabwe." *Race/Ethnicity: Multidisciplinary Global Context* 1 (2): 253–78.
Smith, Daniel. 2006. "Love and the Risk of HIV: Courtship, Marriage, and Infidelity in Southeastern Nigeria." In *Modern Loves: The Anthropology of Romantic Courtship and Companionate Marriage*, edited by Jennifer Hirsch and Holly Wardlow, 135–53. Ann Arbor: University of Michigan Press.
Smith, Ian. 1997. *The Great Betrayal: The Memoirs of Ian Douglas Smith*. London: Blake.
Solidarity Peace Trust. 2005. *Subverting Justice: The Role of the Judiciary in Denying the Will of the Zimbabwean Electorate since 2000*. KwaZulu Natal, South Africa: Solidarity Peace Trust.
Spronk, Rachel. 2003. "Ambiguous Pleasure: Sexual Relations of Young Professional Women in Nairobi, Kenya." Paper presented at the Pan-African Anthropology Association Conference, Port Elizabeth, South Africa, June 30–July 3.
Staunton, Irene. 1990. *Mothers of the Revolution: The War Experience of Thirty Zimbabwean Women*. London: James Currey.
Steady, Filomina. 1981. *The Black Woman Cross-Culturally*: Cambridge: Schenkman.
———. 2006. *Women and Collective Action in Africa*. New York: Palgrave Macmillan.
Stockley, Cynthia. 1903. *Virginia of the Rhodesians*. London: Everyman.
———. 1911. *The Claw*. London: Hurst and Blackett.
———. 1923. *Ponjola*. London: Constable.
Stoler, Ann. 2002. *Carnal Knowledge and Imperial Power: Race and the Intimate in Colonial Rule*. Berkeley: University of California Press.
Sylvester, Christine. 1991. *Zimbabwe: The Terrain of Contradictory Development*. Boulder, CO: Westview Press.
Tate, Claudia. 1983. *Black Women Writers at Work*. New York: Continuum.
Tripp, Aili Mari, Isabel Casimiro, Joy Kwesiga, and Alice Mungwa. 2009. *African Women's Movements*. Cambridge: Cambridge University Press.
Urban-Mead, Wendy. 2004. "Religion, Women, and Gender in the Brethren in Christ Church, Matabeleland, Zimbabwe." PhD diss., Columbia University.
Van Allen, Judith. 1976. "'Aba Riots' or Igbo 'Women's War'? Ideology, Stratification, and the Invisibility of Women." In *Women in Africa: Studies in Social and Economic Change*, edited by Nancy J. Hafkin and Edna G. Bay, 59–85. Palo Alto, CA: Stanford University Press.
Veit-Wild, Flora. 1989. "Women Write about the Things That Move Them: Interview with Tsitsi Dangarembga." *Matatu* 6 (3): 101–8.

Vera, Yvonne. (1992) 1994. *Without a Name*. Harare: Baobab Press.
———. 1993. *Nehanda*. Harare, Zimbabwe: Baobab Press.
———. 1996. *Under the Tongue*. Harare: Baobab Press.
———. 1998. *Butterfly Burning*. Harare: Baobab Press.
———. 2002. *The Stone Virgins*. Harare: Weaver Press.
West, Michael O. 2002. *The Rise of an African Middle Class: Colonial Zimbabwe, 1898–1965*. Bloomington: University of Indiana Press.
White, Aaronette M. 2007. "All the Men Are Fighting for Freedom, All the Women Are Mourning Their Men, but Some of Us Carried Guns: A Raced-Gendered Analysis of Fanon's Psychological Perspectives on War." *Signs* 32 (4): 857–84.
White, Luise. 1990. *The Comforts of Home: Prostitution in Colonial Nairobi*. Chicago: University of Chicago Press.
Whyte, Beverly. 1989. "No Need to Feel Nervous." *Mahogany* 12–14:48.
Wilson, Carter. 1995. *Hidden in the Blood: A Personal Investigation of AIDS in Yucatan*. New York: Columbia University Press.
Win, Everjoice. 2004. "When Sharing Female Identity Is Not Enough: Coalition Building in the Midst of Political Polarisation in Zimbabwe." *Gender and Development* 12 (1): 19–27. http://www.jstor.org/stable/4030589.
Zimbabwe Women Writers. 2000. *Women of Resilience: The Voices of Women Ex-combatants*. Harare: Zimbabwe Women Writers.
Zimbabwe National Statistics Agency. 2010–11. *Zimbabwe Demographic and Health Survey*. Calverton, MD: ICF International.

Magazines and Newspapers

Home and Country: Journal of the Federation of Women's Institutes of Southern Rhodesia
Jekesa Pfungwa/Vulingqondo Newsletter
Daily Telegraph, UK
The Daily News, Harare
The Financial Gazette, Harare
The Globe and Mail, Canada
The Herald, Harare
The Independent, Harare
Megabucks, Harare
Mahogany, Harare
The Mirror, Harare
The Observer, Harare
Parade, Harare
The Standard, Harare

Index

Page numbers in *italics* indicate figures.

affect, and despair, 9, 46, 52
agency, 2–3, 14, 43, 56, 114, 120, 170
AIDS Levy, 100, 104, 109. *See also* HIV/AIDS
appearance (self care). *See* self care (appearance, hygiene)
associations. *See* organized associations for women
attachments, 170–71; conventionality and, 119, 168; Homecraft and, 15, 46; working wives/mothers and, 5, 125–27, 129–31, 133, 166
AWC (Association of Women's Clubs, formerly Federation of African Women's Clubs), 18–19, 42, 106, 173n1, 175n14, 176n28
AWZ (Associated Women of Zimbabwe [pseud.]), 85–87, 94–95, 118; board of trustees of, 88–89, 94, 98–99, 104, 106, 108, 110–12; consciousness-raising and, 91; consensus decision-making and, 103, 112; corruption in government and, 104; cosmopolitan feminism and, 86, 114; democratization and, 109; director narrative and, 87–89, 94, 98–99, 101, 103–5, 107–8, 111–14, 118–20, 168; donors and, 7, 95, 106–10; economic decline and, 7, 85–89, 96, 107–8; equity and, 113; freedom of assembly/movement and, 87, 89–91; gender budget and, 104–5; gender equity and, 113, 120; HIV/AIDS and, 108; labor issues and, 87, 91; laws and, 106, 111; leadership and, 106, 176n28; lobbying and, 88–90, 95–99, 104; married and unmarried women's relations in, 27; media and, 95–96; membership of, 87–89; non-kin relationships challenges in, 27; the personal as political and, 113; political violence and, 7, 86, 98–99, 110; promises of feminism and, 87, 120; protests against state and, 87–94, 95–96; race and, 87, 89, 94, 103, 112; retrenchment plan of, 108–11, 179n9; single mothers and, 27, 93–94, 179n4; state accommodation and, 7, 86–88, 97–98, 105; state elections and, 98–99; state relationship with, 7, 86–87, 91; trauma talk, 113–14; UN and, 94; voices of women and, 91, 94; witchcraft beliefs and, 27; workshop model of, 88, 90–93, *92*, 107–8, 112, 178n2; ZANU (PF) and, 91–92, 98–99, 101, 110

Barnes, Teresa, 19, 21, 33, 146, 174nn9–10, 175n14, 175n20
beauty and modeling contestants ("Pretty"), 6–7, 9, 50, 75–76, 83–84, 170; animate ways of being and, 7, 73; containment of self and, 71; cosmopolitan feminism and, 71, 75; critiques and, 76, 178n21; desires and, 73; educational achievement of, 70; fashions of, 7, 71–73, 77–81; gender equity and, 70; interpersonal relations and, 7, 71; maternal responsibility and, 7, 70–71; media and, 71–73; middle class and, 48–49; Miss Summer Breeze, 79, 79; Miss Zimbabwe/Miss World, 11, 70, 74–80; mixed-race contestants in, 75–76, 178n21; politics and, 76–77; power and, 7, 70, 83–84; progress and, 71; self care and, 74–75; sponsorships and, 73, 77; urban townships and, 48–49. *See also* femininity
Berlant, Lauren, topics of: attachments, 119, 125, 166; cruel optimism, 7–9, 45, 125, 167–68; desires, 7–8; despair, 179n14; good life, 7–8, 45, 119, 179n13; neoliberalism, 87; trauma talk, 114
"better life, a," 168–69; colonial era and, 5–6, 13–14, 39, 173n2; feminist activists and, 1–3, 8–9, 70; Homecraft and, 13–14, 22, 39, 44–46, 148; working wives/mothers and, 125, 148, 165. *See also* cruel optimism; good life
black peril, 34, 175n16
body/ies, of women, 3–4, 11, 19, 113, 120, 160, 163
Bond-Stewart, Kathy, 52, 54–56, 176n5, 178n3
Bourdieu, Pierre, 32–33
British Empire. *See* Great Britain (British Empire, British Commonwealth)

CAF (Central African Federation), *xii*, 36–38; colonial power and, 37, 175n21; cruel optimism and, 44; Homecraft and, 14–15, 25–26; labor issues and, 20, 37–38; partnership between whites and blacks in, 14–15, 36–37, 44, 175n23; progress and, 36–38, 44 capitalism, racist, 44–45

CC (Constitutional Commission), 66–67, 100–101, 158
China (Peoples' Republic of China), 6, 10, 38
Chiroro, Patrick, 151, 155
Christianity, 124–26, 128, 130–31, 135, 151–52, 155, 160
church-related groups: colonial era and, 13–14, 22–24, 173n1; companionate marriages and, 146; Homecraft and, 14, 23, 173n1; Kitchen Teas and, 31; leadership and, 23–24, 174n8; married women and, 24; organized associations' relationship with, 23–24, 174nn8–9; white women and, 14, 22–23, 24, 173n1
civilizing/civilization, 13, 22–23, 26, 33, 39, 41, 45, 174n10
civil society, 105–6
classes, social: among whites, 21; differences in, 13, 21, 26, 168, 174n11; elites and, 39, 48–49, 162, 164, 174n7, 175n14, 176n25, 180n10; gender equity and, 118; Homecraft and, 26, 174nn10–11. *See also* middle class
cleanup program (freedom of assembly/movement law), 1, 61, 76, 87, 89–91, 148
colonial era, 20–22, 36. *See also* Homecraft; Rhodesia; Southern Rhodesia; whites
coloured (mixed-race), 20, 33–36, 75–76, 87, 122, 137–38, 175n17, 178n21
community: colonial era and, 18–23, 26; development of, 2, 6, 27, 36, 43; service to, 18–20, 22
consciousness-raising, 13, 33, 39, 50–51, 53–54, 59, 91, 115
Constitution, 38, 100; CC and, 66–67, 100–101, 158; gender equity and, 101; NCA and, 66–67, 99–101; one person, one vote and, 10, 38, 100; reform of, 66–69, 100–101, 158, 179n7, 179n11; state expropriation of land and, 101
containment (minimization) of self, 3–4, 11, 27, 30–31, 39, 57–58, 71, 115
conventionality, 4–5, 170; attachments and, 119, 168; beauty/modeling contestants and, 7; blacks and, 3, 21, 27, 30–32, 35, 175n19; cruel optimism and, 168; feminist activists and, 2–3, 8; Homecraft and, 5–6; Kitchen Teas and, 30–33; labor issues and, 39; organized associa-

tions and, 33; politics and, 119–20; in postcolonial era, 2–3, 118–20, 119–20; prostitution and, 3, 21, 27, 81; unmarried women and, 27; white men and, 35, 175n19; women combatants/veterans and, 57–58, 60; working wives/mothers and, 7, 127, 156, 165
corruption, 1, 59, 87–88, 90, 96, 100, 104
cosmopolitan feminism, 64, 71, 75, 86, 114
cruel optimism, 1–3, 6–9, 44–46, 82–87, 125, 166–68, 171–72. *See also* "better life, a"
Cvetkovich, Ann, 9, 82

Dangarembga, Tsitsi, topics of, 1, 3–4; agency, 170; church groups, 13; feminism, 3, 85, 114–17, 167, 173n1; gender equity, 114, 116–18; intellectuals, 162; labor issues, 117; liberation, 13, 118, 163, 176n25; "loose" women, 3, 47, 85, 117, 162–63; maternal responsibility, 162; moral superiority, 85, 149–50; patriarchy, 3, 117, 150, 161, 181n20; the personal as political, 117; political violence, 3, 54, 176n25; power/empowerment, 117–18; racial discrimination, 117; self versus security, 1, 3–4, 117, 124; sensuality, 3, 115–16, 162–63, 170; socialism, 117; voices of women, 3–4, 116, 170
—Works: *The Book of Not*, 54, 162–63, 176n25; *Nervous Conditions*, 1, 3–4, 13, 47, 54, 114–17, 149–50, 162–63, 181n20; *She No Longer Weeps*, 3–4, 85, 114–18, 162–63
democratization and, 10, 68, 86, 108–10
desires, 3, 7–9, 13–15, 26, 64, 125–26, 145–46, 162–63. *See also* sensuality (sexual desires)
despair, 9, 46, 52, 55–56, 82, 120, 179n14
divorced women, 11, 129, 132, 134, 137, 141, 162
domestic skills, 2; clothes washing and, 22, 48–49, 143–45, 161, 180n10; colonial power and, 5, 20, 22–24, 26, 36, 173n2; Homecraft and, 11, 20, 22–26, 36, 39, 46; Kitchen Teas and, 29; nationalism and, 38; urban townships and, 24–25; white women's role and, 20, 22–24, 36, 38
domestic workers, 19, 34–35, 45, 143–45, 144, 175n18, 180nn9–10

donor resources: constitutional reform and, 106; democratization and, 108–10; gender and, 68; HIV/AIDS and, 108–9; NGOs and, 7, 86, 88, 90, 106–8
Dorman, Sara Rich, 97, 101, 106

economic decline, 7, 11, 44, 47, 53–54, 83, 85–89, 96, 107–8, 125, 149, 153, 168
economics, 168; income-generating projects and, 2, 26, 33, 42–43, 45, 149; justice and, 3, 66; neoliberalism/marketization and, 87, 148; remittances and, 92, 102, 107, 153, 168
educational achievement, 181n15; of beauty/modeling contestants, 70; in colonial era, 14, 23, 26; of domestic workers, 180n9; of feminist activists, 49; Homecraft and, 33, 35–36; job opportunities and, 168–69; of middle class, 48, *48*, 49, 173n3; NGOs and, 55–56; organized associations and, 24; in postcolonial era, *48*, 173n3; in rural areas, 36, 175n19; in urban townships, 24, *48*; of women combatants/veterans, 49, 54–56; of working wives/mothers, 149, 181n15
elections: fraud in, 11, 69; one person, one vote and, 10, 38, 100; political violence and, 69, 98–99, 106, 177n11; rural areas and, 91, 102; voices of women and, 59, 102–3. *See also* politics and political activism; *and specific political parties*
elite class, 39, 48–49, 162, 164, 174n7, 175n14, 176n25, 180n10
envy, effects of. *See* witchcraft beliefs
equity, and politics, 24–25, 113. *See also* gender equity
ethnicities, 1–2, 97, 125–26, 130, 163

Federation of African Women's Clubs. *See* AWC (Association of Women's Clubs, formerly Federation of African Women's Clubs)
femininity, 11; liberation and, 163; power and, 2–3; prostitution and, 81; working wives/mothers and, 125, 160–61, 163. *See also* beauty and modeling contestants ("Pretty"); masculinity; working wives and mothers ("Mercy"/"Nyasha")

feminism, promises of, 1, 3–4, 8–9, 13, 46, 60, 87, 119–20, 167–72

feminist activists ("Nyaradzo"), 2–3, 6, 9, 13–14, 50, 60–62, 82–84; "a better life" aspirations for women, 1–3, 8–9, 70; consciousness-raising and, 13, 50–51, 115; containment of self and, 3, 115; conventionality and, 2–3, 8; cosmopolitan, 64, 114; cruel optimism and, 2, 7–8, 83; desires and, 3, 8–9, 64; despair and, 9, 46; donor resources and, 67; educational achievement and, 49; fashions and, 81; gender equity and, 6, 11, 50–51, 86, 114, 116–18; HIV/AIDS and, 65; homosexuality and, 63–64; intellectuals and, 60, 63–64, 69, 162; journals for, 60, 63, 66, 177n14; labor issues and, 117; "loose" women and, 3, 47, 85, 117; master's liberation ideology and, 115, 173n1; maternal responsibility and, 69–70, 129; middle class and, 48–49, 66; NGOs and, 60–62, 64–67; patriarchy and, 3, 117, 150, 161, 181n20; political violence and, 3, 54, 112, 176n25; power and, 1, 83–84, 117–18; prostitution and, 70, 81; proto-feminism and, 2, 5, 13, 46; sensuality and, 3, 115–16, 170; un-African narrative and, 3, 6, 10, 61–63; voices of women and, 3–4, 70, 116, 170; women combatants/veterans and, 55–56, 60, 82.

"Flame." *See* women combatants/veterans ("Flame")

freedom: assembly/movement law and, 1, 61, 76, 87, 89–91, 148; black women and, 2–3; feminist activists and, 1–3; Homecraft and, 13, 14–15, 21, 33; Kitchen Teas and, 29; liberation and, 54, 82; self versus security and, 4–5; women combatants/veterans and, 55, 59, 82; working wives/mothers and, 124, 148, 160

FWI (Federation of Women's Institutes of Southern Rhodesia), 20, 34, 36, 43–44, 175n14; AWC and, 176n28; colonial power in context of domestic skills and, 20, 22–23, 36; community service and, 18–19; domesticity and nation relationship and, 20, 22; educational achievement and, 35–36; goals of, 20, 22, 34; Homecraft and, 15, 23, 36, 173n1; income-generating projects and, 26, 45; men as domestic workers and, 19; mixed-race and, 20, 175n17; moral superiority and, 43; prostitution and, 19, 35, 175n17; urban townships and, 18–19, 35–36; white and black women's relationship and, 18–20, 35–36, 42–44; white women's political activism, 15. *See also* Homecraft

Gaidzanwa, Rudo, 63, 67, 71, 130, 144, 147–48, 160–61, 164

gender budget, 68, 103–5

gender equity, 1–2, 170; beauty/modeling contestants and, 70; constitutional reform and, 101; donor resources and, 68; feminist activists and, 6, 11, 50–51, 86, 114, 116–18; Homecraft and, 23; Legal Age of Majority Act and, 101, 118, 147, 179n11; liberation and, 2, 52–53, 134, 149, 176n25, 180n14; NGOs and, 93, 113, 120, 134–35, 179n14; sexual harassment and, 132, 136–40, 144, 164; social classes and, 118; whites and, 13; women combatants/veterans and, 6, 52–53, 56–59; working wives/mothers and, 7, 123, 134–35, 154–55, 176n25; ZANU and, 81–82. *See also* equity; human rights abuses

gender roles, 23, 68, 123, 128–29, 142–43

Gona, Dorothy, 112, 113

good life, 2, 7–8, 45–46, 119–20, 179n13. *See also* "better life, a"

good wife, 5, 7, 14, 125, 128, 155. *See also* working wives and mothers ("Mercy"/"Nyasha")

governmentality, 20, 36

Great Britain (British Empire, British Commonwealth): colonial era and, 21–22; independence movements (African nationalism) and, 24, 36, 44; job opportunities and, 122–23; Kitchen Teas and, 29; UDI and, 15, 38, 105–6; Women's Institutes Movement and, 34, 43–44; women's role and, 166

habitus, 32–33

Hancock, Ian, 174n11, 175n21

hierarchy, among women, 3, 14, 29–33, 175n13
Hirsch, Jennifer S., 146
HIV/AIDS, 3–4, 47, 151, 154–55, 181n16, 181n18; AIDS Levy disbursement and, 100, 104, 109; "corrective rape" and, 155, 177n15; donor resources and, 108–9; hair/health and, 74, 152–54; media and, 154–55; prevention of, 155–56; self versus security and, 3; working wives/mothers and, 125, 150–55, 181n16, 181n18
home as workplace, 142–45. *See also* working wives and mothers ("Mercy"/"Nyasha")
Homecraft, 13–15, 25–26, 28, 33, 42–44, 148, 169, 173n1; attachments and, 15, 45; AWC and, 42, 176n28; "a better life" and, 13–14, 22, 39, 44–46, 148; CAF and, 14–15, 25–26; church-related groups and, 14, 23, 173n1; civilizing/civilization and, 13, 22, 26, 39, 45, 174n10; class differences for blacks and, 26, 174nn10–11; classes outside homes and, 13, 14, 18, 24; clothes washing and, 22; colonial goals and power and, 14, 24, 26; community and, 18, 21, 26; community service and, 18, 20; companionate marriages and, 146; conventionality and, 5–6; cruel optimism and, 44–46; despair and, 46; domestic skills and, 15, 24, 25–26, 39, 46; educational achievement and, 33, 35–36; freedom and, 13, 14–15, 21, 33; FWI clubs and, 15, 173n1; gender and, 23; good wife and, 14; governmentality and, 20, 36; income-generating projects and, 26, 33, 43, 45; "incorporated wife" and, 18, 146, 174n4; leadership and, 15, 33, 39; liberation and, 14–15, 39; married women and, 14, 141–42; maternal responsibility and, 14, 19, 25–26; middle class and, 18, 36, 45; non-kin relationships and, 13–15, 21, 142, 146; polygamy and, 20, 146; professionalism and, 22, 142; progress and, 15, 20, 141; promises of feminism and, 13, 46; proto-feminism and, 5, 13, 46; radio clubs and, 14, 25–26, 33; Rhodesia and, 42; rural areas and, 14, 36; self care and, 19–20, 29, 32, 80, 146, 148; statuses of women and, 15, 25–26, 39, 174n10; traditional practices and, 19–20, 33; UDI and, 15; unmarried women and, 14, 33; voices of women and, 18, 20, 26–27, 38–39, 46; white and black women's relationship and, 14–15, 42–43; white women's roles and, 13, 26. *See also* FWI (Federation of Women's Institutes of Southern Rhodesia); JP/V (Jekesa Pfungwa/Vilingqondo); Shona; whites
homosexuality, 63–64, 111–12, 179n10
human rights abuses, 2, 51, 53, 56, 59, 124, 127, 134, 155. *See also* gender equity
Hungwe, Chipo, 4–5, 71, 121, 157
hygiene. *See* self care (appearance, hygiene)

"incorporated wife," 18, 146, 174n4, 180n12
infidelity. *See under* marriages
intellectuals and intellectual process, 60, 63–64, 69, 162

jealousy, effects of. *See* witchcraft beliefs
jobs. *See* labor issues
JP/V (Jekesa Pfungwa/Vilingqondo), 39, 40, 42–43; independence and, 41; white and black women's relationship and, 43–44; Women's Coalition and, 178n14; Women's League of ZANU and, 41. *See also* Homecraft

Kaler, Amy, 126, 161
kinship: as metaphor, 43; non-kin relationships vs., 13–15, 21, 27, 142, 146; Shona and, 17, 20–21, 26–28, 33, 174n3, 175n13
Kitchen Teas, 14, 29–32, 170; conventionality and, 30–33; hierarchy among women and, 14, 29–33; traditional practices and, 14, 29, 33, 170

labor issues: CAF and, 20, 37–38; conventionality and, 39; domesticity/state and, 20; domestic workers and, 19, 34–35, 45, 143–45, 144, 175n18, 180nn9–10; feminist activists and, 117; income-generating projects and, 2, 26, 33, 42–43, 45, 149;

labor issues (*continued*): job opportunities and, 2, 122–23, 132–34, 180nn3–4; Labour Relations Act and, 111, 134, 136; liberation and, 39; master-servant/whites-blacks relations and, 13–14, 18, 148; NGOs and, 87, 91; racist capitalism and, 44–45; rural areas and, 45, 102, 148; sexual harassment and, 132, 136–40, 144, 164; Shona and, 23; unions and, 14, 24–25, 38, 87, 91, 174n9; workshop model and, 90–91. *See also under* working wives and mothers ("Mercy"/"Nyasha")

land and people, relationship between: in colonial era, 22; liberation and, 87; Shona and, 20–21; Southern Rhodesia and, 36; state expropriation of land and, 11, 13, 59, 101, 106, 109

laws: bifurcate system of, 101, 168; on domestic violence, 68, 86; on freedom of assembly/movement, 1, 61, 76, 87, 89–91, 148; Infanticide Act (1990), 94; Labour Relations Act, 111, 134, 136; Legal Age of Majority Act (1982), 101, 118, 147, 179n11; Private Voluntary Organizations/PVO Act (1995), 105–6; Termination of Pregnancy Act (1977), 179n4; Welfare Organizations Act, 105–6

leadership, women's: AWZ and, 106, 176n28; church-related groups and, 23–24, 174n8; Homecraft and, 15, 33, 39; white women and, 18, 106, 173n1, 175n14; women combatants/veterans and, 39, 57–58

liberation ideology and armies, 1–2, 10, 39, 149, 169; black women and, 11; China and, 6, 10, 38; companionate marriages and, 176n25; consciousness-raising and, 53–54, 59; domestic skills and, 39, 176n27; East Africa and, 52–53; elite class and, 39, 176n25; emancipation and, 1–2, 6, 10; femininity and, 163; food preparation and, 2, 15, 39–41, 53; freedom and, 54, 82; gender equity and, 2, 15, 52–53, 134, 149, 176n25, 180n14; global hybridity and, 2, 6; Homecraft and, 15, 39–41, 176n27; human rights abuses and, 2, 51, 53, 56, 59; JP/V and, 39–41, 176n27; land redistribution and, 87; master's liberation ideology and, 115, 173n1; one person, one vote and, 10, 100; political violence and, 39, 41, 53, 176n25; power and, 1, 54–55; Rhodesia and, 1, 6, 10, 38, 53; rural areas and, 1, 2, 39, 53–54, 177n6; second wave of feminism and, 10, 113, 169; South Africa and, 10; Soviet Union and, 6, 10, 38; stipends for veterans and, 53–55; traditional practices and, 176n25; ZANLA and, 52–53, 176nn26–27, 180n14; ZIPRA and, 52, 176n26. *See also* women combatants/veterans ("Flame")

"loose" women, 4–5, 156; companionate marriages and, 159; elite class and, 162; feminist activists and, 3, 47, 85, 117; media and, 156–58, 181n19; moral superiority and, 85, 159; power and, 160–61; university campus and, 156–57; women combatants/veterans and, 59; working wives/mothers and, 81, 130, 135, 140, 152, 156–61, 163–65. *See also* prostitution

Lorde, Andre, 115–16, 173n1, 179n11

Lyons, Tanya, 52–53, 58, 76, 176n5

majority rule (one person, one vote), 10, 38, 100

Mapara, Jacob, 71, 178n21

marriages: companionate, 5, 8, 124, 145–46, 159, 176n25; "incorporated wife" and, 18, 146, 174n4, 180n12; infidelity and, 5, 150–52, 155, 157; patriarchy and, 145; polygamy and, 20, 146–48, 147; statuses of women and, 15; traditional practices and, 57, 71, 122, 126, 130, 145–47, 155; women combatants/veterans and, 11, 57–59. *See also* divorced women; unmarried women; working wives and mothers ("Mercy"/"Nyasha")

masculinity, 155, 160. *See also* femininity

Mashu, A., 151, 155

Matabeleland, people of, 63–64, 77, 97, 122, 126, 130, 137, 146

Mate, Rekopantswe, 30, 122

Matereke, Kudzai, 71, 178n21

maternal responsibility: femininity and, 11; feminist activists and, 69–70, 129; Homecraft and, 14, 19, 25–26; Kitchen Teas and, 14, 29–32; legislation and, 94, 179n4; liberation and, 1; NGOs and, 64–65; power and, 1, 17; rural areas and,

1; Shona and, 71; statuses of women and, 3, 5–6; traditional practices and, 19–21; working wives/mothers and, 125–26, 129, 150, 155, 162. *See also* working wives and mothers ("Mercy"/"Nyasha")

McFadden, Patricia, 60, 63, 66–67, 69, 177n14

MDC (Movement for Democratic Change), 66–67, 98–104, 109, 177n11, 179n6

media, 71–73, 95–96, 102, 106, 109

"Mercy." *See* working wives and mothers ("Mercy"/"Nyasha")

methodology and research, 3, 9–10, 51, 121–22, 171, 176n5

middle class, 35–36, 168, 175nn19–20; beauty/modeling contestants and, 48–49; class differences and, 26, 48–49, 174n11; educational achievement and, 48, *48*, 49, 173n3; feminist activists and, 48–49; good life and, 45; Homecraft and, 18, 36, 45; "incorporated wife" and, 18, 146, 174n4, 180n12; nationalism and, 41; political violence and, 153; racial discrimination and, 41; statuses of women and, 45; women's movement and, 66; working wives/mothers and, 48–50, 120, 122, 125, 131, 137, 142, 145, 160–61, 164–65. *See also* classes, social

minimization of self. *See* containment (minimization) of self

mixed-race (coloured), 20, 33–36, 75–76, 87, 122, 137–38, 175n17, 178n21

modeling contestants. *See* beauty and modeling contestants ("Pretty")

Moore, David, 174n7, 174n11

moral superiority, 8–9, 170–71; good wife and, 7; "loose" women and, 85, 159; men as irresponsible and, 8, 127–28; moral standards and, 14, 36; NGOs and, 85; working wives/mothers and, 7, 125–30, 149–50, 155, 161, 166

mothers. *See* maternal responsibility; working wives and mothers ("Mercy"/"Nyasha")

Muchena, Olivia, 23, 61, 177n11

Mudim, Leocardia Chimbandi, 52, 54–56, 176n5, 178n3

Mugabe, Robert: on AIDS Levy disbursement, 100; authoritarianism of, 88; biographical information about, 77, 97; constitutional reform and, 68–69, 99; corruption and, 88, 100; economic decline and, 11, 53–54; election fraud and, 11, 69; feminist NGOs' relationship with, 61, 87; freedom of assembly/movement and, 1, 87, 90; on gender equality, 52; and HIV/AIDS, 4, 109; on homosexuality, 63–64, 111–12, 179n10; inclusion politics of, 96–97; and political violence, 1–2, 11, 69, 97; and PVO Act, 105–6; and state expropriation of land, 11, 59, 101, 106; state leadership by, 38, 100; Western support for, 10; wives of, 163–65; ZANLA led by, 52, 176n26; ZANU led by, 176n26. *See also* ZANU (PF [Patriotic Front])

Muhwava, W., 151, 155

n'anga (prophet/witch doctor/traditional healer), 17, 27, *28*, 177n15

NCA (National Constitutional Assembly), 66–67, 99–101

Ndebele culture, 63–64, 77, 97, 122, 126, 130, 137, 146

Nehanda, Ambuya, 16–17, 77

NGOs (nongovernmental organizations), 6–7, 51, 114, 169–70; AIDS Levy disbursement and, 104; community development and, 2, 6, 27; constitutional reform and, 101; corruption and, 90; donors and, 86, 88, 90; educational achievement and, 55–56; freedom of assembly/movement law and, 1, 61, 76; gender budget and, 68, 103–5; gender equity and, 93, 134–35, 179n14; HIV/AIDS and, 65, 108–9; intellectual process and, 90; maternal responsibility and, 64–65; moral superiority and, 85; non-kin relationships and, 27; promises of feminism and, 119–20; PVO Act and, 105–6; rural areas and, 6, 27, 64–65; self-help groups and, 27; social services and, 87; state accommodation and, 2, 7, 86–88, 97–98, 105, 106; state relationship with feminist, 61; urban townships and, 2, 6; voices of women and, 103; witchcraft beliefs and, 27, 64–65; workshop model and, 103–10. *See also specific NGOs*

Nhongo-Simbanegavi, Josephine, 41, 53, 176n27
non-kin relationships, 13–15, 21, 27, 142, 146
"Nyaradzo." *See* feminist activists ("Nyaradzo")
"Nyasha." *See* working wives and mothers ("Mercy"/"Nyasha")

Ogundipe-Leslie, Molara, 62, 129, 166
organized associations for women, 2, 14, 23–24, 28–29, 33; ad hoc groups and, 14, 32; church-related groups' relationship with, 23–24, 174nn8–9; community service and, 18–19; political violence and, 14, 19; self-help groups and, 174n9; Wayfarers/Sunbeams programs and, 24, 36; white women and, 18–19. *See also* Kitchen Teas; NGOs (nongovernmental organizations); urban townships; *and specific NGOs*

Page, Gertrude, 22
patriarchy, 2–3, 11; feminist activists and, 3, 117, 150, 161, 181n20; Kitchen Teas and, 30–32; marriages and, 145; Shona culture and, 16, 181n20; whites and, 35, 175n19; working wives/mothers and, 5, 127, 145–46, 150, 155, 161
Pattman, Robert, 160
political violence, 153, 168, 170; body/ies of women and, 11; constitutional reform defeat and, 69, 99; elections and, 69, 98–99, 106, 177n11; ethnicities and, 1–2, 97, 163; feminist activists and, 3, 54, 112, 113, 176n25; liberation and, 39, 41, 53, 176n25; MDC and, 99, 109, 179n6; organized associations and, 14, 19; postcolonial era and, 1–2, 11, 69, 76; Women's Coalition and, 7, 66; ZANU (PF) and, 99, 110
politics and political activism, 49; absence-presence paradox and, 68–70, 86; authoritarianism and, 83, 86, 88–89, 153; consciousness-raising and, 39; conventionality and, 119–20; democratization and, 10, 68, 86, 108–10; equity and, 24–25, 113; gender budget and, 68, 103–5; liberation and, 39; NGOs and, 114; the personal as political and, 113, 117; political parties and, 59, 177n11; prostitution and, 70; socialism and, 1, 6, 10, 62–63, 110, 117, 169; voices of women and, 59–60; white women and, 15; women combatants/veterans and, 58–59; women's movement and, 1, 7, 64–68. *See also* elections; *specific political parties*
power/empowerment: beauty/modeling contestants and, 7, 70, 83–84; black women and, 11, 15–18; colonial-era women and, 15–18; femininity and, 2–3; feminist activists and, 1, 83–84, 117–18; "loose" women and, 160–61; NGOs and, 114; women combatants/veterans and, 11, 54–58, 83–84; working wives/mothers and, 7, 83–84, 126–27, 129–30, 139, 146–47, 149, 156, 160–64
"Pretty." *See* beauty and modeling contestants ("Pretty")
progress: beauty/modeling contestants and, 71; CAF and, 36–38, 44; feminist activists and, 61–62; Homecraft and, 15, 20, 141; postcolonial era and, 61–62, 118; Rhodesia and, 38, 44–45; Southern Rhodesia and, 36–37; white women and, 15, 20; working wives/mothers and, 141, 146, 155–56
promises of feminism. *See* feminism, promises of
prostitution: conventionality and, 3, 21, 27, 81; femininity and, 81; feminist activists and, 70, 81; freedom of assembly/movement and, 61, 91; politics and, 70; sensuality and, 81; unmarried women and, 27; urban townships and, 19, 35; white women and, 19, 35, 175n17; wife vs., 71, 81; women combatants/veterans and, 58, 60; working wives/mothers and, 81, 141–42, 158–59, 162. *See also* "loose" women
proto-feminism, 2, 5, 13, 46. *See also* feminist activists ("Nyaradzo")

racial discrimination, 13, 19–20, 22, 33, 36–37, 41, 44–45
Ranchod-Nilsson, Sita, 25–26, 39, 146, 174n4, 180n12
Ranger, Terence, 36, 174n3, 175n23
research. *See* methodology and research

Rhodes, Cecil, 21
Rhodesia, 36, 42, 122; beauty pageants and, 76–77; companionate marriages and, 146; economics and, 11, 37–38, 45; JP/V and, 39; labor issues and, 45; liberation and, 1, 6, 10, 38, 53; progress and, 38, 44–45; racial discrimination and, 19; racist capitalism and, 45; UDI and, 15, 38, 105–6; Welfare Organizations Act and, 105–6; white minority government and, 1, 15, 19, 38, 44, 97; Zimbabwe-, 38. *See also* liberation ideology and armies; Southern Rhodesia
rural areas: constitutional reform and, 100–101; educational achievement and, 36, 175n19; elections and, 91, 102; Kitchen Teas and, 29; labor issues and, 45, 102, 148; land and people in, 11, 13, 59, 87, 101, 106, 109; married women in, 175n19; maternal responsibility in, 1; polygamy in, 147, 147–48; power and, 1; remittances and, 92, 102, 107, 153, 168; voices of women and, 102; women's movement and, 65–66
Rutherford, Blair, 27

Schmidt, Elizabeth, 16, 18, 35–36
self care (appearance, hygiene), 51; colonial era and, 20, 38; hair/health and, 74, 152–54; Homecraft and, 19–20, 29, 32, 80, 146, 148; Kitchen Teas and, 29, 31–32; organized associations and, 23; working wives/mothers and, 74, 80, 135, 146, 148, 152–54
self vs. security, 1, 3–5, 117, 124
sensuality (sexual desires): body/ies of women and, 11, 19, 113, 120; feminist activists and, 3, 115–16, 170; Kitchen Teas and, 30–31; prostitution and, 81; working wives/mothers and, 162–65. *See also* desires
sex, instrumental, 139–42
sexism. *See* gender equity
sexual abuse. *See* human rights abuses
sexual harassment, 112–13, 132, 136–40, 144, 164
Shona culture: ad-hoc groups and, 23, 29, 32–33; beauty and, 50, 71; community and, 20–21; containment of self and, 39, 57–58; dance performances and, 77; divorced women and, 162; domesticity and, 15–16, 18, 20–21; Great Zimbabwe and, 16, 173n2; hierarchy among women and, 32–33, 175n13; homosexuality and, 63–64; kinship and, 17, 20–21, 26–28, 33, 174n3, 175n13; Kitchen Teas and, 14, 170; labor issues and, 23; land and people in, 20–21; marriages and, 57; maternal responsibility and, 71; moral standards in, 17; *n'anga* in, 17, 27, 28; "patriarchy" and, 16, 181n20; power and, 15–16, 18, 23, 174n3; public/political roles of women and, 16–18, 26–27, 39, 46; single mothers and, 162; social groups and, 23; statuses of women and, 16–17, 161–62; wife vs. prostitute in, 71; witchcraft beliefs in, 17, 27, 71, 175n13; working wives/mothers and, 71, 122, 126, 130. *See also* traditional practices
single mothers, 6, 51, 57, 93–94, 162, 179n4. *See also* unmarried women; working wives and mothers ("Mercy"/"Nyasha")
social classes. *See* classes, social
Southern Rhodesia, 21–22, 35–37; CAF in, 38, 175n23; mixed-race in, 20, 35, 175n17; nationalism in, 15, 22, 36; UDI and, 15, 38, 105–6; white women's role in nationalism of, 15, 22, 36, 38. *See also* colonial era; FWI (Federation of Women's Institutes of Southern Rhodesia); Rhodesia
Soviet Union, 6, 10, 38
Spronk, Rachel, 72–73, 81, 164–65
statuses of women, 3–6, 15–17, 25–26, 39, 45, 161–62, 174n10
Steady, Filomina Chioma, 62, 129
Stockley, Cynthia, 22

traditional practices: dance performances and, 74–75, 77, 78; Homecraft and, 19–20, 33; intellectuals and, 23; Kitchen Teas and, 14, 29, 33, 170; laws and, 168; liberation and, 176n25; maternal responsibility and, 19–21; moral superiority and, 8; self care and, 19–20; women's movement and, 8, 13; working wives/mothers and, 71, 122, 126, 130, 145–47, 155. *See also* Shona culture

UDI (unilateral declaration of independence), 15, 38, 105–6
un-African narrative, 3, 6, 10, 61–63
UNESCO World Heritage sites, 16
United Nations, 11, 38, 94
United States: class differences and, 168; cruel optimism and, 7–8, 86–87; democratization and, 110; desires and, 7–8; feminism and, 10, 113, 166, 169; good life and, 7, 179n13; job opportunities and, 122–23; neoliberalism and, 87
unmarried women, 14, 27, 31, 33, 141, 157, 161–62, 166. *See also* marriages; working wives and mothers ("Mercy"/"Nyasha")
urban townships, 14, 19, 24–25; educational achievement and, 24, *48*, 49; freedom of assembly/movement and, 1, 61, 76, 87, 89–91, 148; Kitchen Teas and, 14, 29; married women and, 24, 141–42; political activities and, 25, 174n9; polygamy and, 147–48; remittances and, 92, 102, 107, 153, 168; white and black women's relationship and, 18–19, 35–36, 175n14; women's movement and, 65–66

Vera, Yvonne, 54, 59, 124–25, 162–63, 170
voices of women: constitutional reform and, 100–101; feminist activists and, 3–4, 70, 116; Homecraft and, 18, 20, 26–27, 38–39, 46; liberation ideology and, 173n1; media and, 102; NGOs and, 103; politics and, 6, 41, 59–60, 91, 102–3; rural areas and, 102; women combatants/veterans and, 59–60; women's movement and, 70

Wardlow, Holly, 146
West, Michael O., 18, 23–24, 122, 175n19
whites: AWC women leaders and, 18, 173n1, 175n14; and black domestic workers, 22, 34–35, 175n18; black peril and, 34, 175n16; church-related women's groups and, 14, 22–23, 24, 173n1; class differences among, 13, 21; community and, 18, 22; conventionality for, 35, 175n19; domesticity and, 33; domestic skills classes by female, 20, 22–24, 36, 38–39; gender equity and, 13; Girl Scouts and, 24; "incorporated wife" and, 174n4, 180n12; integrationism and, 37; leadership by women and, 18, 106, 173n1, 175n14; master-servant/whites-blacks relations and, 13–14, 18, 22, 148; men civilized by women, 33; mixed-race and, 20, 33–36, 175n17; nationalism and, 15, 22, 36, 38; partnerships between blacks and, 14–15, 18–19, 35–36, 37, 175n14; patriarchy and, 35, 175n19; political power for men and, 24–25; progress and, 15, 20, 141; prostitution and, 19, 35, 175n17; racial discrimination and, 13, 20, 22, 33; urban townships, 18–19, 35–36, 175n14; white peril and, 35; white supremacy and, 34, 175n16; women's organizations and, 33–34; yellow peril and, 34–35, 175n17
wife, good, 5, 7, 14, 125, 128, 155. *See also* working wives and mothers ("Mercy"/"Nyasha")
Win, Everjoyce, 19, 21, 33, 67, 148, 174nn9–10, 175n14
witchcraft beliefs, 17, 27–28, *28*, 64–65, 71, 175n13
women combatants/veterans ("Flame"), 1–2, 6, 9, 50–60, 81–82, 84, 169; divorced, 11; educational achievement of, 49, 54–56; gender equity and, 6, 52–53, 56–59; leadership and, 39, 57–59; marriages and, 11, 57–59; middle class and, 48–49; military training/service and, 6, 11, 51, 57; power and, 11, 54–58, 83–84; single mothers and, 6, 51, 57; social normality and, 11, 51, 55–57, 59–60; urban townships and, 48–49. *See also* liberation
Women's Coalition, 7, 66–68, 101, 106, 178n14
women's movement, 3, 6, 66–67, 86; absence-presence paradox and, 68–70, 86; constitutional reform and, 66–69, 100–101; critiques of, 65–66; democratization and, 68, 86; economy and, 66; NCA and, 66–67; NGOs and, 65–66; politics and, 1, 64–68; promises of feminism and, 1, 3–4, 8–9, 46; traditional practices and, 8, 13; un-African narrative and, 3, 6, 10, 61–63; university

campus and, 63–64; urban townships and, 48–49; voices of women and, 70; Women's Coalition and, 7, 66–68, 101, 106, 178n14. *See also* feminist activists ("Nyaradzo"); laws; Women's Coalition
women's relations: between married and unmarried, 27, 29, 31, 166; between white and black, 14–15, 18–20, 35–36, 38, 42–44, 175n14
working wives and mothers ("Mercy"/"Nyasha"), 6–7, 9, 50, 121–25, *123*, 132, 165–66, 169–71, 180n3; attachments and, 5, 125–27, 129–31, 133, 166; "a better life" and, 125, 148, 165; Christian guidance and, 124–26, 130–31, 135, 151–52; clothes washing and, 143–45, 161, 180n10; companionate marriages and, 5, 8, 124, 145–46, 159, 176n25; constitutional reform and, 158; conventionality and, 7, 127, 156, 165; cruel optimism and, 125, 166; desires and, 125–26, 145–46, 162–63; divorced women and, 11, 129, 132, 134, 137, 141, 162; domestic workers hiring/training and, 45, 143–45, 180nn9–10; economic decline and, 125, 149, 153; educational achievement of, 149, 181n15; ethnicities and, 125–26, 130; femininity and, 125, 160–61, 163; freedom and, 124, 148, 160; gender equity and, 7, *123*, 134–35, 154–55, 176n25; gender roles and, *123*, 128–29, 142–43; good wife and, 5, 7, 14, 125, 128, 155; hair/health and, 152–54; HIV/AIDS and, 125, 150–55, 181n16, 181n18; home as workplace and, 142–45; human rights abuses and, 124, 127, 155; income-generating projects and, 2, 26, 33, 42–43, 45, 149; infidelity and, 5, 150–52, 155, 157; instrumental sex and, 139–42; job opportunities for, 2, 122–23, 132–34, 180nn3–4; labor issues and, 2, 17, 121–23, 125, 132–34, 136–40, 144, 148, 164, 180nn3–4; laws and, 136, 147–48; "loose" women and, 81, 130, 135, 140, 152, 156–61, 163–65; and lovemaking, 5; married vs. unmarried, 27, 166; masculinity and, 155, 160; maternal responsibility of, 125–26, 129, 150, 155, 162; middle class and, 48–50, 120, 122, 125, 131, 137, 142, 145, 160–61, 164–65; mixed-race and, 122, 137–38; moral superiority and, 7, 125–30, 149–50, 155, 161, 166; patriarchy and, 5, 127, 145–46, 150, 155, 161; power and, 7, 83–84, 126–27, 129–30, 139, 146–47, 149, 156, 160–64; professionalism and, 125, 141–42; progress and, 141, 146, 155–56; promises of feminism and, 168; prostitution and, 81, 141–42, 158–59, 162; rural areas and, 147, 147–48; self care and, 74, 80, 135, 146, 148; self vs. security and, 4–5, 124; sensuality and, 162–65; sexual harassment and, 132, 136–40, 144, 164; single mothers and, 6, 51, 57, 93–94, 162, 179n4; traditional practices and, 71, 122, 126, 130, 145–47, 155; unmarried women and, 27, 141, 157, 161, 162. *See also* maternal responsibility

WOZA (Women of Zimbabwe Arise), 69–70, 82–83, 95, 129, 169

yellow peril, 34–35, 175n17. *See also* mixed-race (coloured)

ZANLA (Zimbabwe African National Liberation Army), 52–53, 176nn26–27, 180n14
ZANU (PF [Patriotic Front]), 38, 88, 97, 177n9, 178n1; AWZ and, 98–99, 101; constitutional reform and, 100–101; economic decline and, 99; gender budget and, 104; political violence and, 99, 110; politics and, 59, 177n11; PVO Act and, 106; Women's League of, 91–92, 98, 169
ZANU (Zimbabwe African National Union): corruption and, 59; gender equity and, 81–82; one person, one vote principle and, 38; political parties and, 38, 176n26; Women's League of, 6, 10, 25, 41, 169
ZAPU (Zimbabwe African People's Union), 25, 38, 176n26, 178n1
Zimbabwe, *xii*, 1, 38, 54
Zimbabwe-Rhodesia, 38, 42. *See also* Rhodesia
ZIPRA (Zimbabwe People's Revolutionary Army), 52, 176n26

CAROLYN MARTIN SHAW is a professor emerita of anthropology at the University of California, Santa Cruz, and the author of *Colonial Inscriptions: Race, Sex, and Class in Kenya*.

The University of Illinois Press
is a founding member of the
Association of American University Presses.

———————————————

University of Illinois Press
1325 South Oak Street
Champaign, IL 61820-6903
www.press.uillinois.edu